W9-DGY-397

The
Last Revival

The Death of Christian Civilization
and the Return of Hope,
Martyrdom, and the
New Testament Church

By Robert W. Mears

Title, Author, Copyright, Publisher

*The Last Revival, The Death of Christian Civilization and the
Return of Hope, Martyrdom, and the New Testament Church,*
by Robert W. Mears.

Copyright © by Robert W. Mears, 2000 A.D.
All rights reserved.
ISBN 0-9700117-0-9

Published by Prophetic Services,
P.O. Box 6059,
Lakeport, New Hampshire 03246.

Scripture references and quotations are taken from the New
King James Bible, copyright © 1992 by Thomas Nelson Publishers,
Nashville, Tennessee.

Printed in the United States of America
by Johnson Graphics,
Gilford, New Hampshire 03246.

DEFINITIONS

Recovery: The return of health and strength after a condition of weakness or sickness; the gaining back of what was lost or stolen.

Reform: To form again, to correct deformities, eliminate abuses and corruption, repair or reconstruct and cause to function properly.

Renewal: The return to a state of newness, being like new, beginning again, a reconditioning on the original design or plan.

Restoration: The return of what has been lost, stolen, atrophied, corrupted or decayed, a reconstruction of the original form, bringing back to a normal condition.

Revival: A revitalization; the return to vitality following a period of decline, a reappearance after a time of being in obscurity, a return to integrity after a time of compromise and corruption.

CONVICTIONS

It is written that Christ loved the church and gave Himself for her that He might present her to Himself at His second coming a glorious church without a stain or blemish. I believe He will accomplish what He intends. I believe God gave us a glimpse in the New Testament and especially in the early chapters of the book of Acts—at the beginning—of what such a church is like. I believe that **revivals** play a key role in the purification of the church. I believe that the last five hundred years in particular—known to historians as the modern age—have been in God's mind the age of **reform**. It has been characterized by repeated **revivals**. They have certain features in common but no two are identical. That, I believe, is because God has been working to **reform** the church by the **recovery**, one by one, of the characteristics of the New Testament church that were lost or corrupted in the course of church history—most notably during the time of Constantine.

THESIS

The thesis of this book is that the **reform**—essentially a **renewal**—of the church will be completed in the next and last **revival** by the **restoration** of those qualities of the New Testament church that are still lacking in the contemporary church—for instance, the love, unity, purity and willingness of the early church to follow in the footsteps of Jesus Christ. The thesis is also a prayer to God and a call to His people.

Contents

Outline

1. The need for another revival—the last—to complete the reform of the church.

2. The nature of a New Testament revival

3. The key issue addressed by revivals: the church's fall from New Testament integrity and the promise of restoration

4. Two signs from the1960s indicating that the time of restoration has come

5. Three revivals—Protestant, Anabaptist and Roman Catholic—at the beginning of the era of reform, indicating God's goals and methods

6. The emerging New Testament church in spite of traditional resistance

7. What remains to be done in the last revival to restore the church to New Testament integrity

Acknowledgments

This book is mine in the sense that it was conceived in my heart. I carried the vision and brought it forth in pain and joy like a woman giving birth. It is my responsibility. But there were many "midwives" and counsellors without whose help it might have been aborted, stillborn or deformed. So the book is also a product of the body of Christ because of the help of some of its many and quite different members. They cannot be blamed for its faults, but they deserve credit for helping me bring it to birth and for making it a better book than I could have produced by myself.

So let me acknowledge the many brothers and sisters who read drafts of this book while it was in process and/or gave me counsel and encouragement. I will mention a few: Ted Kirsch (now deceased), a Christian businessman from Southwestern Oregon, a mentor and the first elder I appointed in the church I served there. We remained friends long after I left Oregon, and it was Ted who encouraged me to write a book.

I must mention Roger Dewey, a dedicated servant of Christ in the inner city of Boston—theologically conservative but politically and socially liberal. He read the manuscript, commented in detail, and asked a probing question: "what would a New Testament revival look like?" It changed the focus of the book.

Thanks to Dan Gruber, a friend and colleague, who painstakingly critiqued the manuscript from a Messianic-Jewish perspective; to Phyllis Shoemaker, a member of our first community in the early 1970s and a recent convert to Catholicism, who challenged me from the point of view of the Roman Catholic Church; to Ed Spurlin whose "voice in the wilderness" represented the biblical and prophetic tradition within Protestantism.

Thanks to David Woodward, spokesman for a communal church in Vermont that was raided early one morning in 1984 by the state police. They were armed with real ammunition and blank warrants. I investigated the incident, wrote an article about it and in the process met David. We carried on a long correspondence and through his input I got a surprising glimpse of how a New Testament church might relate to state and society in the U. S. A. today.

Thanks to Terry Sullivan, a non-violent, pro-life activist and a theological non-conformist, for his extensive research and penetrating analysis of the fourth century revolution that hobbled the church from that day to this; to Sue Cook, a light in a dark place, who gave some helpful comments and encouragement; to my daughter, Jennifer Watson, who attends a Presbyterian church and would not let me forget my evangelical roots; to Dave and Carol Usher who encouraged me in the project and offered valuable advice; to Dr. Bill Morehouse of Rochester, N.Y., who suggested I find an editor; and to David Hare who filled that position and more—editor, theological advisor and friend.

Roger Boucher and Leo Lenschow are old friends who rejoiced with us through the revival of the seventies and suffered maybe more than any of us through the eighties and nineties. They were co-leaders who found themselves on opposite sides in a struggle that destroyed their church and plunged them into a long and profound sorrow. For years they didn't speak to each other. Then God renewed their faith and love. They have not only forgiven each other but have been reconciled as brothers and friends. They contributed to this book by providing an exemple in real life of a key part of the vision I have seen and tried to put into words.

Thanks to my wife, Doris, my best friend and partner in life (and during the last few years in a family business in which she is the boss) for her patience with me during the hundreds of hours I spent writing and rewriting this book.

Finally and supremely, I thank Jesus Christ for His grace and patience with me. He put the vision in my heart, gave me the insight and ability to see the obvious in His gospel and would not let me be satisfied with anything less than the truth. He helped me express the vision in words and bring it forth to see the light of publication.

Preface

My book is about revival. That is because God spoke to me about revival—about a particular revival that would come in my lifetime and for which I must prepare. It was the defining moment of my life. I was in my late twenties studying to be a minister. From a musty used-book store I had purchased a book entitled, *Revivals, Their Laws and Leaders,* by James Burns. As I read that volume I experienced a moment of illumination, and yes, revelation.

The Holy Spirit planted in my heart a word, a promise, a call to martyrdom. The word related to a time and season, a day and hour coming sometime in the future. I didn't know when. But I knew I must begin immediately to prepare for it. A revival was coming, one that would profoundly affect the United States and because of this nation's influence, western civilization and the whole world. It would change the way the church related to the world.

Burns' book consisted of a general introduction to the phenomenon of revivals in church history and a series of sketches of particular historic revivals. The one that seized me in that moment some time in the early 1960s was Burns' account of the revival in Florence, Italy, led by the Dominican Friar, Girolamo Savonarola, at the end of the fifteenth century. It left me with the burning conviction that somehow Savonarola and the revival he led had a crucial relevance for me, my own times and the church in the United States.

I will tell Savonarola's story later in the book. For now I will say that he was a biblical scholar, a reformer, the leader of a great revival, a prophet and perhaps most important, a martyr for the faith. God used him in a great revival in Florence. Many were converted and for a while the magnificent Renaissance city was like the city of God. Then came the backlash. Savonarola was rejected and killed. Nevertheless, he inaugurated the period of church reform and what we call the modern era of history. Less than twenty years after his death, the Protestant Reformation broke out in Germany and the long process of reform was underway and unstoppable. That was the message.

Nearly forty years have passed since I received that word. In the intervening time I have come to understand the message, and I have watched the church, the nation and the world change in preparation for its fulfillment. I too have changed. This is the book I have wanted to write ever since I became a Christian, but it took me forty years to gather the information and experience to be able to write it. I believe the message is now ripe, and I have finally succeeded in putting it into words.

The understanding came to me over the years in flashes of insight, illumination and revelation interspersed in long periods of study, practical work in pastoral and prophetic ministry and in the joys, routines and struggles of family life. Understanding came piece-by-piece like a jigsaw puzzle. The picture that emerged as I put the pieces together is a vision of the last revival.

My conclusion as to Savonarola's significance for our times is that the process of reform that began with him more than five hundred years ago will be completed in my lifetime in the last of a long series of revivals. Furthermore, I believe that last revival is now at hand, has in fact already begun, and will soon sweep the country. It will arise in New England, that historic seedbed of revivals, but it will not simply duplicate the revivals that have occurred here in the past. Rather, it will finally accomplish the goal to which all true revivals made their particular and partial contributions. It will restore the integrity of the New Testament church and prepare the way for the kingdom of God, the kingdom of Israel under the Messiah, the son of David and King of the Jews.

Savonarola and the fifteenth century revival in Florence stood at the beginning of the era of reform. The next revival at the end of the twentieth and the beginning of the twenty-first century here in the United States will finish it. But before I say any more about the next revival, I have to say something about the one that preceded it. For I know about that one by experience.

I was part of the leadership team of a church that was born in the revival of the 1970s. We experienced something of the amazing grace that marked the church at its beginning. We believed in those days that we were on the way to reestablishing a New Testament church. We saw some miracles and tasted a little of the love that characterized the early church. It was wonderful and exciting. But the promises of that revival were not fulfilled. We experienced what Bill Gothard calls the death of a vision. We—in particular, we who were the leaders—lacked the experience, the knowledge and the character to build a church on the New Testament pattern. As a result, many were hurt and disappointed and some of them are unwilling to risk being hurt again. I understand that, too, from experience.

As in a divorce, the breakup of those who were once lovers will almost always seem like a betrayal. It is the hardest kind of sin to forgive. That's how it seemed to a lot of us who were part of the revival that swept the nation like a great wave in the early 1970s and ebbed later in the same decade leaving a lot of debris and wreckage behind.

When we have been hurt and disillusioned, we instinctively react by running and hiding. We want a place of safety where we can avoid all risk and danger, at least until our wounds have healed. But the avoidance of risk and danger is the exact opposite of the calling we have received from Jesus in the New Testament, and a key reason for the failure of the revival of the 1970s.

Whatever our pain and disappointment, therefore, it is a mistake to try to protect ourselves by hardening our hearts against God and His people. It is a mistake because God remains faithful whatever the errors and sins of those who claim to represent Him. Furthermore, He has promised to fix the church and make it a safe place for His people, paradoxically, in the midst of great danger. In the New Testament, that promise has special reference to a particular time period. The signs indicate that the time is now at hand, as I will try to demonstrate in this book.

If we clear that first hurdle and are willing to embrace the idea of another revival, we are tempted to forget the one that turned sour, pretend it never happened, and try to begin again assuming that we can avoid the mistakes of the past. I believe that, too, would be a mistake. For in the wreckage of the last revival lie the clues to the underlying problem of the church and the means by which God will restore the New Testament qualities still lacking in the church today. The revival of the seventies and its painful aftermath did not, therefore, constitute a pointless disaster, but a necessary prelude to the last revival, the revival that will complete the reform of the church.

I am certain that if we try to ignore what happened in the revival of the seventies and the debacle of the eighties, we will wind up repeating the same mistakes all over again. For in the struggles of the seventies and the eighties, we—in particular, we who were leaders in it—repeated some ancient mistakes that most of the church—and in particular, its leaders—decided long ago to ignore and pretend never happened. Worse, they tried hard and almost successfully to convince themselves and those who followed that their sins and mistakes were actually a great victory. The result has been that Christians have been making the same mistakes and committing the same sins ever since.

Of course, we have sins and mistakes of our own to confess. But some of the sins that damaged the revival of the 1970s were ancient errors that we inherited along with the church and reproduced like a kind of hereditary disease without intending or wanting to. That does not excuse us, but it explains a lot. I believe God in His mercy rather than His wrath, allowed us to walk through some ancient ecclesiastical errors in order to reveal to us what they were. He let them become our own so that we could confess them, repent of them and lead the church back to the truth.

I am persuaded that if we will take a long, honest and thoughtful look at the sins and errors of the 1970s and 1980s and at the historic root from which they sprang; if we seek God's grace by prayer, confession and repentance; then we—in particular the leaders—can serve God in the coming revival as a part of the solution instead of the problem. I believe the time has come when God will heal a disease of long standing in His church, and prepare us to face the final conflict at the end of the age with the kind of faith that will issue in victory.

In this book I am reaching out with a word of hope to those who have been hurt and disappointed by the revival of the 1970s. Some of them are still in hiding as I myself was for some seven years. I have thought deeply and prayed long about my own struggles and experiences, and I believe God has given me some answers to my questions about what went wrong, why it went wrong, and how He is going to fix it. And because my own struggles were typical of the church as I found it—and as it largely remains today—the answers God gave me are relevant and important. I dare to say that they are relevant and important, not only to the evangelical and charismatic wing with which I identify, but to the whole professing church of Jesus Christ.

I am also reaching out to our younger brothers and sisters who do not remember the revival of the 1970s. They must learn from us and avoid our errors and sins. For we are standing at the door of a new day. The glory of the Lord is rising on us in the midst of a world of deepening darkness. A revival is coming and now is that will challenge us to the core of our being, but will not disappoint us. For when we walk in the truth, the Lord Jesus Who is the truth (and the life and the way) will be with us to the end of the age. The gospel of the kingdom will be preached with integrity to all nations, and then the end will come.

Robert W. Mears

Laconia, N.H., January 2000

Introduction

A revival is a precious thing, more precious than we know. It is the very presence of God among His people for the purpose of blessing them with the highest and greatest gifts and benefits, including eternal life and the forgiveness of sins. You can't buy the presence of God or any of His blessings. He gives us His Spirit freely. But God doesn't want His presence and His gifts to be undervalued. And one way He makes us appreciate the priceless is to give us a taste of it, awaken our sense of need and desire, and then make us wait for it and pray. He makes us wait until we value His presence supremely, until we treat it as the precious thing it is, until we learn to handle it with respect and care, not waste it or misuse it for our own selfish purposes.

God started a lot of His redemptive work with Abraham. God promised Abraham a son and an heir, but he made Abraham wait a long time for the precious heir through whom He planned to bring salvation to the nations. And while Abraham was waiting patiently and still believing, God taught him many things he needed to know about how to relate to God. For instance, He taught Abraham about trusting God as distinguished from human effort. It's a tricky thing for us flawed humans, but we have to learn it.

Abraham wanted the promised son so badly that he tried to make it happen. It was probably Sarah's idea initially. She knew how much Abraham wanted a son and heir. But Sarah was barren, never had a child. And she was past the age of child bearing. So she offered Abraham her maid, her slave. Abraham accepted the offer and Hagar, Sarah's slave, gave birth to a son, Ishmael. Abraham was his father. It seemed to fit God's promise. It was almost right. But it was Abraham and Sarah trying to make God's promise come true with their own human strength and cleverness. The child caused tensions between Sarah and Hagar, and between Sarah and Abraham.

1

A few years later the son of promise was born. His name was Isaac, meaning laughter. He brought joy to Abraham and Sarah from the time he was born. He was right—God's gift, a miracle baby, and the carrier of the messianic seed through whom God was going to bless the nations. But Ishmael, Hagar's son, hated Isaac, and Sarah feared he would harm her boy. So Hagar and her son, Ishmael, had to leave.

Later God spoke to Abraham about Isaac and called him "your only son." What about Ishmael? God promised to bless Ishmael for Abraham's sake. But he was not the son of promise. There was too much of Abraham in him, too little of God. He was the product of Abraham's human cleverness and strength, and his cleverness and strength overrode Abraham's faith.

What was true of Abraham is true of all of us. We may have faith, genuine saving faith as Abraham did. But faith is a fruit that ripens slowly, and we are clever and strong and impatient. We want to help God along and we try to do His work for Him and hurry up the process. But when we do, we produce Ishmaels instead of Isaacs. They are almost right, but not quite. They cause problems and tensions in the family of God, and in time God has to send them away. They are the result of our own efforts, not God's grace.

So it was with us in the revival of the 1970s. There was too much of our own human cleverness and strength in it. But God's promises remain true. Another revival is already on the scene and will soon sweep the nation. Like Isaac, it will bring us joy.

I believe the next revival will be the last, because with it the reformation of the church will be complete. And the church, at last restored to the character of the New Testament original, will complete its task of proclaiming "this gospel of the kingdom...in all the world as a witness to all the nations," so said Jesus, "and then the end will come."[1]

The next revival will be the last revival because when the reformation of the church is completed and the church has been restored to its New Testament integrity, there will be no need for another revival. This revival will continue until the Lord returns. For what we call revival is simply the normal condition of the church. And when the church is restored to normal, the gospel of the kingdom will be preached with integrity in all the world and the Lord will be with His church even to the end of the age.[2]

The next revival will be the last because it will restore the centerpiece of Christian faith, the unique and distinctive characteristic of Christian faith that sets it apart from all other faiths: the cross. This will not be the ornamental cross with which we are all too familiar, but the redemptive cross with which the early church was familiar, including persecution and martyrdom.

Persecution and martyrdom of Christians are facts all over the world—in Muslim countries like the Sudan and in Marxist countries like China. Soon they will be facts in humanist countries like the United States and Canada that were once known as Christian nations.

Today revival tends to be understood as the impetus to world evangelization, the preaching of the gospel to every tribe and tongue and people and nation.[3] The last revival, then, will finish the task of world evangelization. But I have already alluded to the other side of revivals. They have been the instruments for the reform of the church.

Historically, reform came first. It was not until the reformation of the church had progressed to a considerable extent that believers began to recover the burden to evangelize the world. The goal of reformation is to restore the character and integrity that marked the church at its beginning. The revivals in the history of the church have reformed first one thing and then another that were corrupted or lost, qualities that the church enjoyed in wholeness at the beginning. I am not talking about the restoration of a period piece, complete with robes and sandals, but of the essentials of New Testament faith that characterized the church at its beginning. The last revival, then, will restore the last missing piece. It is that revival, the last, which I believe has already begun.

Both of these goals of revival—world evangelization and church reform—are far advanced and within reach of completion today. This has been said repeatedly about world evangelization. Multitudes of believers are hard at work on that task, much of the resources of the church are now being devoted to it, and it has almost eclipsed the other side of revival: reformation. My plea in this book is that reformation not be neglected. I believe it is essential to the integrity of the gospel and of the church.

That point came sharply into focus for me at a missionary conference at Moody Bible Institute in Chicago in 1959 or 1960. The keynote speaker was Allen Redpath, the Pastor of Moody

3

Church at that time. The tall, white-haired Englishman preached to an audience composed mostly of students at the Institute.

In his crisp English accent, Redpath began in measured tones, "The purpose of this conference is twofold: to recruit personnel and raise money for world missions. But I give you this caveat." Suddenly his face was red with passion and the veins stood out on his forehead. "If that's all we do, if we do not first heal the sickness of the church here at home, the only thing we shall accomplish is to spread the disease all over the world."

The reform of the church and the proclamation of the gospel have to go hand in hand. For the church is designed to exemplify life in the coming kingdom of God. Jesus taught equally by His example and His formal instruction. And often His formal teaching was an explanation of His deeds.[4] The church is called to follow in the footsteps of Jesus.[5] The church is the demonstration unit of the kingdom of God.[6] We don't expect anybody to make a serious investment without seeing some kind of a demonstration. We show the potential investor a working model. The church is intended by God to be a working model of the kingdom of God, to exemplify in its lifestyle the gospel of Jesus Christ and the power of the world to come.

This was what Redpath was driving at. If, for instance, the Gospel of the love of God is proclaimed, but without a community of believers who exemplify that love, the message will be largely misunderstood or discounted. For the words will be interpreted according to the lifestyle of those who profess to believe them. To be intelligible, the Gospel of a reconciling God has to be proclaimed by a company of people who are reconciled to God and with one another. If the message of reconciliation is proclaimed by a company of people who are in competition with one another (quarreling with one another about doctrines and methods, divided by class and race and the bitter political rivalries of this present evil world, and whose leaders are involved in power struggles with one another over money and power) there is an inevitable distortion of the Gospel, even if every theological *i* is properly dotted and every *t* is correctly crossed.

And if the gospel of a crucified Messiah is preached by a company of people who are quite comfortable and at home in this world, whose hopes are wedded to the world that now is, and who get along very well in the same evil age and the same corrupt world that crucified Jesus, the message will be misunderstood. Even if the gospel story is told accurately, it will seem unreal. The message may be entertaining and engaging, but if the audience witnesses a scene that is thrilling and dangerous, but does so from a vantage point of comfort and safety; and if those who tell the tale are not themselves in any danger, the whole scene is theatrical. Those who tell it are in the character of actors and actresses rather than apostles and prophets. This too is a distortion of the gospel, and a dangerous one, considering what Jesus had to say about playactors, that is, hypocrites. Jesus had nicer things to say about prostitutes than hypocrites.

I hope it will be clear that I am speaking in love. I do not wish to be judgmental, to put the church down, or to make any claim to moral and spiritual superiority. But I am obliged to say that the integrity of the church is seriously compromised today. For our lifestyle is out of character with the message we preach. In other words, church reform has not kept pace with world evangelization.

I am a part of the church and I am seeking and praying for a revival because I belong to the church and care about it. What I write here, I write with the hope of blessing the church, and of benefiting myself as a member of the church. If I can use an Old Testament analogy, Joshua and Caleb didn't enter into the Promised Land by themselves. They had to wait until all Israel was ready and a generation arose that dared to believe God. We need one another, like stones in the same temple[7] or sheep in the same flock[8] or parts of the same body.[9] We must together constitute the generation that will go into the promised land. When we do, we have the assurance from the Lord that He will never leave us or forsake us. Nevertheless, the church must change.

Precisely because I love the church, I intend to tell her the truth. In the pages to come I will exhibit some representative pictures of the faith as it was proclaimed by Jesus and the apostles, and lived by the church in New Testament times. The disparity between the church as it appears in the New Testament and the church as we experience it today will be clear. I will trace the decline of the church from its New Testament integrity to the source of its decline, or at least to the establishment and institutionalization of the decline, in the silent revolution that occurred in the fourth century. I will show how that revolution in church history has continued to affect the church to this day, for that radical plunge into compromise with the present world was not touched by the Protestant Reformation. I will indicate the way by which the Lord has promised in the New Testament to recover the church's integrity and return her to the image of the New Testament original. And finally, I will try to show what we can do to establish a more normal relationship to the world and the state (normal, that is, from a New Testament perspective).

The change has been in process for a long time. The illusion of Christian states, nations and civilizations has been exposed and repudiated by Christians, non-Christians and anti-Christians. The attempt to Christianize the devil's world has proved an impossible task, and profoundly disappointing from whatever angle one looks at it. For more than a generation the death of Christian civilization has been generally acknowledged as fact. Today it has reached critical mass. An explosion of persecution can be expected in the near future. All that is needed is an incident to detonate it.

This changed relationship to state and society is one we will find threatening, dangerous, and offensive enough to cause many to abandon the faith. We must be prepared for it. The temptation we shall face as Christians is to distance ourselves from persecuted believers, melt into the anonymity of the crowd and disappear, like the "disciples" who objected to the "hard sayings" of Jesus and walked with him no longer.[10]

Jesus established the criteria for His disciples when He said, "If anyone desires to come after Me, let him deny himself, and take up his cross daily, and follow Me, For whoever desires to save his life will lose it, but whoever loses his life for My sake will save it."[11] In other words, the call of Jesus was a call to martyrdom. It will be heard in days to come in the plain, literal sense in which it was heard and understood in the first century. That call will be proclaimed in all the nations, including the United States.

America was discovered as the period of reformation began, has been the scene of many revivals, the location of much of the work of church reform and an important base for world evangelization. I believe it will be the scene of the completion of the church's reformation, and a launching pad for the fulfillment of the Great Commission.

The revivals of history have been well chronicled. So I will not deal with most of them. I will discuss the revival of the seventies because I know it, and through it stumbled across an ancient sin that is still established and dominant in most churches. In addition, I will highlight three key revivals that came at the beginning of the

6

period of reform and restoration, and indicated the goal toward which authentic revivals move and the principles on which they proceed. My focus will be not so much on what has already been accomplished in past revivals, although that is much and significant, but on the last missing piece, the part remaining to be restored to the church in the next and last revival. I believe God is now ready to confront the issue that established and confirmed, if it did not exactly cause, the church's decline in the first place. It is the last issue to be addressed in the long process of reformation, and the least understood.

P.S. In spite of my best intentions and efforts, some of the material in this book gets a little technical and detailed. Some of the situations I address are complicated, and I had to put in enough facts and details to make the argument clear and to demonstrate the validity of the conclusions. A little extra effort and study may prove rewarding. But I think the book can be read with profit without dealing with all the details. So if you get bored or confused with a chapter or a section, skim it or skip it and go on to the next. You can come back to it later. Some of my readers will need the details, some won't. They are there if and when you need them.

1

Revival And Debacle

The classic description of revival was put so well by James Burns that I will not try to improve on it, but quote him. In 1909 Burns wrote,

> In the history or religion, no phenomenon is more apparent than the recurrence of revivals. At certain intervals there sweeps over certain districts a passion of repentance. Large numbers of persons who have been dead or indifferent to spiritual realities then become intensely awakened to them. They are arrested in the midst of their worldly occupations; they are suddenly seized by a terror of wrong-doing, and fear as of an impending doom haunts their minds. Flinging all else aside they earnestly seek a way of escape, and cry out for salvation.

> These movements, when once begun, are found to spread with amazing rapidity. They pervade the atmosphere like a contagion, and burst out in unexpected places as if carried by unseen hands. They often produce phenomena of the strangest character, and awaken forces at other times quiescent, or too faint to be recognized.

> Frequently these movements are local and limited in their area, but sometimes they sweep over whole peoples, and produce the most momentous results.[1]

In the early 1970s we experienced a revival. It began on the West Coast, rapidly spread across the country and reached the East

Coast in 1971. There were cover stories on the Jesus movement in LOOK, TIME, and LIFE magazines. The revival was fresh and innocent. Gospel songs like "Amazing Grace" made it to the top of the charts in pop music. The whole world was singing, "Put your hand in the hand of the man from Galilee." And everybody became acquainted with a Sunday School song, "Jesus loves the little children of the world." It was a New Testament revival: counter-cultural, announcing the second coming of Jesus, reaching out to others with the gospel, and characterized by the love the converts had for God and for one another.

Young people who had left home, hitch-hiked across the country, and had become involved in drugs and risky sex, were met on the streets by young evangelists who offered them hope, faith and love through Jesus. Christian coffee houses sprang up everywhere, like "His Place," operated by Arthur Blessitt on the Sunset Strip in Hollywood, where the young people could have a sandwich and a cup of coffee while they listened to Christian music and heard the word of God preached in a way that made sense to them.

There were Christian communities like the Lighthouse Ranch in Eureka, California. There Jim Durkin and his staff of fervent young Christians—formerly pill-popping, pot-smoking hippies, and still wearing long hair, flannel shirts and bell-bottom jeans—offered the young wanderers a primitive shelter and nourishing food for three days while they made up their minds whether they wanted to follow Jesus or not. If a visitor decided to become a disciple and join the community, he or she learned a job, studied the Bible, and shared the gospel with other young people on the streets. Soon teams of young believers were trained and sent out to preach the gospel and start churches in other places. Sometimes whole hippie communes became Christian community houses almost overnight as the college-age young people turned from pot and illicit sex to Jesus and a strict Christian morality.

The revival found a more conventional expression in the charismatic renewal which reached an older and more conservative generation. The Spirit of God broke into main-line denominations and made dedicated and enthusiastic Christians out of many people who had previously been among the lukewarm or indifferent church members or who had stopped attending church services altogether.

We had both kinds of converts in the church that formed in our community in the Lakes Region of New Hampshire. There were a lot of young Jesus people. In a period of two or three months, my family and I left the traditional Baptist church of which I had been Pastor and my wife and I became overseers of a Christian community house in a nearby city. A Christian business woman who had been renewed by an experience with the Holy Spirit, felt directed by God to offer us the use of her big old farmhouse for a "Jesus People's church." Soon it was full of young people eager to learn about God. We became part of a church that was experiencing a spiritual renewal. In that church there were a number of older believers who had recently been touched by the charismatic renewal. Ours was one of dozens of churches in New England that sprang up with the revival in the early to mid-seventies, like wheat fields after a warm spring rain.

In 1975 several of the men from our church attended the Shepherd's Conference in Kansas City. It was convened by an association of charismatic teachers with national ministries. They felt led by the Holy Spirit to join together as a means of providing accountability and mutual help for themselves and their ministries, as well as taking a step toward unity in the body of Christ. The national leaders were Bob Mumford, Derek Prince, Charles Simpson, Don Basham and Ern Baxter. They all took on disciples and formed hierarchies that were linked together by the partnership of the five leaders. Originally, the headquarters of the new association were located in Fort Lauderdale, Florida where "New Wine" magazine was published. The magazine presented the vision for the association and the latest teachings.

The shepherding movement was an attempt to bring some cohesion and order to the revival, to conserve its fruits, and to make of the disorganized mass of converts something like a disciplined army. The Kansas City conference was a gathering of men—leaders and potential leaders—and we had the sense that this was an historic event, and that this meeting represented a movement capable of changing history. At one point in the conference, Ern Baxter led the thousands of men assembled in the auditorium in a thunderous shout that reverberated through the hall, "Jesus Christ is Lord! Jesus Christ is Lord! Jesus Christ is Lord!" It reminded me of film clips I had seen of the Nuremberg rallies of the NAZI party in Germany during the Hitler years. "Today Germany," they said in the 1930s and 40s, "tomorrow the world!" Hitler came close to conquering the world. And I thought, *what the Nazis did in Germany for evil, the Christian revival will do in the United States for good.* It was a dangerous thought, a temptation, but I didn't know it at the time, and so it did not even occur to me to resist it.

At the conference we gathered in groups according to the regions we came from. We met fellow believers from New England and the Northeast, and after the conference we began to meet periodically. The Northeast Elders provided wonderful fellowship, encouragement and practical help. But all was not well with the shepherding movement.

There was a national reaction against the new movement after the Kansas City conference. There were concerns about an unbiblical authoritarianism that troubled many. Some said that those who were designated "shepherds" and collected tithes from their "sheep" or disciples, were taking advantage of people and depriving them of the normal decision-making that was their right and responsibility. It was said that the shepherds were taking the place of Jesus in the life of believers. We began to hear horror stories of the abuse of authority and the misdirection of trusting disciples, some of whom received and acted on counsel contrary to their own consciences and convictions. Our own church pulled out of the movement a year later. A couple of our leaders were counseled by someone in the hierarchy who attempted a diagnosis of our church and prescribed a harsh remedy from thousands of miles away. His counsel was based on hearsay and intuition. It was clear to us that he didn't know what he was talking about.

The fellowship of leaders in the Northeast region grew and prospered. I became the coordinator, planned meetings and sent invitations and newsletters. Some of the concepts of the shepherding movement continued to influence us. We were preoccupied with our ministries. We heard and preached hundreds of messages on what we called the equipping ministries, as listed in Ephesians chapter four, of apostles, prophets, evangelists, pastors and teachers, to equip the church for its work of service. We thought God was as fascinated with our leadership as we were. It was in fact our time of temptation like that of Jesus.

After He received the Holy Spirit, the Lord was led by the Spirit into the wilderness to be tempted by the devil.[2] It is uncanny how our temptations followed the course of the temptations Jesus faced. The issue was, now that you have received the Holy Spirit, what will you do about this wonderful source of power? Will you use it to do the will of God, or to satisfy yourself?

First, the Lord was faced with the temptation of bread. He was hungry from fasting. The devil suggested that Jesus use the power of the Holy Spirit to satisfy his hunger, to meet the needs of his body by turning stones into loaves of bread miraculously. The leaders of the revival of the 1970s also faced the temptation of bread, the temptation to use the power of the Holy Spirit to create bread and all that it symbolizes—the satisfaction of material needs. Some succumbed to that temptation For instance, there was the teaching that Christians are king's kids, that they ought to travel first class and enjoy the very best. That attitude led to extravagance, waste, the misappropriation of funds, and to absurdities like solid gold bathroom fixtures for one prominent minister and an air-conditioned doghouse for the pet of another.

The second temptation of Jesus was to throw himself down from the pinnacle of the temple. Why? Because God had promised in the Bible to protect His servants. Jesus should use that text to protect Himself from the consequences of taking a risk that God had not commanded Him to take. The leaders of the 1970s faced a similar temptation. All they had to do was "name it and claim it," that is, quote a biblical promise, believe it, and God would certainly fulfill it, was in fact obligated to fulfill it.

Finally, there was the temptation of power. The devil showed Jesus the kingdoms of the world and all of their glory. He promised to give them to Jesus if the Lord would only worship him, the devil. That was the temptation we faced in the shepherding movement. We felt that we had the power to take the kingdoms of the world. Oh yes, we would be taking them for Jesus. But we didn't consider the corrupting influence of the world's power or the compromises it involves that result in serving not God but the devil. Three years later we saw where that course could take a man.

One of the most sensational news stories of the decade concerned a minister who succumbed to the temptation of power. It was front page news over the Thanksgiving weekend in 1978. An American Pastor, Jim Jones, had became a Marxist demagogue. Accused of exploiting his followers, Jones was being investigated by a U.S. Congressman. Under that pressure Jones led more than three hundred followers in a mass suicide in their Guiana colony. Jim Jones began as a Christian minister with a remarkable gift. But he misused his authority, exalted himself and exploited his people. In Jonestown (the colony he founded in Guiana) his word was law and his people were ready to lay down their lives for him. The unfolding story of a deadly "communion" service of grape Kool-Aid mixed with cyanide, sent shock-waves through the world. Terms like *cult* and *cult leader* became familiar to everyone. The story raised chilling fears and suspicions in regard to religion, particularly any religion that made serious demands on its members or featured a strong and charismatic leader.

The media spotlights were trained on religious leaders. Concerned parents hired "de-programmers" to kidnap their children who had become involved in church and religious groups that were suspected of exercising an unhealthy influence on their converts. The de-programmers subjected the young people to a kind of "brain-washing" to counteract the indoctrination they had received.

In the 1980s it was clear to everyone that the revival had turned sour. The images from that era tell the story: Jim Bakker, the head of the PTL (Praise the Lord) network, leaving the courtroom and getting into the vehicle that would take him to prison for fraud and misappropriation of funds; Jimmy Swaggart's tear-streaked face, and his confession, "I have sinned," on national television. His story included a competitive struggle with other TV preachers he helped to topple, and his own fall in a scandal involving a prostitute and his personal addiction to the pornography he denounced publicly.[3] Televangelist Pat Robertson's 1988 presidential campaign collapsed in the South where he expected to win, a sign of the eroding public confidence in ministers of Christ. Televangelist Oral Roberts became the source of jokes on late-night television for announcing to his viewers that if he didn't raise the money to complete a certain project at Oral Roberts University, God was going to take him home; that is, he would die.

These were the prominent ministries, but the same thing happened throughout the body of Christ. Where there were character weaknesses among leaders, they came to the surface. Greed, lust, and ambition were exposed. As with Moses, David, and Peter, God did not protect His leaders from public humiliation but exposed their weaknesses and sins. Ministers were caught in moral lapses, financial indiscretions, and selfish ambition. These weaknesses and failures led to power struggles, doctrinal and procedural disputes and church splits. The revival of the 1970s gave way to the debacle of the 1980s.

As one of the founders and leaders of a church that was born in the revival and experienced the debacle, I struggled with the questions: Why? What happened? How was the revival derailed, a revival that seemed destined to restore the New Testament church? My answer must begin with myself. I was allured by power. I understand the temptation of a vision of the kingdoms of this world and their glory, a temptation peculiar to leaders. And the gifts of the Holy Spirit that God gave me to serve Him as a minister of Jesus Christ, gave me an ability to grasp and make use of power.

I could write and speak, and as a local elder and a coordinator of a gathering of elders in the Northeast, I had the opportunity to do so regularly. I remembered the auditorium in Kansas City filled with men—all of them leaders and potential leaders—and I knew that if they could ever work together in unity, they would have a decisive influence on the nation. That was the vision of the shepherding movement as Bob Mumford expressed it in his keynote speech. He was well aware of the potential power of the revival movement, not only from a spiritual perspective, but from a political and cultural point of view as well. If all of the people who claimed to be born-again believers could speak with one voice, work together and vote for the same ticket, they would be the decisive force in the nation. The thought was expressed often in the seventies.[4] I myself expressed it frequently. And it was not fantasy, it was a real possibility.[5]

I didn't realize at the time that the vision I wanted and pursued—the vision of power and glory in the present evil world—appeared in the New Testament as a temptation presented to Jesus by the devil, a temptation which He resolutely refused. In common with many, if not most other Christians at the time, I saw it, not as a temptation to be resisted but as a great opportunity to be grasped.

In the pursuit of that vision and in trying to grasp that opportunity, I became involved in exalting myself and my ministry. Consequently, I found myself locked in power struggles with other leaders who had similar ambitions and similar visions.

15

But I knew the New Testament. Why didn't I recognize the obvious? Why did I see a temptation to sin as an opportunity for service? Why the blind spot? Richard Wurmbrand pointed to the answer to those questions. He suffered unspeakable things as a Christian prisoner in Rumania during the Communist era. After fourteen years he was released and came to the United States in the 1960s. He was grieved to find church leaders in the West who compromised with communism but he resisted the temptation to blame them. "The evil comes not from them," he wrote. "It is much older. These leaders are themselves the victims of a much older evil. They did not create the mess in the Church. They found it...."[6] Wurmbrand found the answer to my questions in the "underground church" he represented. He said that the persecuted churches were "like the church of the first centuries."[7]

The difference between the early church as it appears in the New Testament and the church as we see it today has been noted again and again. It is a familiar theme throughout most of church history. But what specifically is the difference? Even as a new convert in the mid-1950s, I noticed three major differences. First, the early church had miracles; we didn't. Second, the early believers loved one another; we didn't. Third, the early church was persecuted; we weren't.

I belong to the evangelical Protestant wing of the church. I use the term evangelical broadly to include all who look to the Bible as their authority and seek to proclaim the Gospel of Jesus Christ. One distinctive feature of evangelical Christianity is revival. I often heard the early church set forth as the standard by which to measure our present churches. And I heard many calls for revival with the hope of purifying what was corrupted or restoring to the church today the lost characteristics of the early church.

There have always been groups within the evangelical tradition that have sought to restore the miraculous to the church. The Pentecostals and Charismatics are modern representatives. Most evangelicals have sought to restore brotherly love. The Methodists carried that banner for generations. But it is not characteristic of evangelicalism as I have known it, in spite of its commitment to the New Testament, to expect that a revival in our churches would result in persecution for us today as it did for the early church. I have got the impression over the years that the whole subject of persecution is one evangelicals prefer to avoid. I can understand that; nobody wants to suffer. But persecution is so crucial a feature of New Testament Christianity, that to overlook it or explain it away is to misunderstand the faith in its central and distinctive feature: the cross.

I always figured there was a connection between the miracles, the love and the persecution the early church experienced. In the history of the church they all faded away together at about the same time. And I have always thought that a thoroughgoing reform and revival would restore all three characteristics of the early church.

The main difference between the early church and our modern churches is obvious. In New Testament times the offense of Christ and of the cross was so glaringly obvious that nobody could miss it. Those who confessed that Jesus was the Messiah, the chosen heir to the throne of King David, were expelled from the synagogues in disgrace.[8] To join Jesus and His disciples was to expose oneself to persecution, including conflicts within one's own family.[9] Judean leaders condemned Jesus and stoned Stephen to death. As to the Apostle Paul, the Jews declared themselves quite clearly: "Away with such a fellow from the earth, for he is not fit to live!"[10] Those who confessed Jesus as the Messiah were considered enemies of God and subversive of established authority.[11] They were not in a position of power in their society, and it was not their intention to try to grasp it. They expected persecution in this world and power and glory in the next.

The apostles were arrested and brought before the Sanhedrin for preaching Jesus as the Messiah. They were jailed, threatened and beaten by the authorities. Scripture says, "So they departed from the presence of the council, rejoicing that they were counted worthy to suffer shame for His name. And daily in the temple, and in every house, they did not cease teaching and preaching Jesus as the Christ."[12]

The early Christians had an attitude toward suffering that we often celebrate but do not share. They rejoiced. Why? They had been counted worthy to suffer shame for His name. If we are not suffering for the name of Jesus, we must ask ourselves, why not? According to the text, the probable reason is that we are not worthy. Why not?

The answer from an evangelical point of view has to be this: our revivals and reforms have not gone far enough. They have not yet taken us to the cross. We want to exercise power in this world.

And so, more or less consciously, more or less deliberately, we have stopped short of a revival that would restore the New Testament church.

In the next and last revival, things will be different. The church is going to recover her first love.

2

First Love

The last revival will be a New Testament revival, one that will restore the kind of vibrant, dynamic faithfulness unto death that characterized the church at its inception. For this reason the New Testament church has a claim on every believer.

The term revival carries with it as an essential element, the idea of a restoration of the faith and fellowship of the church at its beginning. Typically, revivalists compare the condition of the contemporary church with that of the church as it appears in the New Testament, and call on the people to repent and return to the faith, hope, love, unity, zeal, and commitment of the early church. This is as it should be.

The New Testament church was not perfect, but it was, and I believe it was intended by God to be, exemplary. The attempt to portray the early church as primitive, as if it needed some kind of evolutionary development to reach its ideal form and effectiveness at some later time; or infantile, as if it needed to grow up before it reached maturity and the fullness of power and grace at some later point in its history, simply doesn't work. Church history doesn't read that way. There is no point in the history of the church when it exhibited more clearly the comprehensive grasp of truth, the winsome grace, the awesome presence of God, the miraculous power, love and unity that it had at the beginning. And every genuine revival, whether implicitly or explicitly, is an attempt to restore to the church one or another feature that the early church already exhibited at the beginning and then was lost somewhere in the course of its journey.

The well known story of Thomas Aquinas when he visited the Vatican illustrates the point. The great schoolman was taken on a tour by a dignitary of the church, who showed him the wealth and treasures in the Vatican vaults, and remarked, "You see, Thomas, no longer need the Church say, 'Gold and silver have I none.'"

"True," Aquinas retorted, "but neither can she say to the cripple, 'In the name of Jesus Christ, stand up and walk!'"[1]

The church has been richer, more comfortable, and more prominent in the world than it was at the beginning; it has never been as holy. And that is why the goal of every genuine revival is the restoration of the church to what it was at the beginning. The Lord had to make this emphasis early in church history at the end of the New Testament era late in the first century.

The letter to the church of Ephesus in the book of Revelation reveals a zealous church, a church that was doing a lot of things right. But the Lord Jesus had something against that church. And that something was serious in His sight. This church had already begun to drift from its first love and its original commitment. That was serious enough that the Lord Jesus threatened to remove that church's lamp stand from its place if the church did not return to its first love. The lamp stand in the prophecy represents the church.[2] The Lord said that the church would be removed from its place unless it repented and did the first works.

What then is this first love? In personal terms, first love is the pure and all-consuming love of the newly converted believer. It is a love that glimpses the Lord and sees Him as he is: worthy of the soul's complete devotion. It is a simple and innocent love without reservations. It is a devotion to death akin to that of the Lord Jesus Himself during His time of humiliation here on earth at His first coming. "He humbled Himself and became obedient to the point of death, even the death of the cross." So says that wonderful passage in Philippians 2.[3] It is introduced by the words, "Let this mind be in you which was also in Christ Jesus..." So it was not only the attitude of the Lord Jesus, but it is the proper attitude of every Christian, too.

There is, I believe, a moment in the life of every believer when one sees the Lord as He really is. And the believer offers the Lord God one's whole heart in that moment. It is a moment like that in which a young man and woman fall in love. When love is true they speak words of promise to each other from their hearts. They use words like *forever*. They give and want to give everything for the sake of their love. No sacrifice is too great. No suffering is too hard. The beloved is worth whatever labor must be extended, whatever sacrifice must be made to keep that relationship of love inviolate, to have and to hold the beloved for as long as they both live.

But romantic love is only an analogy. Freud wanted to reduce devotion to God to an idealized sexual urge. The opposite is true. The sexual urge at its highest and purest is only a dim likeness of the love of the awakened heart for God.

First love comes at the moment of conversion and commitment. And whenever that moment occurs, that is the moment of the soul's first love. It is a moment of insight, of understanding, of pure worship, of truth and commitment. The believer sees the Lord as He really is and falls in love with Him. The soul responds to the embrace of God, and makes its commitment until death, even if death comes with suffering and alienation.

The first love commitment has to do with the rest of one's life. Implicit in it is a promise that pertains to the future. It does not refer only to how one feels now. It has to do with how one will behave tomorrow and the next day and forever. We have seen something, and because we have seen it and embraced it, we have been changed forever. We have discovered a treasure and we will not rest until we possess it.

Is the emotional intensity of that moment of conversion capable of being sustained for a whole lifetime? If human love is a valid analogy, then the answer is no. The initial passion and vision fade at times and may lose intensity when the convert takes on the practical responsibilities of life. But the passing of time and the involvement in practical duties do not mean that the vision is no longer true or the love is no longer real. First love is the birth of hope which is never fulfilled in this life. But neither is it forgotten. It remains as a fixed point, like the north star, a reference point for the whole of one's life thereafter. A navigator charts his course by the north star, even though he doesn't expect to reach it. The covenant is a covenant of promise. It assures us of what will one day be, and that hope is the star that keeps us on course.

In a marriage the covenant leads to faithfulness to the promises a man and woman make to each other. That is the reason for the marriage covenant, the vows, and the promises. The covenant confirms and validates the first love and preserves it for as long as both partners live.

When he was in a NAZI prison during World War II, the German theologian Dietrich Bonhoeffer wrote a wedding sermon for his niece. In it he gave his niece and her husband this important counsel: "It is not your love that sustains the marriage, but the marriage that sustains your love."[4] It is true of human romantic love. It is also true of the romance of the soul with Christ. As marriage sustains a couple's first love, so God preserves the believer's first love by a covenant of promise. The covenant assures us of the truth we saw with clarity and embraced with passion at the beginning. For the truth remains valid even when we are not able to see it clearly. The sun shines even on cloudy days, and God is present for us even when we cannot see Him. His covenant promises remain in force. They are given because God knows we must walk by faith and not by sight. The covenant preserves our first love by means of a commitment that embraces all of the future. God provided a covenant to keep our first love inviolate, and to create the atmosphere of trust in which first love can be refreshed and renewed.

Scripture likens marriage to the covenant between God and His people[5] because God makes covenants. It is His way. He makes commitments to His people, confirms them with an oath, and puts them in writing so that His people can have a solid hope and the certainty that they can safely rely on Him.[6] He promises and does not change. And by means of the covenant He establishes the original promise and vision. He keeps the promises He made at the beginning of the relationship, and confirms the first love. He calls us to keep our covenants, too, and as we develop character by keeping our covenant promises our confidence in God grows.[7]

The routines of life, the crises, the trials and struggles, the highs and the lows, the suffering and death, are the means by which the original vision is worked into our souls and blended into every part of our lives like the ingredients in a mixing bowl. As the vision is mixed into our lives, our commitment deepens and godly character is formed.

Yes, our feelings will change. Our circumstances will change. We ourselves will change. But true Christians will not leave their initial commitment or abandon their first love; we will die first. If we slip, we will return. That, indeed, is part of our commitment. For if we change our commitments with the changing circumstances, our lives will be chaotic, like a sailboat without a rudder. It is blown here and there with every change in the wind. The inevitable result will be shipwreck. The covenant is the rudder that keeps us on course in spite of the changes of the winds and tides, in spite of the storms and currents.

Let us remember the covenant, for God surely does. And that covenant will sustain our first love through the changes, the struggles, the troubles and tribulations that arise because of our faith.

God has bound Himself to us by covenant, a kind of contract. He keeps His commitments, and He has committed Himself to those who believe in Him by means of an eternal covenant. In this covenant God has promised to give us "all things that pertain to life and godliness."[8] He has confirmed this covenant of promise by an oath. Jesus died in the act of confirming that covenant of first love and promise, and sealed it with His blood. God has shown us how He values His covenant. In Christ, He was faithful to it even to death. And He has given us assurance that the promise holds even when things get hard, the romance seems to fade, and the excitement is lost in the difficulties of practical problems of life and the troubles that come precisely because of our faith and hope in God and Christ. That is the nature of a covenant or contract.

The covenant assures us God hasn't forgotten. And the covenant reminds us when we forget God. In this way—not only in the hour of revelation or mystical ecstasy, but in the ordinariness and weariness of everyday life, in the times of temptation and persecution, of doubt and the "dark night of the soul"—the first love is preserved. The covenant is the super glue that holds us in the bonds of faith and hope through the tough and discouraging times, so that we stick around and are still on the scene when the times of refreshing and renewal come. For they do come, as surely as trials and temptations come.

There are moments and times of refreshment when the Spirit of God renews our emotional intensity, and we feel again the love as we felt it at first. But the covenant remains even when the emotion fades. Yes, it holds even when we sin, when we fail and are disappointed with ourselves and sometimes with God, and we get discouraged. The covenant holds. The promises are still good. God has sworn and He cannot lie.

What is true for the individual believer is also true for the church and the kingdom. God knows us as individuals, but He also knows us as a collective entity. The church represents the kingdom of God. An individual, an ambassador, for instance, can and often does represent a kingdom. But a kingdom is a collective entity, and is best represented by a collection of people in relationship to their king first of all, and then in relationship to one another. And there are some ways in which only a collective entity can represent God's kingdom. The warning of the risen Lord in the book of Revelation was issued to a church. The call to repentance was made to a church. Jesus sees the church as a body made up of individual parts;[9] it functions something like a team.

God Himself is like that. The Bible tells us that the Father is God,[10] that Jesus Christ is God,[11] and that the Holy Spirit is God.[12] Yet together they make up one God.[13] Marriage makes an individual man and an individual woman into one flesh, a complex unity of two persons joined by God.[14] And the church, too, is a complex unity. Human beings were intended to function together as a society.[15] As the poet John Donne wrote, "No man is an island, entire of himself."[16] We belong to one another as members of the body of Christ. And that belonging is not only true of our relationship to the believers now living on the earth, but applies equally to all those who have gone before. The church spans time and space, and the church too had a beginning and a first love.

We can look back in our personal history to our own first love when we first "saw" the Lord, believed and committed ourselves to Him and His kingdom. But we can also look back as a church to the moment of collective first love when at Pentecost the believers were baptized by the Holy Spirit into one body and became the collective bride-to-be of the Son of God.

When we believe we are baptized into the same body of Christ.[17] We tap into the same stream of love that the church experienced at her beginning when her love was new and she too saw her Lord and how utterly worthy of her love He was. In that day the church collectively loved Jesus and became engaged to Him. And the members of the church loved one another with a new and innocent love.[18] It was the church's first love, and a sign of the coming kingdom of God recognizable by all people.

The New Covenant was announced by the prophet Jeremiah in the Old Testament as a promise to Israel and Judah.[19] It was proclaimed by Jesus, the Mediator of that covenant, at a Passover supper that the Lord shared with his disciples.[20] There He

24

proclaimed the fulfillment of the Passover by His death and the shedding of His own blood for the forgiveness of the sins of all who believe in Him. There He instituted the Lord's supper, the communion which confirmed the New Covenant to those who accepted Jesus as God's Son and Israel's Messiah and king. It was a sign of their union with Jesus as Messiah and with one another as members of His body. It was a collective event representative of the coming kingdom.

The New Covenant revelation is a sort of constitution of the kingdom of God. And the disciples, because of their faith in God's king, Jesus, are a sign of that kingdom. The New Covenant belongs to the future kingdom of God, but it is already in effect. It was put into effect by the death, resurrection and ascension to heaven of Jesus. He took the gift of the Holy Spirit from the Father and bestowed it on the disciples. The Spirit burst into the experience of the believers on the day of Pentecost. The power of the world to come filled the believers gathered in the upper room and they in turn offered it to the Jews gathered in Jerusalem for the feast. Three thousand believed and were baptized. Others joined later.

The New Covenant is Israel's and Judah's contract with God and mediated by the Messiah whose blood sealed and confirmed it. And these disciples represented Israel and Judah in God's sight. The kingdom was theirs because they believed in God's Messiah, the lawful king of Israel and Judah who would unite those two peoples in one.

But the kingdom was not yet established in power and glory on the earth. God intended to take the kingdom to the nations of the world. Meanwhile, as a nation-state, Judah went on its way in unbelief, and those Jews who confessed Jesus as the Messiah, gradually became separated from the main body of their countrymen. They were rejected by their fellow-Jews and called by God out of the main body of Judea, out of the majority. And that was the origin of the church—the *called-out ones.*

Without the institutional power, the official authority, or the coercive force of a state, they nevertheless represented God and His future kingdom, like a political party out of office. They proclaimed the good news that the Messiah had come. They enjoyed already in the present evil world a measure of the blessings and the power of the world to come. And they demonstrated in their fellowship the lifestyle of love and truth that will characterize the future kingdom of God. These Jewish believers were later to discover to their amazement that God welcomed gentiles (non-Jews) into Judah like wild branches grafted into the trunk of a cultivated tree. They became something like naturalized citizens, but more than that, for they became family by a spiritual adoption. And that is how they became heirs of the New Covenant promised to Israel and Judah.

The believers, natural Jews and adopted Jews, became the church, a kind of nation-within-a-nation with a distinct identity but not as yet given the coercive power of a state. For the time had not yet come for them to rule with the Messiah, but only to represent Him and proclaim His kingdom. Nevertheless, with the appearance of the Messianic King, that kingdom already existed, and it was the church's duty to proclaim that it would one day be in power on the earth. The church was to demonstrate the power of the future kingdom by its love, its unity and by its miracles. They were to call people from every nation to repent, believe in Israel's Messiah and become part of that kingdom, truly the kingdom of God. The early church announced the coming of the Messiah, first to suffer for sins and to purify a people who could comprise a righteous society. They also proclaimed His second coming when He would rule and reign over the entire earth. The early church, like its Lord and Head, Jesus, suffered for that kingdom, and rejoiced in the vivid hope of reigning with Him when He returned. That was the task assigned by the Lord to His church, and the early church did it in a remarkable way, an exemplary way.

There is, I believe, an inevitable interest that all believers in Jesus have in the church as it appears in the New Testament and particularly in the book of Acts in which her beginning is recorded. We cannot help being fascinated by and drawn to the early church. For that is where the church started. Her first love is our first love. The love of God we experience is the love of the Holy Spirit that was poured out initially at Pentecost. That outpouring established the bond of peace which we are responsible to maintain. There, we instinctively believe, is the depth and purity of love that is our own birthright as a church.

Pentecost was the moment of the church's first love. As members of the church, that first love is ours as well as theirs, although we are separated by centuries and cultures and languages from those first believers. Across all these barriers, we are brothers and sisters of those early believers in the Lord Jesus. The covenant the church entered into at the beginning is the same covenant into which we enter when we believe in Jesus. And the privileges she enjoyed in those early days likewise belong to us. They are our heritage.

Therefore, the call to recover our first love comes not only to the church in Ephesus in the first century, but to all of us as members of the church of Jesus Christ. It calls us all back to our beginnings. The early church has a claim on us. Her example is compelling.

The church in Ephesus had fallen from its first love. How is the first love lost? It happens when our initial commitment is modified. I think this kind of thing happens almost routinely when a new convert makes a commitment to Jesus Christ, the kind of commitment that new converts understand instinctively by the Holy Spirit is without reservation. And then this person joins a church and finds that the kind of whole-hearted commitment the new convert has made is not required by the church, is not characteristic of church members, and in fact is regarded as strange and unwelcome by leading members. The convert settles into churchly routines, conforms to the church's lower (and easier) standards, and the convert's first love lapses.

Another example is that of a young man called by God to the ministry. He finds that the kind of sacrificial commitment he wants to give to the Lord is not required by the church as he finds it. Instead, there are academic requirements and social duties that are more or less irrelevant to the New Testament but are high priorities for the church. The young minister conforms to the institutional requirements and in time his original commitment to the Lord and His service is lost amid the multitude of mundane tasks required by the church. He is compensated financially but compromised spiritually.

First love is lost by a church when it discovers that the uncomfortable tension between the church and the world in which it lives can be relieved by conforming to and cooperating with the state and society. Instead of representing the future kingdom of God and Christ, the church offers itself and its services to the presently reigning political, cultural, and commercial authorities. The church becomes a partner with the state in governing the society and maintaining peace and order. This new and comfortable alliance with the powers now reigning in this present evil world is then justified by new or modified doctrines, traditions, and policies that are subsequently regarded as "orthodox."

But in truth, men cannot change the character of the church with their theologies. The passage of time does not validate deviations and distortions of the church's character. God does not accept our human revisions of His truth by traditions or teachings that have attached themselves to the church like barnacles to the hull of a ship during its journey.

There was a beginning to the church, a moment when she entered into the New Covenant, a time when her character was revealed for all time. It was the moment of her first love when the New Covenant was implemented in her.

Jude wrote in the first century of the faith that was already "once delivered to the saints."[21] The apostle Paul wrote about the covenant which God made with Abraham, and made the point emphatically that when a covenant is once made, nobody adds to it or takes from it.

The church in her first love is the church we are bound to. The church that is normative for us is not the church of the nineteenth century or the eighteenth century or the sixteenth century or the fourth century. It is the church of the first century, the church as she appears in the New Testament.

I believe the Holy Spirit is calling us as He once called the church in Ephesus, back to our first love, with the warning that, unless we return, the lamp stand will be removed. It is not that religion will cease or that religious institutions will necessarily cease to exist. There is plenty of religion in the area where the church of Ephesus once existed. Today that religion is Islam. The lamp stand of the church of Ephesus was removed. The temptation the church has always faced is to become simply a power of this present evil world instead of a representative of the future kingdom of God. If the church serves this world it comes under the power of one of the principalities in the heavenlies, and in the service of the prince of this world and eventually of the anti-Christ. The churches are being called back to their first love, and that means, back to the kind of love and commitment that characterized the church at its beginning.

In returning to our first love, the Scriptures are crucially important. They contain the original covenant, the common bond that holds us together. No one adds to or takes from a covenant or contract once it is made and sealed.[22] And the New Covenant scriptures are written down. They have been preserved. The word of God is in our hearts, but it is also written in a book, by the design of God. As a result, we know what it says, in spite of the passing of time, the change of circumstances, and the deviations of a compromised church.

The Scriptures have not always been interpreted honestly and applied accurately. But they have, at least, been preserved. And from time to time the Lord has raised up prophets and apostles and teachers and pastors and evangelists who have dared to read the New Testament and interpret it honestly, whatever the cost to them personally. And they have consistently called the church back to her first love and to the covenant that was sealed with the blood of the Son of God and put into effect by the love and power of the Holy Spirit.

God will not be satisfied until we read that covenant honestly and return to our first love. And in our hearts, neither will we.

Let us then resolve to repent and return to our first love, regardless of the cost. That is the goal of every genuine revival. It is a goal that has been fulfilled in increments in the course of history, particularly in the last five hundred years. The next revival, which I believe is the last, will see that goal finally achieved. The church at the end of the age will reflect the character of the church as it was at the beginning.

But what exactly was the character of the church at its beginning? And what can we expect from a New Testament revival? We will address those questions next.

3

What Can We Expect
From A New Testament Revival?

I believe our church experienced a genuine revival. We knew something of the wonderful power that marked the church at its beginning. There were miracles and there was love. But something was missing, for after a while the miracles stopped and the love turned sour. Questions arose and troubled my heart like a throbbing wound. I could not avoid searching for answers. And the Lord supplied them. The prophet Isaiah wrote these words concerning the Messiah, but in a measure, the experiences of the Messiah became his own. And to a degree, they have also become mine.

The Lord GOD has given Me the tongue of the learned, that I should know how to speak a word in season to him who is weary. He awakens Me morning by morning, He awakens My ear to hear as the learned. The Lord GOD has opened My ear; and I was not rebellious, nor did I turn away. I gave My back to those who struck me, and My cheeks to those who plucked out the beard; I did not hide My face from shame and spitting. For the Lord GOD will help Me; therefore I will not be disgraced; therefore I have set My face like a flint, and I know that I will not be ashamed.[1]

The key to the blessings of God comes in the shape of the cross. And without the cross, the blessings, even if they come, do not come in their purity or last for long. The revival we knew was therefore not a full-blown New Testament revival. I believe the revival impending now will be.

What, then, can we expect from a New Testament revival? That is the question I begin to address in this chapter. The answer to that question will bring some surprises, not from any vagueness

31

or confusion in the New Testament, but from the ambiguity of the church as we have inherited it.

What is written here is both well known and unknown. I don't really have anything new to say. I intend to point out the obvious: teachings and behaviors that are on the surface and in the heart of the New Testament. On the other hand, what I have to say is largely unknown. I will be dealing with truths about Jesus, the Gospel, and the church that were perfectly obvious in the first century. Unfortunately, they are anything but obvious in the twentieth. They are truths that have been neglected and obscured by a kind of "gentlemen's agreement" of long standing.

In regard to revival, I will say what most Christians will nod and agree with. I believe the greatest revival in history occurred in Jerusalem in the first century in connection with the appearance of Jesus, the Messiah of Israel, the Son of David and the legitimate heir to his throne, and with the formation of the church. And then I will point out the practical results of that greatest of all revivals. Most Christians know that, too. But Christians who believe in and pray for revival, as I have done for most of my life as a believer, are almost all expecting from revival something that first century revival did not produce. And they are not expecting and do not want some things that first century revival did produce.

What was the impact of that greatest of all revivals on Jerusalem and Judea? We know from the New Testament record that no fewer than 3,000 were converted and baptized on the day of Pentecost alone.[2] There were a hundred and twenty disciples who gathered for prayer prior to that momentous event. Probably there were many more who believed who were not at the prayer meeting. And there were many more who believed after the Pentecostal explosion.

There was an amazing display of the supernatural: miracles of healing, the raising of the dead, an explosion of love and a demonstration of unity among the believers that was astonishing and appealing to those who witnessed it.[3] But among those who believed that Jesus was the Messiah, there was also an awful presence of the holy God that made hypocrisy and sin mortally dangerous. There was great joy among the believers and there was great fear. Unless people were really converted and embraced a life of holiness and truth, they kept their distance, lest they be struck dead for their secret sins as were Ananias and Sapphira. Their story was well known in the city and beyond.[4]

Furthermore, the prominent leaders among the Christians were in and out of jail. The Messianic movement was proclaiming the kingship of a man who was executed because he was regarded by the establishment as a false teacher, a deceiver, and a threat to the nation. The reigning authorities were hostile to the upstart sect. And the people who shaped public opinion defined the new Messianic movement as a cult and dangerous. It was risky for that reason, as well, to belong to it.[5]

What then was the effect of that revival on Jerusalem and Judea? Did the church "take the city" as our contemporary revivalists are telling us we should take our cities for God? Not if taking a city and nation means to convert them. For the city of Jerusalem was not converted, and the nation of Israel did not turn to Jesus.

Jesus marched on Jerusalem accompanied by a crowd of unarmed disciples. He entered the city riding on a young donkey, thereby fulfilling the prophecy of Zechariah concerning the Messiah, the son of David and king of Israel.[6] Jesus made his confession before the Sanhedrin and the Roman Governor Pilate that He was indeed God's chosen Messiah.[7] Pilate posted a sign declaring Him to be king of the Jews, but in his mind it was bitter sarcasm directed at the Jewish leaders and the whole Jewish community.[8]

Jesus was denounced, ridiculed, condemned and crucified. His claim, of course, was rejected by the authorities, but God raised Him from the dead, overruling the decision of the reigning powers. Jesus ascended to the right hand of God and sent the Holy Spirit on the waiting disciples. In the power of the Holy Spirit, Peter and the other apostles declared Jesus to be Lord and Christ on the day of Pentecost.[9] By His obedience unto death the Lord Jesus was given authority by the Father over Jerusalem and Israel. In fact, all authority in heaven and on earth was granted to Him.[10]

Yes, He took the city and the nation. That is what our faith teaches us. It is there in the New Testament for all to read. But He has not to this day claimed the prize He won by His suffering and obedience unto death; neither has He taken control and begun His reign there or anywhere else. That will take place at His second coming and not before.

The revival associated with the outpouring of the Holy Spirit on the day of Pentecost, mighty as it was, did not convert the city of

Jerusalem or the Jewish nation to God and His Son and king. The religious establishment in Judea rejected Jesus. In a mockery of justice, a hastily convened tribunal found Him guilty of being a deceiver, and engineered his crucifixion. When the church refused to let the issue of Jesus as Messiah die with the death of their leader, the authorities persecuted the church. Many believers were driven out of the country. A few church leaders were beaten, incarcerated or put to death. Many believers and confessors were likewise beaten or put in prison.

A great number of Jews, including a few of their leaders, became believers in Jesus. But the revival under Jesus and the first apostles did not turn the Jewish capital or nation to Jesus Christ; it polarized Jewish society. The Judean establishment led the majority of Jews into the rejection of Jesus' Messianic claims. Out of the crisis in Judea precipitated by the Gospel, the church eventually emerged as a distinct society. Believers were hated and persecuted by fellow Jews and many were driven out of Judea and into the nations of the earth where they preached the Gospel to the non-Jewish nations.

In the pagan countries where the Gospel was preached there was a similar result. Some believed. There were many in Corinth, for instance, who were converted to Christ and revealed to be the people of God. There were very few in Athens. Churches were established in Rome, Greece, Macedonia, Spain, and in a number of towns and cities in Galatia and along the coast of Asia in what is now Turkey. Everywhere they went the believers were persecuted. There is not a single example in the New Testament of the conversion of an entire city or town, let alone a nation. Rather, there was a church which was a kind of island of truth and light in the midst of pagan darkness.

A New Testament revival can be expected to produce the same results as in New Testament times; that is, the polarization of society, the emergence of the church as a colony of God's kingdom suspect and unwelcome in the devil's sinful world.

If there was any nation on earth that might be expected to be converted as a nation to the faith as proclaimed by the Messiah of the Jews, it was Judea. And that nation was not converted, even though there is Scriptural basis, in both the Jewish and Christian Scriptures, for hope that such a national conversion of the Jews will one day take place. But I believe it will happen at the second coming of the Messiah when a remnant of the Jews, survivors of a great persecution at the time of the end, will "look upon him whom they pierced and mourn for him as one mourns for an only son."[11] It is evident that the conversion of "all Israel" did not happen at the first coming of the Messiah.

There is no basis in the New Testament for the expectation that any other nation will be converted as a nation prior to the second coming. But our Protestant and evangelical tradition has given us other expectations for the revivals they talk about and pray for. This position is well represented by my good friend, Dr. Richard Lovelace, an evangelical scholar who has written and spoken extensively on revival. He looks back to the revivals of the seventeenth, eighteenth and nineteenth centuries which, in the wake of the Protestant Reformation, dominated the culture and controlled the civilization in which they occurred. He speaks longingly of the days when an evangelical coalition was large enough and influential enough to control practically the whole English speaking world. "In those days, friends," he said once in a conference, "evangelicals owned the store." And he believes it could and should happen again.

It's true. Evangelicals did pretty much run things in those days. It's an alluring and exciting vision. But it is not a New Testament vision. That's why for years, whenever I preached on revival, I always used Old Testament texts. The fact is, I couldn't find anything in the New Testament that supported the kind of revival I was preaching about. I couldn't find it because it isn't there.

The redemptive instrument of God in this age is not the nation-state of Israel or any other nation-state. It is the church, not a state, that represents Jesus Christ in this age. An individual may represent Jesus Christ, or an agency devoted to one or another aspect of the church's work. But such an individual or agency is in reality acting as a part of the church, the body of Christ, whether consciously or not. The chief difference between the church and a state is that a state is empowered to make and enforce laws in the present age. The church represents the future and has not in this age been given the coercive instruments necessary to dominate society and its institutions. The response the church seeks for its message has to be free and cannot be coerced or pressured. The use of threat, torture, lethal force and even the more subtle pressure of cultural domination such as evangelicals have practiced in the past, is counter-productive for the gospel. It does not have the sanction of the New Testament.

35

According to the New Testament, the church is a remnant from every tribe and tongue and people and nation. The New Testament scriptures consistently and without exception contemplate the church as a minority in every nation for as long as this age lasts.[12] The New Testament everywhere presupposes that the church will be a despised and persecuted people, that the way is and in this age will continue to be the narrow way that is taken by a few. That is to say, the church will remain a despised and persecuted minority *if* it remains faithful to the Lord Jesus and walks as He walked.

When the church becomes dominant it can only be because it has compromised itself and exchanged its New Testament purpose and calling for something more compatible with the surrounding world. When that happened, however, the church forfeited her purity and power, and soon lost her love and unity. Revival is God's activity to restore to the church what was lost. In His mercy God has given a measure of His grace and power back to the church in answer to the fervent prayers of many believers. But for reasons which I will address later in this book, the revivals we have experienced up to now have come short of restoring the church to what she was in the New Testament.

It is my firm conviction that an authentic New Testament revival is coming, that it will restore the church to its New Testament integrity and purity, and that many will be converted. But when it happens, the church will no more carry the United States, for instance, into the kingdom of God during this present age than the first century revival carried Judea into the kingdom of God at the beginning of the church age. On New Testament grounds we can expect an authentic New Testament revival to have a significant impact on a city and a nation. But the New Testament leads us to expect that impact to polarize the nation, not to convert it, and that the majority in this age will reject the church and the gospel it proclaims.

I believe we can and will win our cities and our nations for Jesus Christ. But if we are faithful to represent the Lord Jesus accurately, we will do it in the same way Jesus won Jerusalem and Judea. His claim to the throne of Israel will be validated on the day when He returns, for He was faithful unto death to the Father. And the claim we make in His name to our cities and nations will likewise be validated when the Lord returns, if we have been faithful unto death as Jesus was. Those who have suffered with Christ will reign with Him on the earth in that day. But there is nothing in the New Testament to suggest that the church will take charge of cities and nations or shape the dominant culture during this present age. If we follow in the footsteps of Jesus and are faithful to the gospel, we can expect the same results that Jesus and the early church achieved in Jerusalem and Judea and the other nations to which the Gospel came in the early days.

The result we must expect from a New Testament revival is that the church which is faithful to her Lord will be rejected and persecuted by the world. Jesus predicted that His people would be hated and persecuted in all nations as He Himself was hated and persecuted in the land of Judea, his own nation and homeland.[13]

We can also expect that the church which experiences this kind of revival will be approved by God, and filled with the joy of a living hope. And the church will know the witness of the Spirit and of a clear conscience that it is walking in integrity and prepared for the return of her Lord.

Richard Wurmbrand wrote about the underground church in Communist Eastern Europe, "I can never describe the beauty of this Church! Often, after a secret service, Christians are caught and sent to prison. There Christians wear chains with the gladness with which a bride wears a precious jewel received from her beloved. The waters in prison are still. You receive His kiss and His embraces and you would not change places with kings. I have found truly jubilant Christians only in the Bible, in the underground Church and in prison."[14]

His words have the authentic ring of the New Testament. There we are instructed to look to "Jesus, the author and finisher of our faith, who for the joy that was set before Him endured the cross, despising the shame, and has sat down at the right hand of the throne of God."[15]

The early church was filled with the joy of hope to a degree we can hardly imagine today. Clearly, the early believers had something to live for that was worth dying for, something they wouldn't lose by dying. On the contrary, they grasped it by laying down their lives in this world. I believe it is God's intention in the coming revival to restore to the church her blessed hope in the coming kingdom of God, and her powerful witness to that glorious kingdom.

4

Hope And Witness

The historian Edward Gibbon, author of the classic, *THE DECLINE AND FALL OF THE ROMAN EMPIRE,* made this observation on the ancient Christians. They "were animated by a contempt for their present existence and by a just confidence of immortality, of which the doubtful and imperfect faith of modern ages cannot give us any adequate notion." [1] He was referring to the Christian belief in the second coming of Jesus. Gibbon cited this hope as a key reason for the rapid spread of the Christian faith through the Roman Empire in the early days of the church.

The rapid spread of the faith and the growth of the church were two features of what we today call a revival. Gibbon was right in identifying the church's hope as an important feature of that revival and a key cause of the growth of the church. He was also right when he said that the doubtful and imperfect faith of modern ages cannot give us any adequate notion of the importance of hope to the early church.

It is my conviction that a New Testament revival will restore the hope of the New Testament both as to its content and its intensity. For the willingness of the early believers to risk their lives for Jesus and the gospel was directly connected with their hope. They were so sure of the reality of the kingdom of God and the resurrection to eternal life at the coming of the Lord Jesus—and so sure that they had a personal stake in the future kingdom—that they were willing to lay down their lives in this world for Jesus and the gospel. Their hearts were set on a city with foundations that God was preparing for them.[2] It was because of that hope that they became such effective witnesses.

The word for witness in the New Testament Greek is *martyr.* A martyr came to be identified with one who sacrifices his life for a cause he believes in, because so many witnesses lost their lives. The two ideas were brought together by the Christian Church. The lifestyle of the church was one of voluntary suffering and death in the interest of a better world to come. The willingness, and often eagerness, of the early Christian believers to lay down their lives, testifies to the strength of their hope. This was an astonishing disregard for the first law of human nature: self-preservation.

They won a grudging respect from the pagans. And they aroused a tremendous curiosity by their unnatural lifestyle. Doctrine alone would not have done it. There were plenty of interesting and strange religions in the Roman Empire in the early days of the Christian church. There were myths about dying heroes who rose again, following the cyclical pattern of the seasons, the deathlike winter giving way to the new life of spring. Mystery religions grew up around these fictional tales that nevertheless communicated a sort of truth. One could derive a measure of natural encouragement and hope from such myths, some consolation that helped people cope with the frustrations of life. The pagans typically did.

But you didn't find the pagans risking their lives for the sake of those beliefs. You did find Christians doing it for theirs. The Christians had what we would call factual history on their side, for their faith was built on events which they believed were real, historical, and verifiable—particularly the resurrection of Jesus Christ. There were many witnesses who had left credible records of actual conversations with Jesus after His resurrection. Consequently Christians took their faith literally, and with a seriousness that was alien to the easy-going paganism of the day. That was the marked and unmistakable difference between Christianity and paganism, even if both made reference to deaths and resurrections. The Christians had factual documentation for their story, the pagans did not. The Christians were willing to risk their lives for the truth of their beliefs, the pagans were not.

Among themselves, Christians were known for the One they worshipped. They worshipped the one true God of Israel, and His Son, the Anointed One, the Messiah of Israel, Jesus Christ. They believed that Jesus fulfilled many of the prophecies of Scripture that promised a coming Messiah. They believed that Jesus would come again and fulfill all of the Messianic prophecies of Scripture. That was a volatile issue among the Jews. But outside of Judea, the confession that Jesus was the Messiah would not in itself have brought upon the Christians persecution, suffering and martyrdom.

The Christians were known among their pagan neighbors for what they did *not* worship. They absolutely refused to worship any other god than the God and Father of Jesus Christ, their Lord. The pagans, on the other hand, could worship the god of their favorite myths and the gods of other people's favorite myths. And they could worship the emperor, too, or the genius of the emperor. All that was required in connection with emperor worship was the recitation of a short formula and the offering of a handful of grain. It was the ancient equivalent of a loyalty oath. All it meant was that they were loyal to the Roman Empire in which they lived and to the reigning emperor.

The attribution of deity to the emperor did not have to be seriously believed. Some of the Emperors themselves did not take their "deity" seriously. There was no way to test for hypocrisy, anyway, and no real intention to do so. The little ceremony meant something like the affirmation required in the U.S.A. during the "cold war" that one was not part of a conspiracy to overthrow the government by force and violence. The Roman authorities wanted the assurance that their subjects accepted that some divine agency had established the Emperor and the Empire in authority, and that the citizen or resident of the Empire would respect that authority and obey it.

The Christians would not offer that worship. At the risk of their lives, they refused to offer such worship. They were not in fact disloyal; that is, they were not plotting the overthrow of the Empire by force and violence. But they believed the empire was corrupt and that one day Jesus Christ would return and overthrow the Empire and replace it with the kingdom of God. Christians would not worship something corrupt. And they would not attribute deity to a man who wasn't God, who wasn't even righteous from a Christian point of view.

By refusing to give the minimal worship demanded by the Empire, the Christians put their lives at risk. They created an issue and put their lives on the line for the sake of that issue. It was not their worship of Jesus Christ that got them into trouble. It was their refusal to worship anything or anybody else, including the Emperor.

Historian William Ramsay wrote that "Roman Imperial policy...treated religion as a part of the machinery of government", and that "refusal to comply with the prescribed forms of respect to the Emperor was a refusal to be a member of the Roman unity, and constituted disloyalty and treason....Christianity was, under Domitian, treated as treasonable."[3]

By that act of defying a command of the government and refusing to do a patriotic duty, the early Christians became involved in civil disobedience and made targets of themselves. By refusing to offer sacrifice to the Emperor, the Christians were perceived as disloyal to the Empire. Jesus was the Lord, the only Lord and Messiah, the only One established by the one true God. They would worship Him and Him alone. Had they been willing to worship Jesus *and* the other gods, Jesus *and* the emperor, they would have been welcome in pagan Rome. One more god, what did it matter? The pagans already had a pantheon of gods. But the Christians refused to treat the pagan gods or the emperor as equals to Jesus. They would lay down their lives rather than compromise on that point.

That was what they believed, and the Christians were not content to have their faith remain a private matter between themselves and God. They were open and public about their faith. Had they maintained a discreet silence about what they believed, they could have lived in peace. Instead, they intruded their faith into the public square, and debated it in the forums of the ancient world. Those who did not actually preach the gospel, provided help and comfort for those who did. They visited them in prison when they were arrested, provided food when they were hungry, clothing when they were naked, aid, comfort and shelter when they were sick, needy or on the run from the authorities. And so they put themselves at risk equally with the more vocal and public members, as accomplices, and were liable to the same punishment. According to New Testament Scripture, they could also expect the same reward on the day of judgment.[4]

The public, uncompromising and exclusive attitude was characteristic of Christian faith from the beginning until the fourth century. In this context it is understandable why the apostle Peter wrote as he did. "But sanctify the Lord God in your hearts, and always be ready to give a defense to everyone who asks you a reason for the hope that is in you, with meekness and fear; having a good conscience, that when they defame you as evildoers, those who revile your good conduct in Christ may be ashamed. For it is better, if it is the will of God, to suffer for doing good than for doing evil."[5]

The uncompromising behavior and attitude of the early Christians provoked questions from their unbelieving neighbors. Those questions related to the Christians' hope. They suffered for the sake of that hope. They created problems for themselves that they could have avoided by a modest accommodation to the conventions of the surrounding society. But they would not make those accommodations. They insisted on making a witness, that is, maintaining a distinct identity and a public stand. They were different and they magnified their difference. They didn't dress differently or adopt an outlandish lifestyle. But they saw themselves as citizens of the future kingdom, and they conformed to the moral and spiritual principles of that future society. Furthermore, they refused to conform to the immoral and unjust conventions of the earthly society in which they lived. They served another king, Jesus, and by doing so the Christians became aliens in their own lands.

Most people, including the leaders and authorities of the society, reacted with resentment and abuse. The Christians endured the abuse with patience and faith. They refused either to compromise or retaliate. That attracted the attention of the pagans. The more severe the punishment they received, the more the Christians rejoiced in the hope of a better world to come. That puzzled their unbelieving neighbors and provoked questions. In spite of themselves, the unbelievers respected, if not the convictions themselves, at least the courage, constancy and joy with which the Christians held those convictions. Their interest was piqued, their curiosity was aroused, and they asked the Christians questions about their hope.

This was the opportunity the believers had to bear witness to Jesus Christ and to their hope of a better world coming soon. Their witness grew out of their lifestyle. They lived in such a way as to raise questions in the minds of those who saw them. They asked questions, and the Christians answered their questions respectfully and graciously. And so other people were instructed in the faith and some became believers.

While the entire book of 1 Peter relates to the sufferings of believers who were trying to follow in the footsteps of Jesus, one passage should illustrate how the early Christians lived out their faith. Peter exhorted slaves to be submissive to their masters, not only to the good ones, but also to those who are harsh and unjust.

He supported his exhortation this way:

> For this is commendable, if because of conscience toward God one endures grief, suffering wrongfully. For what credit is it if, when you are beaten for your faults, you take it patiently? But when you do good and suffer, if you take it patiently, this is commendable before God. For to this you were called, because Christ also suffered for us, leaving us an example, that you should follow His steps.[6]

It was the element of unjust suffering that raised questions. Nobody wants to suffer. People endure it if they have to. But the suffering of the Christians was voluntary. It was avoidable. It was not imposed because of the faults and sins of the Christians or because of their ancestry, over which nobody has any control. They were innocent. And they were Christians by choice. All they had to do was not confess Jesus Christ and conform to the unbelieving society in which they lived, and they could easily have avoided persecution.

But they had a hope. Hope was elevated to a preeminent doctrine in the early church. Even the well known passage about faith in the eleventh chapter of the book of Hebrews, defines faith as "the substance of things hoped for, the evidence of things not seen."[7] It was faith about the future, or hope. It was a promise that had not yet been fulfilled, and hence, not seen. The early Christians laid hold of that promise and hope and they were able to let go of this present evil world. For the sake of that hope they gladly endured suffering, persecution, and martyrdom. It was this willingness of the early Christians to suffer for their hope that raised questions in the minds of their unbelieving friends and neighbors and opened up an opportunity for the Christians to bear witness.

The lifestyle and convictions of Christians here in the U.S. today doesn't usually raise questions in the minds of their unbelieving neighbors. Today's Christians typically don't have a costly issue for which they are willing to suffer and die. There is no clear and obvious point on which believers refuse to compromise. There is nothing about their faith that makes Christians seem in any sense like aliens to their worldly neighbors. There is little in their lives that is all that different from other people who live for the pleasures and goals of this present world. There is little, therefore, that points unambiguously to a hope in the coming kingdom of

God. There isn't much of anything that needs explanation. And so there isn't much in the contemporary scene that corresponds to the witness made by the early Christians in the first three hundred years of the faith. Our witness today does not have the meaning it had in those early days when witness and martyr were equivalent terms, when one put one's life on the line to make that witness. This is a serious matter.

Luther made a distinction between a *profession* and a *confession* of faith. He said, "If I teach every article of Christian faith except precisely that article that the world and the devil are now attacking, I am not *confessing* Christ, however loudly I may be *professing* Him." It is an accurate distinction. In a confession of Christ there is the element of risk and danger that is missing in a mere profession.

It is a serious matter because salvation is connected to the confession of faith in Christ, and not to a mere profession. The apostle Paul wrote, "that if you confess with your mouth the Lord Jesus and believe in your heart that God has raised Him from the dead, you will be saved."[7]

In the New Testament there were many who heard Jesus speak and were said to believe in him, but it was clear that their faith was tentative; Jesus did not accept it at face value. For instance, the Gospel of John records that "many believed in His name when they saw the signs which He did. But Jesus did not commit Himself to them, because He knew all men, and had no need that anyone should testify of man, for He knew what was in man."[8] The Lord could easily discern the difference between a profession and confession of faith in Him. A key part of His evangelistic ministry was to confront those who had "believed" in Him with the costly and dangerous call to confess Him.

The idea of confession goes beyond religious opinions about doctrine. There is a passion that marks a true confession of Christian faith. A true witness not only believes something, but resolutely refuses to believe something contradictory. The true witness not only worships the living God, but absolutely rejects false worship. The witness discerns false worship and stands against it even if that false worship is supported by social custom and law and all that the world calls holy, even if the false worship is supported by legal sanctions, yes, even if refusal to worship it carries the death penalty.

The element of risk is essential to witness. If one may *profess* faith in Christ without putting one's life at risk, one cannot *confess* Christ without risk. True faith in Jesus is a commitment unto death. One's life may not be required immediately, but it must be offered up with sincerity and with the understanding that the appointed time may come at any moment when it will be required. That, it seems to me, is essential to the New Testament idea of a saving confession of faith. For Jesus surely calls every believer to take up his cross and follow Him. As Dietrich Bonhoeffer said, "When Jesus Christ calls a man, he bids him come and die."[9]

The emergence of the NAZI state in Germany during Bonhoeffer's lifetime brought that truth to light in a sudden and shocking way. Most German Christians in the NAZI era were unprepared to face a New Testament situation in which faith in Jesus Christ put one's life in jeopardy. We must not allow ourselves to be caught off guard when a similar situation arises in our times and in the United States. Too much is at stake. Furthermore, we have been warned by what happened in German history.

When something similar happens here, we must be prepared not only to profess Christ, but to confess Him, and with the confession of faith in Jesus to renounce all that is contrary to Him. Surely in a society as corrupt as that of the United States today there is a witness to Jesus Christ to be made by believers, something to believe, and something to reject and disbelieve. I have thought of a few issues that might involve risk and danger for any believer who might speak out as a witness to Jesus.

1. Abortion. Christians have been arrested, subjected to police brutality, fined, sued, and jailed for holding sit-ins or "rescues" at abortion clinics. In the 1980s I led a number of protest demonstrations and was arrested once in a sit-in, found guilty of trespassing and fined. For a year I was a kind of outlaw, because I refused to pay the fine. I was not sent to jail but that possibility was always present. It was my first experience of being on the wrong side of the "law" because of my Christian convictions. I engaged in an ongoing public debate and was subjected to ridicule in a local paper. During that time I was given an understanding of the New Testament I had never had before. I experienced in a small way the tension with the state and society that the early Christians lived with continually.

46

2. Lawlessness in society and government. The chief accomplishment of the Pro-Life movement was to keep the issue before the public and force the politicians to take a stand. It was not something they wanted to do. Who, after all, wants to come out in favor of declaring open season on unborn human beings? But politicians found that they could represent the murderous procedure as a facet of liberty and women's rights, could vote for abortion and still get elected. In fact, abortion emerged as the cornerstone of the feminist movement, and more often than not, the militant feminists were successful in electing candidates who supported their agenda.

As politicians learned that they could tap into the coalition of the lawless and succeed politically there was less and less reason to pretend to Christian values. Soon even the appearance of government-by-law will erode away. The checks and balances of our constitutional system will be gone. To address this issue, particularly after the impeachment of President Bill Clinton ended in failure to remove him from office, will be an exercise in futility. Not only will it fail politically, it may be dangerous. But the church has a prophetic (as distinct from political) duty to speak the truth. What is required is faithfulness, not success. In the near future faithfulness in addressing the issue of governmental lawlessness may be life-threatening. One can be a professing Christian and not handle that hot potato. To confess faith in Jesus Christ involves denouncing evil.

3. Homosexuality. The activist homosexual community is determined, apparently well financed and influential. Homosexuals and lesbians have pretty much succeeded in getting their perversion accepted as an "alternate lifestyle." It is not an interest of Christians to try to deprive homosexuals of civil rights. If the state and society choose to grant them equal rights, or even a species of affirmative action to compensate them for past "discrimination," that is their business, and they will be accountable to God for their decisions. But it is the church's business to keep itself clean. And it is unacceptable to allow an unrepentant homosexual to become a member of a Christian church or to serve as a minister in a Christian church. Homosexuals regard that as discrimination and a deprivation of their civil rights. If they pressure the state to use its coercive power to force a church to open its membership and its ministry to homosexuals, the faithful church will have to refuse, whatever the consequences. The consequences could come from the state or from a gang of lawless homosexuals, the state unable or

unwilling to control them. I can see danger in taking a public stand on that issue. But I see no way to avoid it and still confess Jesus as Lord.

4. Economics. There has been no backing for American currency for a generation and more. The economy is like a balloon that keeps on being inflated, beginning in the 1930s and continuing at an increasing rate until now. Why that balloon hasn't burst yet, nobody knows.

It is the policy of government officials, news reporters, and even educators to treat inflation as if it were a phenomenon like an earthquakes or the weather—something that simply happens and is beyond human control. But it is not so. Inflation is government policy. It happens because somebody decides to make it happen. And it is dishonest. It is the deliberate debasing of the value of money.

Paper money is like a check. It is valuable only if there is money in the account to cover it. The time was when the American dollar was redeemable for gold and silver, just as a check can be cashed. For every dollar printed there was a dollar's worth of gold or silver to cover it. This is no longer the case. It has not been the case for a generation or more. The Federal government and the Federal Reserve system have been writing bad checks. They are lying to you, telling you, in effect, that there is real money in the account when in fact there is not. We are trading with worthless pieces of paper whose value is illusory. If you and I write bad checks, it is a crime punishable by fine or a prison sentence, but the government and the Federal Reserve do it routinely and the politicians and the news media speak of it as if were an act of God, like a tornado or a hurricane.

It is not an act of God. The true God does not deal in falsehood. Even the forgiveness of sins is not a debasing of the moral currency. When God forgives He does not simply cancel the debt, He pays it. The apostle Paul made that point emphatically in the letter to the Romans. He said that God set forth Jesus Christ as a propitiation "to demonstrate His righteousness because in His forbearance God had passed over the sins that were previously committed."[10] His argument runs along these lines. He is saying that God's forbearance in time past appeared as a letting down of the standards of righteousness. How could God be just and not punish sin, the violation of His laws? Does not His failure to punish sin constitute an invitation to break the law? The answer is no,

48

because the sacrifice of the Son of God pays for the broken law. God does not cheapen the moral currency. He does not bankrupt the bank of heaven by freely forgiving our sins, because Jesus has paid every penny. His sacrifice was of such infinite value that it paid the price in full for every offense against God's holy law. God has not lowered His standards. He can forgive us without compromising His justice in the least, because God Himself has paid the penalty for sin. In the moral realm, then, God has not established a policy of inflation. The gospel establishes His righteousness in spite of forgiving sins, because the price of sin is not simply cancelled, but paid.

In preaching the Gospel, the early Christians pointed out the sharp contrast between the righteousness of God and the unrighteousness of men. They did not hesitate to point out the contrast between the justice of the Son of God and the injustice of the rulers of this world and of this age. So it must be with us.

Richard Wurmbrand, when he was released from prison, was warned by the Communist officials not to speak against Communism. He could preach the gospel all he wanted; he must not speak against the Communist government. The Communists threatened him with death and slander if he did. Wurmbrand decided he could not preach the truth without denouncing lies, could not preach Christ without exposing the evils of Communism. He decided to take the risk.[11]

5. Islam. Christians in the West do not really understand this religion which holds as a cardinal doctrine that their faith is properly propagated by force and violence. Secularists are offended by the use of persuasion by Christians. They talk about having had religion "crammed down their throats" as children in Sunday School. They know nothing of real coercion in religion. Islam enforces its religion at the point of a bayonet, with bombs, machine guns and machetes. This is orthodox Islam, not an intolerant deviation from it.

Where Islam is in power, to convert from Islam to Christianity is to come under the sentence of death, not mere excommunication. Some orthodox Jews hold a funeral for one of their family members who becomes a baptized Christian. They treat the person as if he or she were dead. Orthodox Islam dispenses with the "as if" whenever possible. Muslims kill other Muslims who become baptized Christians. And it is a capital crime to evangelize Muslims in Islamic states. To point out the errors of Islam is life-threatening.

Where Islam is in power Christians are denied the right to practice or propagate their faith, or even to defend themselves against a Muslim in an Islamic court of law.

We should make no mistake. The Muslims are enemies—deadly enemies. And yet, they are sons of Abraham, and so they are also our brothers. Abraham is the father of many nations, and the Arabs are one of those nations, and beloved for Abraham's sake. Yes, Ishmael, the father of the Arabs, was rejected, but only in the sense that he was not chosen to be the carrier of the Messianic seed; that came through Isaac. But Ishmael and his descendants are among the "all nations" which were to be blest by that Messianic seed. The descendants of Ishmael are redeemable. They are enemies, but they are enemies who must be loved in a special way. For there are centuries of unresolved bitterness between Christians and Muslims, and the fault is not all on the Muslim side.

Muslims must be evangelized, but it will take more than words to win them. The truth will offend them and they will surely retaliate with deadly force. Miracles and obvious answers to prayer will get their attention, but it will take love to win them—the kind of love that does not retaliate, but blesses, returns good for evil, blessings for curses and kindness for cruelty. There are Christian martyrs in Muslim lands and there will be more. There will be martyrs here in the United States at the hands of Muslims. But martyrdom is the only strategy that will win Muslim hearts.

These are just a few examples of issues to be addressed in our times.

In the 1970s when the Jesus movement reached the East coast my wife and I found ourselves almost overnight in charge of a Christian community. The Lord sent us a number of young people who had been converted to Jesus Christ and were eager to learn everything they could about living the Christian life. They were in earnest and they responded enthusiastically to our teaching of the word of God. We all lived together in a big farmhouse. My wife and I became a spiritual mom and dad to a lot of young people.

There was a modest economic recession in the 1970s, and we learned to live pretty efficiently and economically in the community. It wasn't strictly necessary at the time. We could have survived economically without the community. But we learned some important lessons by living together, lessons I always thought would one day become necessary for survival.

We learned about planting a garden and burning wood and storing food. And we learned how to get along together, about praying and trusting God when the rent came due or the septic system failed or a car needed repairs. We learned from community what our grandparents and great grandparents grew up knowing and what our parents learned during the Great Depression. Families came together, pooled resources, sacrificed, did without, and survived somehow. In the 1970s we came together as God's family and He taught us some basic lessons. We survived and had a good time doing it. From the experience, I learned something about witness.

Our witness grew out of our lifestyle. We were different. We had different convictions from most of the people in the city where we lived. We had a hope most of them didn't understand. And our convictions and our hope were expressed in our different lifestyle.

Did a house full of young Christians eager to become disciples raise questions in the minds of our neighbors? You bet it did! Many of our neighbors supplied their own answers out of an unreasoning suspicion and fear. Some were afraid that a Christian community in their neighborhood would undermine the value of their property. Some assumed we were pot-smoking hippies. We were referred to for a while as "Marijuana Ranch." But some people were really curious and a few had spiritual needs and honest questions. And of course, our communal lifestyle raised questions in the minds of the families and friends of the young believers. For they didn't simply change their opinions when they became Christians, they changed their way of life in a radical way. Friends, neighbors, and especially family members wanted to know why. They asked questions and we answered them with courtesy and respect. In the process we preached the gospel to them. We didn't force it on them, they asked for it. Some of them believed and joined us or other groups like ours. At least they became thoughtful about the faith.

I expect it will be like that again when the going gets rough. The Lord will bring His people together in the power of the world to come. And out of our life together we will give a credible witness to Jesus Christ and the gospel of the kingdom of God. For our way of life will be an illustration of our faith and hope. Our witness will arise out of our way of life and explain it.

In the 1970s, without telling us what He was doing, God was putting together a little colony of the coming kingdom of God. We didn't have a church in the traditional sense, but in the New

Testament sense of the word. We were not trying to fix the present world, but looking forward to and representing the future kingdom of God, and bearing witness to our coming King.

5

Choosing The Future
Or Fixing The Present?

In answer to the question the disciples asked about the signs of His coming in power and glory and the end of the age, Jesus answered, "...as the days of Noah were, so also will the coming of the Son of Man be. For as in the days before the flood, they were eating and drinking, marrying and giving in marriage, until the day that Noah entered the ark, and did not know until the flood came and took them all away, so also will the coming of the Son of Man be."[1]

Well, then, what were the days of Noah like? They were days of impending judgment. The whole civilization was corrupt. The earth was filled with violence. God had already pronounced His sentence against it and determined on its destruction. It was doomed. But despite the presence of Noah, a preacher of righteousness, in their midst who was busy preparing an ark against the threat of a civilization-wide flood, nobody was prepared for it. They went about their business oblivious of the doom that was approaching with deliberate speed.

Why were they not prepared? Probably because Noah was not the only preacher in those days. Jesus said that one mark of the last days would be false messiahs and false prophets who would mislead many.[2] We can infer that in the last days before the flood it was the same. It is pretty clear that Noah didn't convince his contemporaries in spite of a serious effort over a long period of time. Whoever it was who had the ear of the people convinced them that Noah was some kind of a kook who was not to be taken seriously. Nobody did...until it was too late to do anything about it. Noah convinced his wife, his three sons and their wives. That was all.

53

Noah is the one we remember because he survived to tell his story. But since his family was the only one that survived, the conclusion is inescapable that somebody else had the attention of the people who lived before the flood. Another philosophy prevailed than the one Noah preached and lived. It was wrong. But it was almost universally believed. That philosophy could be called uniformitarian, a cyclical view of nature and history that corresponded to the normal changes of the seasons. It allowed for gradual, evolutionary and natural changes, but categorically rejected the sudden catastrophic view represented by Noah. What the people expected, clearly, was more of the same kind of thing they already knew or could infer from observation: spring, summer, fall and winter, erosion. They were prepared for processes like that. They were not prepared for a catastrophe that would destroy their entire civilization.

They didn't want to think about that. And there were plenty of learned and persuasive men around to assure them that they didn't have to think about or prepare for a catastrophic interruption of their routines. Whatever was the means of communication in those days—the assemblies of the elders in the city gates, travelling bands of merchants, wandering teachers, local and peripatetic bards, singers, preachers of religions, poets—Noah was no match for these ancient counterparts of our anchor men, reporters, scholars, preachers, commentators, comedians and entertainers. Every one of them summarily dismissed or ignored the foreboding message of Noah. He must have been known, but apparently he was regarded as a crank. His idea that a flood was coming and his efforts to build a monstrous, water-tight box, must have been dismissed as craziness or fanaticism. I can imagine the jokes and wise-cracks, as well as the erudite put-downs and the angry epithets directed at Noah, his doctrine of catastrophe and judgment, and his weird building project. Having convinced the people and carried the day with their propaganda, the wise men of his world ignored him. And that was that.

Noah belonged to the future; he didn't fare so well in his own generation and in the civilization before the flood. So shall it be for the disciples of Jesus Christ in the last days just prior to His return in power and glory. In the pages of the New Testament, the Lord said that's how it would be in the last days.

Christians have struggled with the same rejection Noah endured from the opinion makers of our world. Ours is a civilization which seems to have put behind it as unbelievable and unacceptable the idea of a final judgment. And while it is frequently mentioned that disasters (hurricanes, earthquakes, famines, droughts, epidemics, volcanic eruptions, floods and forest fires) are increasing in frequency and intensity, the idea that they might have something to do with retribution, with the wrath of God coming in judgment against human sin, is never mentioned seriously in any news report. Every explanation of the causes of these disasters is a natural and scientific explanation that deals only with secondary causes, and never with God.

Those who, like Noah, speak of divine judgment are represented in the media as comical or ridiculous. If such a position is represented in the media at all, the reporters will pass by ten Christians who present a reasonable argument and train their cameras on some wild-eyed, incoherent ranter who can be easily dismissed as a mindless fanatic.

Modern society has done a brilliant job with communications. Cinematic technique has never been so highly developed or its practitioners so highly skilled. Propaganda has become almost a precise science. In a thousand ways, very convincingly, and everywhere, the point is made again and again that man, not God, is in charge of things on the earth. Religion is reduced to a dispenser of peace of mind, a method by which some people can be helped to cope with the disappointments and disasters of natural life. The fear of God, the warning of coming judgment, the call to repentance and the hope of salvation in a better world to come, have been bulldozed off the public square, discredited and ignored.

Christians have tried hard to overcome this dismissal of their gospel message by a desperate search for relevance. We should consider the story of Noah in this regard. What would we have Noah do when the people ignored him? Modify his doctrine to make it more appealing to the men and women of his times? Perhaps he should have used his building skills in a way that contributed materially to the realization of the aims and goals of the civilization around him? Should he have demonstrated to the people of the world that he could succeed in life along with the best of them? If there was no interest in his floating box, perhaps he should have built something else that would appeal to his contemporaries. Maybe he should have taken a more positive and compassionate attitude toward the people among whom he lived? I'm sure Noah must have been tempted to do all of the above.

But Noah continued to build his ark after the initial curiosity had worn off, when the preacher-builder was no longer news, when the last judgments had been pronounced and the last jokes had been cracked, and he wasn't interesting any more even for the sake of ridicule.

Noah did what he should have done. For the word of God was that the Almighty had already pronounced judgment. There was no way to salvage that civilization. What?! Even though there were mighty men on the earth in those days? Even though there was an advanced civilization? Even though there was a united people who spoke the same language and understood one another and were able to work together with skill and efficiency? Yes, in spite of all those things, God had pronounced the doom of that civilization. For when a people has adopted the wrong goals and taken off in the wrong direction, the greater their strength and skill, the greater their speed and efficiency, the more confident they are in their own righteousness and ability, the worse things are. That civilization was evidently successful enough to have developed an invincible self-confidence. Nothing could stop them. They had overcome all their enemies, natural and human. The earth was theirs. Nothing stood in their way now...but God. And they had forgotten about God. Noah was a forlorn reminder.

They didn't kill Noah. They didn't have to. They had discredited him, alienated him, marginalized him. It didn't matter what he said or did, nobody believed him. The propaganda of that civilization, like everything else they set their minds to, was powerful and effective. It was also false, but plausible, and it seemed to hold together because it was almost universally believed, and it seemed to be confirmed by the palpability of the present. Then, like now, men believed what they could see.

Noah was the exception to a rule that was almost universal. He acted in the present on the basis of something that was revealed to him about the future, something neither he nor anybody else could see. What he did was reasonable in connection with the unseen future; it made no sense at all with reference to the present age in which Noah was living. There was nothing in the historical experience of mankind to prepare people for the kind of thing God had determined to bring on the earth. Noah was prepared for it by revelation and revelation alone.

Scripture says that Noah condemned the world by building the ark.[3] He was preparing for a future disaster that would wipe out the present world. He gave his energy and time to a task which was of no benefit to the existing society. He was not contributing to its improvement or even its survival. He was not going to leave that world a better place; he was a sign to that civilization of its doom. He was preparing for the disaster that would wipe out that whole civilization. With every peg he hammered into the ark, Noah was announcing the doom of the very world in which he lived.

It was not an activity calculated to make him popular with his contemporaries. To the degree that they understood what he was up to, to that degree they must have hated him, or maybe pitied him. But his message was their only hope. If they had taken him seriously, they would either have repented or killed him. Some at least might have been rescued. But they took refuge in a deception; nobody took him seriously. Convinced he was a harmless nut, they let him live and pursue his strange work. So Noah continued to tell them the truth despite their rejection of him and his message. He did what he could for them. Perhaps some had their moments of doubt, but whatever their doubts, their practical decisions were based on what seemed certain to them, based on their experience of the present world. Noah, on the other hand, was responding to a message from beyond, from the future.

But how far can you press an analogy? Has our society reached the same state of irreparable corruption as the civilization before the flood? Hasn't the Lord sent us to be salt and light in the world; salt to retard moral and spiritual decay, light to dispel darkness? And has not the church done that? Has not the preaching of the gospel postponed the threatened judgment again and again during these nearly two thousand years since Jesus came into the world? The preaching of Jonah brought Ninevah to repentance and postponed the destruction of the wicked city for many years. Will not another revival, a spiritual awakening, accomplish the same thing for us in our times?

It is true that the church has often turned back the tide of judgment that seemed certain to engulf the world. Time and again when the judgments of the last days seemed about to fall, a spiritual awakening has intervened to turn people back to God, and the result was that judgment was postponed. And in fact, Christian faith has influenced societies, nations and cultures profoundly, and has brought into being a high degree of civilization. Presumably it could happen again as it happened in England, for instance, in the eighteenth century when the Methodists preached the gospel to the poor and brought enough people to repentance that the character of the nation was altered and judgment that seemed inevitable was turned back. Some historians are convinced that it was the revival led by John Wesley and George Whitefield that spared England the kind of bloody revolution that devastated France in that century. Multitudes of Christians are convinced that it will happen again, and have given themselves tirelessly to try to bring about that very effect. But that was not what Wesley and Whitefield were trying to do, and if they had they would have failed. Their aim was to bring people to salvation and prepare them for the future kingdom of God. The change in the national character that affected both England and the United States was a byproduct of the revival and not its essential purpose.

We have no word from God that revivals will always have that effect. And we have no command from Jesus Christ to try to promote a revival for the purpose of postponing the day of judgment. Our hope is not in a series of postponements of the final judgment, or in the temporary reformation of a society, a nation or a whole civilization; our hope is in the kingdom of God which will come after the judgments of the last times.

There is no promise anywhere in the New Testament that a revival will save this present world or put off the judgment already pronounced against it.

The revival led by Jesus and the first apostles, as we have already seen, did not result in a national repentance for Israel, but rather precipitated judgment, because the Jews rejected the revival and their Messiah. We also know from the New Testament that the last revival will be like the first century revival. That is, it will not postpone, but precipitate judgment. It will be a time like Noah's.

The famous faith chapter in the New Testament (Hebrews 11) goes on to tell us that Noah, by continuing faithful to his calling in spite of the universal rejection by his contemporaries, became an heir of the righteousness which is by faith. He conformed to a kind of righteousness that was unknown in the violent and immoral world in which he lived. His primary source of reference for his values and his lifestyle was the unseen future. In that future world the kind of behavior that was considered normal in his corrupt times would be judged and destroyed. In that future world a different and higher quality of righteousness would prevail. That was only partly a matter of the kind of behavior acceptable in the future world. It was primarily a matter of the source. Noah's righteousness was rooted in God, dependent on God, honoring God. It was a righteousness radically different, not only from the lifestyle of the contemporary civilization but from all its assumptions and underlying beliefs. It was not a matter of acts alone, but of faith and motivation. Noah not only did the right thing; he did it for the right reason. He loved God. And his love for God resulted in a life work that glorified God and functioned in perfect harmony with God's plan for the future, though it put him out of step with his contemporaries and alienated him from them.

Noah demonstrated by his life and work that he belonged to the future, and not to the present. The ark was a serious and sustained investment in the future that he could see only by faith. But he had God's word that it was coming and he believed it.

The people who lived before the flood ignored Noah. But a whole shipload of animals was saved. It was a strange revival but a real one. God told Noah to build the ark and when he built it, the animals came to him. The only people on board were Noah and his family. But the craft was full to overflowing with animals of every kind.

It is a wonderful story and a remarkable illustration of the Scripture that God chooses the foolish things of this world to shame the wise and the mighty.[4] The people were too smart and self-reliant to listen to Noah. So God called giraffes and elephants, sheep and cattle, lions, tigers, rabbits and geese to salvation.

How? We don't know. I suppose it was by the instinct we observe in homing pigeons and salmon. God programmed the instincts of chosen animals and brought them to Noah and the ark in order to save them from the flood. However God did it, it was His doing, a supernatural act, as it is whenever a person comes to Christ. "No one can come to me," said Jesus, "unless the Father who sent me draws him."[5]

I believe the calling of the last revival will be as clearly supernatural as the calling of the animals to Noah's ark. All the authentic revivals have been recognizable as works of God that could not be accounted for by reference to the human agent involved. Yes, God used human instruments in all of them, but the results were so much greater than the human effort expended, that man's works could not account for them. They were wonders attributable only to God. How else, for example, could Gideon and his band of three hundred have defeated an army of a hundred and twenty thousand troops?[6]

What corresponds to the animals who came to Noah and his strange craft? In the 1970s God targeted the college-age young people. In these times He seems to be calling our attention to the high schoolers. The shocking incident at Columbine High School in Littleton, Colorado, on April 20, 1999 is a dramatic example. Boys dressed in black trench coats and carrying automatic weapons walked into school and fired on their classmates. Two girls who were killed in that bizarre outbreak of apocalyptic strife were asked by the black-coated boys if they believed in God. The girls confessed that they believed and both were shot to death. They were martyrs, who gave their lives to make their witness. They were young, but they were involved in the great apocalyptic conflict between good and evil, God and Satan, Christ and antichrist. There were some young people there who were precocious in evil and others in godliness. High school young people committed unthinkable crimes. But in that same high school were a few saints and two martyrs who laid down their lives for the gospel and the kingdom of God. There is good reason to believe Columbine is a typical American high school. It is evident that the devil had his agents there. But God had His chosen ones there, too. He will call many disciples from among today's high school age young people, and from among them will come apostles and prophets, saints and martyrs: soldiers of Jesus Christ.

Noah didn't fix the civilization in which he lived; he prepared the divinely ordained means of escape from the judgment and destruction that struck that civilization. For Noah it was the ark. For us, it is the kingdom of God, and specifically it is whatever task God assigns us to do in serving our king and representing His kingdom. But for us as for Noah, our hope in the future gives direction and meaning to our labor in the present.

The story of Noah teaches us to give our attention to building with materials that are durable with the resilience of eternity. And we must do it with care and precision. For whatever we build must be able to survive the terrific pressures and stresses of the time of the end. We are headed into the unprecedented severity of the storms and judgments of the apocalypse. The world as we know it will be destroyed. It is not fixable. But we belong to a kingdom that cannot be destroyed.

In our service to the Lord Jesus a pretty good job won't be satisfactory. In fact, our human best will not be good enough. It is frustrating. You try and fail and reach the point of despair, for your performance isn't good enough and it's never going to be. That is what it takes to do God's work. Something dies inside. You start praying, not as an exercise in spiritual mastery, or self-made humility, or religious duty, but as an absolute necessity. You learn after trying and failing that you can't do this thing you are called to do. And that's how you learn to pray. Because you must. Because it isn't going to be your work even when you do it. As Jacques Ellul said, the incarnation does not mean that man does God's work; it means that God does man's work. It isn't really you or I who are doing this work of revival and the restoration of the New Testament church, although we are involved in it. Jesus builds His church[7] and He is its Head.[8] There is no easy way to learn this lesson. Because there is no easy way to die.

Revival is a precious thing. It is the presence of God, of Jesus Christ in our midst building His church, and using us as His instruments. A church restored to its New Testament integrity and hope is likewise precious, something God's prophets, saints and martyrs have longed for and prayed for and passionately desired for centuries. God only trusts such labor to those who have died—not only to their sins, but on a still deeper level, to themselves. Those who do God's work have not only died to those things that are wrong and evil, but to those things that are good and noble—to their own good ideas and noble aspirations, even to what is excellent if it has its origin in their own human character and resources, independent of God. For those who work for God on this project will have given up on their own honor and achievements. They will have learned to trust in God rather than men.

I have lived long enough to tell the difference between something that is well built, and something that is carelessly put together with inferior materials. I am sure that Noah built the ark with the best materials and careful, precise workmanship. But the plan was God's. The materials were chosen by God. And Noah worked by the guidance of the Holy Spirit, with God-given strength, skill, and attention to detail. When it was finished, the animals came to him.

All authentic revivals have been works of God that could not be accounted for by any merely human agency. I believe that if we are careful to build on His pattern in the New Testament, for His purposes and glory, God will see to it that His people come and are part of it, just as He brought the animals to the ark, by a miracle. We must labor with such attention to His voice, each of us using the gifts He has given us in precisely the way He directs us, that the work is His rather than ours. And when it is finished, the ark of the restored New Testament church will be seaworthy. The storms and floods will come, but Jesus will be on board and at the helm, and He will bring us all to safe harbor in the kingdom of God, our true homeland.

6

Loyal To The Coming Kingdom

The New Testament teaches us that our citizenship as disciples of Jesus Christ is in heaven. Our loyalty is to the future kingdom of God and is established by the cross. In New Testament times one entered the kingdom of God—and the church which was a kind of embassy of the kingdom of God in a hostile world—by means of the cross; that is to say, by death. Believers in New Testament times understood that when they identified with Jesus Christ by faith they were cutting themselves off from their old life and their former loyalties as surely as if they had died.

Jesus told each disciple to take up his cross and follow Him. In that ancient setting there was no alternative. It was determined very early in the New Testament era that if anyone identified himself with Jesus he was thereby expelled from the synagogue.[1] No other questions were asked.

That was a serious matter in the religion-driven society of first century Judea. To be expelled from the synagogue was to be an outcast, an alien in one's own country and neighborhood. One's friends and family shunned him. The important people spoke against him and used their influence to make life hard for him. In a dispute he was presumed to be wrong and criminal without a trial. Children were excused for being impolite and disrespectful to such a person. There was in his case a suspension of normal human rights, for he was regarded as having violated the sacred code of the community.

We must never forget that Jesus was regarded as a criminal. That's why He was executed. And we must try to understand that the theological reasons for the death of Jesus—which many of us learned as children as if they were the only reasons—were neither known nor understood by most people in first century Judea. They only knew the sociological and political reasons. Their information came from the propaganda of the times which was largely controlled by the Jewish and Roman authorities, the people who had crucified Jesus. So, to confess Jesus as the Messiah was to stand against the movers and shakers, the people of influence, power and wealth in one's own society and nation. Often that meant being alienated from one's own family, friends and acquaintances.

Confession was a public act of identifying oneself with Jesus as a believer and a disciple. Confessing Jesus as Messiah in first century Judea meant being ostracized by one's own culture and community and relinquishing one's rights as a human being and a citizen. But Jesus and the early church leaders after Him didn't let anyone off the hook. Confession of Jesus as Messiah was essential to salvation. The apostle Paul wrote, "...If you confess with your mouth the Lord Jesus and believe in your heart that God has raised Him from the dead, you will be saved. For with the heart one believes unto righteousness, and with the mouth confession is made unto salvation."[2]

Some of the Lord's teachings that may strike us as harsh make sense in the light of the religious, cultural and political reality of those days. For example, Jesus said, "If anyone comes to Me and does not hate his father and mother, wife and children, brothers and sisters, yes, and his own life also, he cannot be My disciple. And whoever does not bear his cross and come after Me cannot be My disciple."[3] Tons of printer's ink have been used to explain away and soften the impact of these words on generations of Christians who never experienced the rejection that the early Christians knew so well.

Why did Jesus speak that way? It was necessary to harden oneself against the tenderest relationships, to be prepared for rejection and not to be deterred from one's resolve to follow the Lord, even to death. Jesus took that path Himself and made it clear that the same thing was required of all His disciples as well. He didn't hide the bottom line. It was part of His presentation of the word of God. He spelled it out from the beginning and His disciples understood well what He was saying. They faced the ultimate issue right from the start. It was a life or death issue. When someone identified with Jesus and confessed Him as Messiah openly and publicly, he signed his life away in this world. But that was the only way to find eternal life in the world to come. The early church understood Jesus literally rather than metaphorically when He said,

"He who finds his life will lose it, and he who loses his life for my sake will find it."[4]

And so the Lord concluded his teaching on this subject by saying, "For which of you, intending to build a tower, does not sit down first and count the cost, whether he has enough to finish it—lest, after he has laid the foundation, and is not able to finish, all who see it begin to mock him, saying, 'This man began to build and was not able to finish.' Or what king, going to make war against another king, does not sit down first and consider whether he is able with ten thousand to meet him who comes against him with twenty thousand? Or else, while the other is still a great way off, he sends a delegation and asks conditions of peace. So likewise, whoever of you does not forsake all that he has cannot be My disciple."[5]

When a person made a commitment to Jesus Christ in that New Testament context he knew from the start that he had to be ready to die for his faith. If he wasn't ready to die, he stayed away from Jesus and the community of believers. If he did decide to follow Jesus, he needed a strong hope in the coming kingdom, because he understood that life in this world was going to be hard and painful and, very likely, short.

The body of Christ functioned effectively in the early days, for one had to pass through the cross in order to get into it. The cross filtered out the flesh. Joining the church in those days was like signing one's own death warrant. A believer risked his life to get in. But once one came in on those terms, the flesh was effectively checked. It was not that there was never any sin; there was, and it was serious. There was Judas who betrayed the Lord,[6] and Ananias and Sapphira who conspired to lie to the Holy Spirit.[7] There was a case of immorality in Corinth.[8] But in each case the sin was dealt with effectively. The body of Christ had an immune system that could deal with sin and keep the body in a healthy condition.

The situation of the church today is quite different. In America today the cross no longer functions as a filter to screen out the flesh. There is no cost to count when entering the church, no risk to take in confessing Jesus as the Christ. People are enticed into the church without a thorough repentance, and the faith of sincere believers is weakened. The church is overwhelmed with more fallen flesh, more sin than the body's immune system can handle. Poisons that in the early church were filtered out at the start or dealt with immediately and effectively as soon as they appeared, now find easy entrance to the body of Christ and comfortable accommodations once they settle in. They come into the church like viruses and attack her vital organs. Typically, human considerations determine church policies, doctrines and traditions. That makes room in the church for self-indulgence, self-exaltation, sexual misconduct, power struggles among leaders, greed for money, glory and pleasure. Such things result in church splits, heresies, divisions, confusion, heartbreak, disappointment and apostasy. I am convinced that the reason our revival of the seventies turned sour was that we, in common with generations of Christians before us, tried to enjoy God's blessings without the cross.

In the church today persecution is not a threat. If it is mentioned at all, it is misrepresented. It is considered something that happened in the early days, but is no longer applicable because of the supposed "triumph" of Christianity. Or Christian leaders talk as if they were being persecuted because the state no longer gives official recognition to the church, or grants her leaders the same sphere of influence in political, social and cultural affairs that church leaders used to enjoy. But there is no real persecution of Christians in the United States. Today the church in America is comfortable, but it is not in a normal and healthy condition from a New Testament perspective.

New Testament faith involves a new loyalty to the future kingdom of God. And the cross is the way by which we choose the future over the present. We die to the present, evil world. We no longer look to the world to satisfy our needs and desires. We are called to die to the world's attractions. We cease to be terrified by its threats. We embrace death in advance, so that death holds no more terrors for us. We are not afraid to lose everything we have in the world, because we have already relinquished it all: reputation, wealth, success, influence, admiration, comfort, pleasure, in the hope of eternal life in the world to come.

That was where Jesus began. Finding himself in the form of a man, He humbled himself and became obedient unto death, even death on the cross.[9] And that's where He finished. He gave up his reputation, laid aside his wealth and power in the interests of a future fulfillment in another, better world, and gave himself to suffering and death in this present evil age.

Jesus was called to be the sign that was spoken against.[10] Faith in Jesus was intended to set a man against his world, even against his father and mother, for it is often in one's own family that the world impinges upon a person in the most telling way. Faith in

Jesus set a man in a right relationship with God, but immediately upset his relationship with this world, at least with his part of the world.

The apostle Paul wrote of what faith in Christ meant to him. To Paul, a Jew, believing in Jesus Christ meant the loss of everything that gave him standing in Jewish society. "Circumcised the eighth day, of the stock of Israel, of the tribe of Benjamin, a Hebrew of the Hebrews; concerning the law, a Pharisee; concerning zeal, persecuting the church; concerning the righteousness which is in the law, blameless. What things were gain to me, these I have counted loss for Christ."[11]

Everything that brought him recognition, approval and status in his world (the Jewish community) was flesh and amounted to rubbish. He lost it all and was glad to lose it for the sake of the excellence of knowing Christ Jesus. We need to translate that statement culturally into something that in our society today corresponds to those marks of recognition, reputation, honor, and security. If we did, we would have to say something like the following. What is gain to me—my family connections, my academic degrees, my financial and business successes, my record of personal achievements, my resumé, sometimes even achievements in the realm of religion and morals, whatever my claim to respect in my community—are garbage, mere flesh. All of that will be lost or at least put at risk by embracing Jesus Christ.

That is to say, for the apostle Paul, flesh was not just the gross sins his society considered wicked and unacceptable, but also the refined and cultured selfishness that most people today consider goodness, including everything that gave him standing in his community, everything that made his life comfortable, happy and successful. He sacrificed it all and had to sacrifice it, in order to embrace Jesus Christ. Because he couldn't have Jesus and those status symbols of this world, even the religious status symbols of this world, for Paul's world was a religious one.

Faith in Jesus must mean the same to us today as it meant to believers in the first century if our faith is to have the same quality and the same efficacy as did the faith of Christians in the first century. For the cross must accomplish the same for us that it accomplished for the early believers. It separated them from their world, made them outsiders, almost outlaws. That is the essential meaning of the cross. To function effectively in our time, the cross must sever us from our own world. Jesus Christ separates a person from his world. Insofar as this world was concerned, the apostle Paul was a dead man. "God forbid that I should boast, except in the cross of our Lord Jesus Christ, by whom the world has been crucified to me and I to the world."[12]

The apostle Paul was a Roman citizen. He also belonged to the nation-state of Judea. But his true loyalty after his conversion was to the future kingdom of God. His Roman citizenship gave him a political lever that he used once or twice to enable him to survive to carry on his work in the kingdom of God. His Jewish heritage was important because it taught him about the Messiah, the king of the Jews, and the coming kingdom of Israel. But his Roman citizenship was not his primary loyalty. And his Jewish loyalty was expressed in his faithfulness to Israel's Messiah who had been rejected and condemned by the presently existing state of Judea. Paul was faithful unto death to the kingdom of Israel, but that kingdom was not yet established on the earth. And his faithfulness to that future kingdom put him at enmity with the Judean state that did exist at that time on the earth. The fact is, Paul was considered a criminal by the rulers of that Judean state precisely because of his loyalty to Jesus and the future kingdom of Israel. His sense of patriotic commitment, therefore, was not to any domain existing on the earth at that time. He considered the whole world evil.

Neglecting even to mention his earthly citizenships, Paul's own words on the issue of loyalty were these:

> For our citizenship is in heaven, from which we
> also eagerly wait for the Savior, the Lord Jesus
> Christ, who will transform our lowly body that it
> may be conformed to His glorious body, according
> to the working by which He is able even to subdue
> all things to Himself.[13]

This kind of commitment is not typical among Christians in today's Western culture. The church's edge has been blunted. A New Testament revival will sharpen it again. That is the good news. But when it happens it will restore the tensions and hostilities that existed between the church when it accurately represented the future kingdom of God, and the state which represents and administrates this present evil world.

7

GOD OR CAESAR?

The first century revival that came with the appearance of Jesus and His claim to be the Messiah of Israel, the son of David, and the nation's lawful king, resulted in a conflict with the authorities who were already in power. It was inevitable. Jesus warned the disciples that it was coming. He told them precisely what would happen. He would be betrayed into the hands of sinners and crucified. They understood the political realities of their situation.

When Jesus told his disciples that they were going to Jerusalem, Thomas groaned, "Let us also go, that we may die with Him."[1] Judas saw what was coming and began thinking of some way to get off this sinking ship before it went down. They were headed for disaster and they all knew it. As for the resurrection, they heard Jesus talk about that, too, but it was hidden from their minds. Nothing in their past experience prepared them to understand such a thing. They didn't know what He was talking about.[2]

During the last days before his death, Jesus was involved in an increasingly tense dialog with his enemies. They tried to catch him in a verbal blunder in order to discredit and destroy him. It was in this connection that he was asked the diabolically clever question, "should we pay taxes to Caesar or not?"

There was no good answer to that question. Whatever he answered, yes or no, would be wrong. If he said, *yes, pay taxes to Caesar*, he would have been made to look like a collaborator with the enemy, the Roman conquerors of his homeland. If he said *no, don't pay taxes to Caesar*, he would have been identified as a public enemy of the Romans, and a target of their overwhelming political power. The question was a trap designed to make him stand either with the hated Romans, in which case He would have forfeited the confidence of his own people, or with the militant Jewish Zealots who preached armed revolt against Rome. Jesus could then be reported to the Roman authorities as an enemy of Caesar and a potential revolutionary leader. It was dangerous to have one's name on the Romans' blacklist. The answer Jesus gave revealed a third way, a way that most people didn't know existed. It was brilliant.

"Why do you test Me, you hypocrites? Show me the tax money." So they brought him a denarius. He held the coin up so they could all see it.

"And He said to them, 'Whose image and inscription is this?'"

"They said to Him, 'Caesar's.'"

"And He said to them, 'Render therefore to Caesar the things that are Caesar's, and to God the things that are God's.'"[3] I imagine the Lord tossing the coin back to its owner as he said this, his offhanded manner revealing the small value He placed on money.

There was nothing in his words that anybody could fasten an accusation on. But, on the other hand, He declared Himself with a brilliant clarity. By His response He demonstrated the relative value of both money and political power. In the Lord's hierarchy of values, the coin comes somewhere near the bottom. God and His kingdom are at the top. Here is what that answer implies: you can give Caesar what belongs to Caesar, a piece of metal with the Emperor's image and a political slogan stamped on it. Neither the money nor the political message represents an ultimate and lasting value or truth. God alone is the real value and the true purpose of men. You, yourselves, are created in the image of God. Give the coin to Caesar, but give your heart and your loyalty to God.

Jesus made it clear that He didn't stand with the Zealots. He did not advocate the overthrow of Caesar with revolutionary violence and bloodshed. His message was, serve God with all your heart, take up your cross, and God will take care of Caesar. At the same time, Jesus distanced himself from the Pharisees and the Herodians who concocted the question. In answering them, he called them hypocrites, playactors, whose purpose in asking the question was not to find out the truth, but to embarrass Jesus before the crowd.

There was a distinct difference between Jesus and all the rest of them—Romans and Jews of whatever party. Jesus was really concerned about God and truth. The rest of them were all playing to the crowd. They were concerned with the image, not the truth,

with how things appeared in the public forum, not how [were?]
were in God's sight. And the name of the game for all o[f?]
political power, money, and social standing in the w[orld?]
righteousness or truth or love or hope or faith in God.

Jesus won the debate at that point. And it was not ε .. unfair
fight. Jesus didn't defeat His opponents with His deity, but in His
humanity. The fascinating thing about the incarnation here is that
Jesus is not so much revealing the nature of Almighty God as He is
true manhood. When He became a man Jesus laid aside the rights
and powers of His Godhood. So the Lord didn't overwhelm His
enemies with omniscience; He responded as a man, with faith and
trust in God. He looked to God as a man does, in a quick and silent
prayer, and received an answer from God for those who sought to
discredit Him and ruin Him with a trick question. Jesus won the
debate, not because He was God and of course could outsmart His
human enemies; He won it as a man because He was better than
they were.

Purity of heart results in clarity of thought. The Lord's mind
was not darkened by selfish ambition, jealousy, and fear; He would
not resort to dirty tricks in reacting to the dirty trick they had just
played on Him. He was sincere in putting God first. The real issue
was character and faith, not intelligence and quick-witted ability in
public debate. His was not just a clever answer to a trick question.
Jesus gave a true answer, a sincere answer, to an insincere and
unfair question that was designed to destroy Him. And His answer
was not designed to destroy His enemies but to save them. He was
free to do that because He was not afraid to die.

Jesus had a vital hope in the coming kingdom of God. He
believed that kingdom was coming, not by the strength or clever
manipulation of men but by the will of God, not by human
propaganda but by the truth of God, not by posturing before men
but by trusting in God's ability and His determination to keep His
promises and fulfill His oaths. The kingdom would come in spite of
anything that men could do to resist it; it would come even if they
killed the One to whom the promises pertained. Ironically, Jesus
had to die in the struggle to bear witness to that kingdom, by doing
the will of God and speaking the truth of God.

That was the secret weapon Jesus always had with Him. He
loved God and was committed to His kingdom, His will, His truth,
even to death. And so He was not afraid to tell the truth or to walk
in the truth. He loved the Father and had already consented to lay

down His life. He believed the promise of resurrection and of a new world of justice, truth and love that was coming. He knew that God would triumph in the end; He knew that He would rule and reign in that coming kingdom in the name of God; and He knew that nothing sinful men or fallen angels or the devil himself could do would be able to stop it.

Jesus had already embraced the cross; that is, He had already chosen the future over the present. He had not completely rejected Caesar or the authorities of Judah, but He had certainly put them in their place. Jesus the man worshipped the God of truth and love and justice; His citizenship was in the coming kingdom of God. It was a dangerous position to take, but Jesus was ready to face the danger.

In another debate with the authorities of Judea, Jesus told the well known story about the good Samaritan. A man was walking along the road that goes from Jerusalem to Jericho. On the way he was waylaid by ruffians who beat him, robbed him, stripped him of his clothing and left him lying at the side of the road half dead. A priest walked by on the other side. A Levite did the same. But a despised Samaritan found the man, administered first aid and took him to an inn. He paid the innkeeper to look after the man and promised to come by and pay any additional cost on his return trip, if more care was required.[4]

I will pass by the obvious point of the story—an act of love toward a man in desperate need by an unlikely neighbor. What I want to focus on here is the way Jesus set up the story. I believe it is significant that the Lord had the priest, the Levite and the Samaritan discover the wounded man after the evil deed had been done. They did not come on the scene while the robbery was in process. There was no heroic, violent intervention to stop the robbery and deliver the victim with his life and property intact. When we read the account, we don't witness the excitement of hand-to-hand combat as our movies do, with five or six minutes of a well choreographed slug-fest, complete with flashing swords, splintering wood, gushing blood and shattering glass. Jesus did not resolve the problem caused by violence by means of more violence. The Samaritan found the man lying half dead at the side of the road. The help he administered was not that of a hero, but the ordinary efforts of a neighbor.

As Jesus told the story, the good Samaritan did not come into conflict with the criminals. Rather, His story set the Samaritan in contrast to two Jewish officials with comfortable lives and honorable positions in society. The officials enjoyed the wealth and honors of a high station in life, but neglected the concrete responsibility to show mercy to a neighbor. The way Jesus told the story, the villains were the priest and the minister who walked by on the other side of the road and neglected to help the man lying in a pool of his own blood. The Samaritan, an outcast racially, probably poor, whose religious doctrine was flawed, gave the wounded man the help the public officials failed to give.

This is not the kind of story we would tell today. In the twentieth century, and particularly here in the United States, the point that would be made is that something should be done about the Jericho road. First, the authorities should increase police protection on the road. Then, the police should find the muggers and put them behind bars. Third, the legislature should mandate tougher penalties for this kind of crime. Fourth, the judges should impose harsh sentences on the perpetrators of such acts. Finally, the government should establish a fund from the public treasury to provide medical care and living costs for the victims of such crimes during their recovery. These are all political solutions—public acts supported by tax monies and administered by professional agents of the government.

Jesus avoided all those things that our politicians and editorial writers would think of first. He assumed the existence of evil and injury in a wicked world. He assumed the inability of the political system to prevent the crime and the unwillingness of public officials to help the victim. The only help came from a private citizen without a public position, without a badge, without a salary, without access to public funds, without a place of honor or even respect in the community. He was an outsider, a foreigner, somebody who was not a part of the system. Jesus did not command, suggest, or even expect a public, political solution.

I once heard a preacher give our modern wisdom on the story of the good Samaritan. He said, "it is better to build a fence at the top of a cliff than a clinic at the bottom to treat those who fall off of it." The political orientation is so much a part of our thinking that the preacher didn't even notice that his solution was not the one Jesus was offering. The point the preacher made was logical from our twentieth century point of view, but it was close to the opposite of what Jesus was saying.

The point is, the Lord was not trying to improve this present society. He ministered to those who were victims of this world's injustice. But He did not try to make over this world into a society of justice. He did not look to the political and religious establishment or to the authorities who operated it, to do what He wanted done. Neither did He plot to throw the rascals out and take their places. He did not aspire to public office Himself in this world and this age or try to install His disciples in public office so they could solve these problems by making the system work better. Rather, He commends the personal and private deed of a despised outcast. It was the hated Samaritan who did the will of God. Out of love for God and man, the Samaritan did what he could to relieve the suffering that is inevitable in this evil world whose real prince is the devil.

The Samaritan represents the church—unofficial, alien during the whole course of this evil age, representative of God's future kingdom, authorized by God's word and moved by the compassion of the Holy Spirit, but without official standing in the community or even respect in this present world. On his own initiative, on his own time and at his own expense, the Samaritan helped the injured man. In his story Jesus showed his approval of the Samaritan's private initiative, even though such private acts would never solve the problem systemically in this age. And He told a lawyer, a public functionary who wanted to discuss a theological point with the Lord, to go and do as the despised Samaritan did.

Why did Jesus respond as He did? From a New Testament perspective the answer is obvious. He responded as He did because Jesus always gave the ultimate answer, the final solution. He anticipated the most far-reaching and complete renovations imaginable. He had a living hope in the future kingdom of God. He had no interest in reforming this present corrupt world, because He believed God was going to destroy the world system and replace it with the kingdom of God in which the righteousness, truth and love of God are the foundational principles and the dynamic powers. So it was written in Daniel's apocalyptic visions, and so Jesus believed.[5]

Furthermore, the Lord Jesus was calling men to shift their loyalty from this present world and its systems of economics, politics and propaganda, to the coming kingdom of God. He asked His disciples to embrace the future and let go of the present. On the other hand, He never commanded His disciples to destroy the present system. He believed God would do that supernaturally at the time of the end. Nor was He calling on His disciples to replace the present system with a "Christian" system. The hope Jesus set before His disciples was uniformly and consistently His second coming, the final judgment, and a complete renewal at the end of the age. Jesus did not have a program for the reform or renovation of the present evil world. His program for the present evil world was to call people out of it and into the kingdom of God.

Jesus and the apostles who followed Him were content to let the established institutions stand. In fact, they acknowledged a certain minimal responsibility that believers owe to this present evil world and its government. The New Testament commands believers to give some of their money for taxes to support a limited political system, however inadequate and even evil it may be.[6] But never in the New Testament is the established authority represented as the agent of God's redemptive purposes or the decrees of the state as the infallible expression of the will of God. The state, although established by God to maintain peace and order in a fallen world, is not regarded as good or holy; more often than not, Scripture represents the authorities as agents of the devil.[7] Nevertheless, the rulers and authorities of this world are proper subjects for prayer.[8] Their function is sharply limited by the New Testament, but within those narrow limits of their legitimacy, they are to be obeyed.[9] They are not, however, expected to understand or be sympathetic to the church or its mission. Rather, the church must expect persecution from the authorities as a general rule.[10] The mission of the church was carried on without the permission or the help of the established powers and more often than not, in spite of their active resistance.[11]

I say that Jesus taught and exemplified a strictly limited state authority in this present age. He continually taught and acted with reference to the authority of God, and often disregarded human authority. He took it upon Himself to correct the authorities in regard to their understanding of Scripture, particularly in reference to the Messiah. He ignored their sabbath rulings, their ceremonial washings, their traditions. These were not what we call religious practices; they had the force of law. To violate them was to risk a fine, imprisonment or possibly stoning. Jesus broke these laws because in His mind they were wrongly interpreted or wrongly applied. He trained His disciples to do the same kind of things He did. By His teaching and example, He thereby imposed limits on the government.

It goes without saying that this was not the concept the authorities held about themselves or their functions. The state demanded then and demands now a loyalty, obedience and a sphere of influence far in excess of the legitimate and limited role assigned to it by the New Testament. What then did Jesus and the early believers do about the excessive claims of the government?

By His authority as Messiah, Jesus decided what the limits of civil government were and are.[12] When the reigning powers and authorities claimed an authority that had not in fact been given to them by God, Jesus simply did what God commanded and ignored the claims of the authorities.[13] Following Him, the early church did the same. They did not rebel against the authorities, because the authorities had a legitimate function that was established by God. But when the authorities overstepped the line of their legitimate authority, Jesus and the early church pointed out their errors, corrected them and did the will of God in spite of what the authorities demanded.[14]

Whenever they discerned that there was a conflict between the laws and rules of the earthly government and the will and commands of God, Jesus and the early church obeyed God rather than the established authorities.[15] In practice, they ignored the authorities, evaded them, went around them, and over their heads. But unlike our American Declaration of Independence, Jesus and the early disciples never claimed the right to alter, abolish and replace the reigning powers. They did not take up arms and fight against the established authorities. They did not attempt to overthrow the existing government either by revolutionary violence or any other political methods. But neither would they obey an unjust or ungodly law simply because the government demanded it. The believers had Jesus as their example and teacher. They were prepared to suffer and die for the sake of the gospel and the kingdom of God; they were not prepared to maim and kill in the name of God, His kingdom and His righteousness.

When they were punished by the authorities for disobedience, they spoke the truth, but did not resist the unjust punishment; that is, they did not return evil for evil, curse for curse, or blow for blow.[16] They expected persecution and willingly accepted suffering and unjust punishment, trusting in God. That was their consistent practice and teaching. There is no other method given by Jesus to

His apostles or passed on by the apostles to the church in dealing with official injustice—none.[17]

The attitude expressed by the church in the New Testament toward the state and its established institutions is one of wariness and caution. At best, the state operates far below the standards of God's righteousness and truth, at worst it is in open rebellion against God, a persecutor of God's saints. But the New Testament concedes that until the kingdom of God is established on the earth, during the whole interim period, bad and inept government is better than no government.[18]

The powers that be are established by God and accountable to God. They are ultimately under the control of God. Although they are sinful and rebellious against God, they can never escape from God's overruling authority. And although the evil they can do is terrible, God has them on a leash, and is able to protect and bless His faithful ones however bad things get.[19]

There are times when a believer cannot and must not obey the authorities, for Jesus insists that the believer's heart belongs not to the state but to God and to the Messiah who will reign on the earth in that future time when God's kingdom comes on earth as it is in heaven. We are citizens of the kingdom of heaven[20] and that is where our hope lies. When Jesus returns in power and glory—but not before—there will be good government on the earth.[21]

When it came to representing God's kingdom, Jesus did not look to the established powers and authorities, but to people who were outsiders to the system as He was. He chose for His apostles men who were not trained experts in religion or law, but what we would today call laymen—fishermen, tax-collectors, laborers. They were regarded by the establishment leaders as "ignorant and unlearned men."[22]

Jesus favored the despised Samaritan, the hated tax-collector, the prostitute, the adulteress. He called them to repentance, yes, but the righteousness to which He called them was not righteousness as defined by the establishment. His goal was not to make His converts good citizens of this present, evil world, but of the coming kingdom of God. He was not trying to make the present reigning powers successful or their work easy. It was not part of His purpose to make the rulers of this world look good. During His time on the earth Jesus operated outside of the religious and political establishment of Judea, without its approval or authorization, and in spite of its active opposition.[23] He embarrassed them in debate, made them jealous by His miraculous powers and His appeal to the common people, and angered them by His teaching. They rejected and murdered Him.

The Lord Jesus demonstrated His right to rule in the name of God by His obedience unto death to the will of God the Father.[24] The other side of the coin is that He exposed the pretensions of those who were in power. In their dealings with Him their injustice and incompetence were unmasked. The religious and political authorities were jealous, corrupt, and unjust. Jesus called them blind leaders of the blind.[25] As if to confirm the Lord's judgment that they were both evil and incompetent, they crucified the Son of God.

The method of operation used by Jesus and the early church was obvious in the New Testament setting. It was so obvious that the authorities hated Jesus and His disciples, considered them a threat to their power and position, and persecuted them.

There is nothing in the New Testament to suggest that He changed His method of operation, or that He planned or authorized a change at some future date. For as long as the present age lasts, until the day when Jesus returns and the kingdom of God is established on the earth in power and glory, we must expect that Jesus and the church which faithfully follows Him, will operate outside of the establishment. He operated outside of the establishment because the established powers did not and do not represent the interests of God.[26]

What then should the church do? It should organize its life according to the ways of the coming kingdom, for the church's hope is in the world to come,[27] lives by the power of that future world,[28] and represents it here and now in this present world.[29] The church should teach the truths by which that kingdom operates, model the lifestyle of that kingdom by its works of mercy, and exhibit in its witness the power of the world to come. The church should proclaim the good news of the coming kingdom as Jesus and the early believers did. Its power was the power of the truth and of the Holy Spirit. The church was taught to expect to suffer in this present world as Jesus did in the world at His first coming, and reign with Christ in the future when He returns.[30] The Apostle is constantly referring to "that day."[31]

Jesus sent the disciples out two by two without securing the credentials or the approval or even the permission of the world or its governing authorities to do so. He didn't even inform the authorities beforehand of His intentions. He anticipated trouble when He did this, and told the disciples that they must expect persecution.[32] The church must take this tack today. It is not being obtuse or troublesome; there is a reason for it.

To accept a license from the state is to acknowledge the state's authority to regulate the church's activities. If the state can grant the church permission to exist and do its work, then the state can also deny that permission and revoke that license, if it so chooses. And it can tell the church what its duties and responsibilities are whether by subtle influence and suggestion, by granting or withholding privileges, or by direct dictatorial command and coercion.

Most Christian leaders do not realize that when they incorporate their church, they make it a creature of the state. To do that compromises the church's integrity. The state owns the church by granting the church its charter, a limited liability, tax exemption, the protection of the state, and other benefits.

The point is, the church's authorization comes from a higher source, from God and His Messiah, who sits at the right hand of God, and from the anointing of the Holy Spirit and the word of God, which is the church's constitution. You may say that the church belongs to God, with or without incorporation papers. But when you incorporate with the state, you make a legal and public acknowledgement of state authorization and therefore of state control. You may hope that the state does not seize your church's books or close and padlock the doors of your Christian school. In fact, the state rarely does that at present. But it has the legal right to do so with a corporation it charters. The church and the state have a contract in which the church acknowledges the authority of the state. It is a legal instrument giving the state the power to control the church, and whenever the state chooses, it can exercise that right. It is all perfectly legal. Where do the authorities of the state get that right? The church gives it to them when it requests and accepts incorporation by the state. Most American churches are "registered" churches. They belong to the state. That is their official witness—signed, sealed, and legal—whatever they may say from the pulpit.

Many American churches display the American flag in their sanctuaries in the place of highest honor ("the marching right, the flag's own right, or an observer's left facing the flag").[33] According to state regulations, that's where it ought to be; it's the law of the land. And if there is a flag representing the kingdom of God, it is on the left of the U.S. flag, (to an observer's right facing the flag). But to be theologically accurate, the national flag, if displayed at all, should be underneath or to the left of the flag of the kingdom of God. For God is Most High, supreme, and the highest authority. Jesus Christ is the King of kings. Any banner that symbolizes His kingdom should be displayed in the position of highest honor.[34]

Some think these symbols don't have any real importance, but they do. Even if most people are not aware of the significance of the positioning of a flag, some are. And the angels and the demons know very well what it means. We are giving a false witness to Jesus Christ if we honor any other authority with a higher dignity than we show to Him and His kingdom. We compromise the church's integrity by subscribing to a legal form that denies the truth of the word of God. We proclaim Jesus as King of kings, but the official symbol places Jesus under the authority of the state. It is idolatry. Whether we realize it or not, we are dishonoring our Lord. We say one thing with our lips and deny it with our symbols. When we look for the causes of the spiritual weakness of the church, we need to look at these factors and their implications, for they are far-reaching.

To Jesus and the early church, their authorization by God rather than men was an important point, an indispensable point. They put their lives at risk to make that point. It was not negotiable. It may seem puzzling to a compromised modern church that is at home in this corrupt world and at peace with its authorities (and with the principalities and powers in the heavenlies who rule over the authorities of this fallen and rebellious world system), but Jesus and the early believers suffered persecution and death rather than compromise or modify that conviction.

That refusal to compromise with the establishment, the refusal to cooperate with the power structure of this corrupt world is the basic reason why Jesus and the early Christians were persecuted. That is the essence of the cross. In the final analysis, persecution occurs by the policy or permission of the state, that is, by the established authorities who wield the power in any society. The authorities either look the other way and passively allow it, or they actively promote persecution by law or custom.

The conflict with the established authorities was the most striking feature of the New Testament church. It is the normal relationship between the church and the state. If you are looking for the point at which the church's power is drained away, and the reason for the ineffectiveness of the church as we experience it today, in comparison with the New Testament church, look right here—in the church's relationship to the state.

In the United States today the church is comfortable and compromised precisely at the point where the early church had its greatest conflict. No wonder, then, that Christians today overlook the obvious and misunderstand the cross.

8

The Weakness
And Foolishness Of God

The great revivals in church history typically came in
connection with the preaching and living of the cross. That is
logical. For the cross is the first thing to go in a time of spiritual
decline. The cross is offensive. It is offensive because it is painful.
Human nature instinctively avoids the cross. But when the cross is
avoided, the power wanes, love drains away, hope dissipates, and
all that remains is religion with its doctrines, rules, rituals, and
organizational structures.

The surest way to restore the love, the power and the hope is to
restore the cross. The restoration of the cross is hard to accomplish,
however, because the offense and the pain are also restored.
Blunting the edge of truth, particularly in regard to the cross, is a
constant temptation for Christians. The early church pioneered the
way of the cross by facing the temptation head on.

In the first letter to the Corinthians, the apostle Paul defended
the gospel against the charges made by the Jews that it represented
God as weak, and by the Greeks that it was foolishness. It was the
preaching of the cross that provoked the charge of weakness and
foolishness against the gospel.[1] Paul didn't try to explain away the
apparent weakness and foolishness of God; he stood his ground and
responded by saying, "the foolishness of God is wiser than men,
and the weakness of God is stronger than men."[2]

The reproach about the weakness of God, of course, came
because Paul represented the Messiah as a loser in this world. Jesus
challenged the rich and powerful without an army and received
what a man can expect to receive who dares to challenge the
powers of this world without adequate force. He ended up

condemned, hanging on a cross and dying. The idea that the Son of God should suffer and die was offensive to the Jews and nonsense to the Greeks.

As Christians who have been steeped in twenty centuries of atonement theology, we are sometimes inclined to shake our heads and wonder what the problem was with the Jews and the Greeks. Why didn't they get it? I am convinced that if we don't understand why the gospel was offensive and appeared foolish in the first century, we won't really understand the gospel, ourselves. We're just used to it, familiar with it. If Christian faith does not seem like foolishness to us in the late twentieth century, it may be because we have not seriously considered that this man who seemed bent on destroying himself asks us to follow his example. He teaches us to live for the future kingdom, to turn our backs on this present evil world, and to do all we can to persuade others to do the same.

> From that time Jesus began to show to His disciples that he must go to Jerusalem, and suffer many things from the elders and chief priests and scribes, and be killed, and be raised the third day.[3]

Jesus' teaching was interrupted by Peter, who rebuked Him. Peter understood the offensiveness of the gospel; he himself was offended. Jesus silenced him with a stinging rejoinder, "Get behind Me, Satan! You are an offense to Me, for you are not mindful of the things of God, but the things of men."[4] Then the Lord continued his discourse.

> If anyone desires to come after Me, let him deny himself, and take up his cross, and follow Me. For whoever desires to save his life will lose it, but whoever loses his life for My sake will find it. For what profit is it to a man if he gains the whole world, and loses his own soul? Or what will a man give in exchange for his soul? For the Son of Man will come in the glory of His Father with His angels, and then He will reward each according to his works.[5]

The apostle Paul explained the lesson the Lord taught the apostle Peter that day: the basic incompatibility of the wisdom of God and the wisdom of this world. Paul wrote,

> ...we speak wisdom among those who are mature, yet not the wisdom of this age, nor of the rulers of

this age, who are coming to nothing. But we speak the wisdom of God in a mystery, the hidden wisdom which God ordained before the ages for our glory, which none of the rulers of this age knew; for had they known, they would not have crucified the Lord of glory.[6]

The reason the rulers of this age didn't understand the wisdom of God is because the wisdom by which one rules in this age of sin is fundamentally different from the wisdom by which God redeems people from sin and its consequences. What's more, this remains true during the whole course of this present age. It isn't as if the rulers of the first three centuries of the Christian era didn't understand the wisdom of God, and then at last the rulers of this world understood it and embraced it. No, the wisdom of this age remains what it is for as long as the age lasts. The wisdom of God, which functions effectively for redemption, is foolishness when it comes to ruling in this present age.

For instance, Jesus told a rich young ruler, "Sell all that you have and distribute to the poor, and you will have treasure in heaven; and come, follow me."[7] The rich young ruler turned away in sorrow. He immediately understood the foolishness of such a proposal, for he understood the present age, just as we understand it. He was unwilling to take such a foolish course, although he was attracted to Jesus and Jesus to him.

It was not at all difficult to figure out what Jesus meant by such teaching. All one had to do was watch him and the disciples who followed him. It was quite clear that Jesus wasn't seeking this world's wealth. He didn't ask the rich man to give his money to Jesus and his disciples; He told him to give his wealth away to the poor. Jesus seems to have considered that the possession of wealth was a hindrance rather than a help in doing the will of God. Jesus was a poor man who trusted God to meet his needs, and regularly gave away most of the money He had to the poor. He challenged others, particularly the rich, to give away their wealth and follow him.

Jesus wasn't seeking this world's power. When He miraculously fed a crowd, they came to him in an attempt to take him by force and make him their king.[8] All Jesus had to do was say *yes* and he would have had what he needed to become a political force to be reckoned with. That crowd represented a potential power base from which to shake the existing system, bring it down

85

and take over. What did he do? He left the crowd of willing supporters and hid in the mountains alone.

Jesus had the audacity to speak the truth to the rich and powerful. He marched on the capital riding on a young donkey in fulfillment of Jewish prophecy of the advent of the Messiah-king, the son of David.[9] He was claiming the kingdom of his ancestor, King David. Jesus boldly strode into the temple and challenged the authorities there, disrupting the routines, driving out the peddlers of sacrificial animals and the exchangers of common currency for the temple coins.[10] He infuriated the chief priests. But his only weapon was the truth. His disciples and followers were unarmed, uneducated, mostly poor, including fishermen, farmers, carpenters, and slaves, their wives and children, and a number of sick people hoping to be touched by him and healed.

Jesus made enemies of the most powerful people in the Jewish establishment. He won the hearts of the poor people who had neither power, nor influence, nor wealth.[11] But then His public pronouncements—most especially His demonstration in Jerusalem—forced the wielders of power to do something about him. Jesus had no intention to resist the reaction He provoked from the establishment. When Peter produced two swords—a totally inadequate arsenal—and attempted to use it in the Lord's defense, Jesus commanded him to put it away. The Lord did not even implore the help of angels.[12]

According to the political wisdom of this world, to provoke an attack and then refuse to retaliate when it comes, was the wrong way to claim a kingdom. It was the wrong way to do it in the first century; it is the wrong way to do it today in the twentieth century or the twenty-first; and it was the wrong way to do it in every century in between.

Unarmed, without powerful allies or a treasure chest, Jesus was a sitting duck. Within a week the movers and the shakers of Judea had tried him, condemned him, and hung him on a cross to die. If that does not seem like foolishness to us in the late twentieth century, it may be because we have not seriously considered what was happening in that setting, the hopelessness of the situation from a human perspective, and the fact that this man who seemed bent on destroying himself asks us to follow Him.

This strategy makes no sense at all in regard to this present age and what works in this present world. Only in reference to the future is it seen to be the wisdom of God. The apostle Paul said it very clearly in his letter to the Corinthian believers in which he deals with the return of the Lord and the resurrection of the bodies of believers.

> If in this life only we have hope in Christ, we are of all men the most pitiable...why do we stand in jeopardy every hour? I affirm...I die daily. If, in the manner of men, I have fought with beasts at Ephesus, what advantage is it to me? If the dead do not rise, 'Let us eat and drink, for tomorrow we die!'[13]

And that, as everybody knew in the first century, is the reason why many Jews and Greeks, who often argued with each other, were in agreement about this, that the Gospel of Jesus as the Messiah was foolishness. It represented God as weak, a loser, and his doctrine and lifestyle foolish. Why then should anybody believe in Jesus? Above all, why should anybody follow Him?

If this is the only world there is, there would be no reason for believing in Jesus. Faith in Jesus makes sense only with reference to the future. In that day it will be clear to all men that Jesus is the Messiah. Then it will be obvious that believing in Him was the wisest thing any man could do.

But Jesus asked his disciples to follow Him in this world and in this age when it was crystal clear that following Jesus was hazardous to one's health. Believing in Jesus in the first century was to put one's life in this present world in jeopardy in the interest of the world to come. And so the wise and the mighty of this world— and those who aspired to be wise and mighty in this world, and those who feared the wise and mighty of this world—considered it foolishness.

It was. And it is.

The preaching of the cross is the same today at the end of the twentieth century. That would be clear to all Christians if they stopped to think about it. But typically Christians today don't stop to think about it.

There is a reason why issues that were uppermost in the minds of early believers are seldom raised today. That reason is rooted in the history of the church and in a silent revolution that changed the public face of Christianity a long, long time ago, in an Empire far away. We will consider that revolution in the following pages.

9

When Hope And Integrity Were Lost

The year was 312 A.D. The place was the city of Rome. It was a momentous occasion for both the Roman Empire and the Christian church. Constantine had just become Emperor of the Western half of the Empire. He had defeated his rival, Maxentius, at the battle of Milvian Bridge. Incredibly, on his shield and the shields of his troops, was emblazoned the sign of the cross. It was incredible because the Roman Empire had been the deadly enemy of Christianity for more than two centuries.

Persecution of the Christian church had been state policy from the time of Nero (64 A.D.)[1] up to and including the reign of Diocletian (284-305). Diocletian retired from office and there was another power struggle which ended with Constantine on top.[2] Within the memory of most people alive at that time, Diocletian had instituted the bloodiest persecution of Christians in the history of Rome and of the church. Now Constantine, the man who had just become the new Emperor in the West, was displaying the sign of the cross.

In 313 Constantine and Licinius, Emperor in the East, ended the persecution of Christians throughout the Empire with the Edict of Milan.[3] It is ironic that the cross became the symbol of Christian faith at precisely the time when persecution ended in the Roman Empire.[4] The cross was transformed from a harsh but redemptive reality for believers in this present age into an ornament, a reminder of a glorious heroic era in the history of the church, an era that was suddenly and unaccountably over. It was the beginning of confusion both in the church and in the state that has not been resolved to this day.

Constantine displayed the sign of the cross, but his triumph was nothing like the way Jesus triumphed by the cross. Constantine's victory did not come by following Jesus in suffering and death. The only blood Jesus shed was His own. Constantine won the Empire in the way of the world, not by shedding his own blood as a witness to the truth, but by shedding the blood of his enemies and competitors. He was not different in kind from Attila the Hun or Adolph Hitler. Constantine's warfare was fleshly, not spiritual; his victory was political and military. He became Emperor the way most ambitious men attain to power in this world: by the sword. He increased his power in the same way.

In 324 there was a struggle between Constantine and Licinius, Emperor in the Eastern half of the Roman Empire. Licinius was killed and Constantine took control of the entire Empire. Constantine sat at the pinnacle of worldly power in the mighty Roman Empire without rival or peer. He attributed his success on the battlefield and in his political maneuverings to Jesus Christ, in the same way that past Emperors had credited their military and political successes to Jupiter and the other gods of pagan antiquity. Constantine was the first "Christian" emperor of Rome. He was the first to establish an alliance between the church and the state, that is, between the symbol of the cross and the reality of the sword.

In his book, *Christianizing the Roman Empire, A.D. 100-400*, Ramsay MacMullen observed that the Roman army served under Constantine, a professed Christian. Later, the army served as well and as loyally under Julian, a professed pagan. Julian, who labored to restore the old pagan faith, kept on his general staff the high ranking officers who had been appointed by Constantius, a Christian. After Julian's death the army chose first a pious pagan. He was too old, so they chose a Christian, Jovian. MacMullen concluded "that faith counted for nothing , or not much, in the high command."[5]

There was nothing specifically Christian in the strategy or tactics of the Roman army under Constantine and his successors. The religious faith of the commanders and the troops was irrelevant to their military task. Constantine defeated Maxentius and Licinius because he was the better general and his troops were battle-hardened and loyal. They were better at killing and shedding blood than were their counterparts in the rival armies. Constantine did display the sign of the cross and he probably prayed to Jesus Christ to give him the victory in battle. But the character of that battle was not decided with reference to the commands Jesus gave to His apostles in the New Testament. Constantine considered himself an apostle of Jesus Christ. If so, he was a very different sort of apostle than the New Testament describes, and the Christ he served was also quite different from the Jesus of the New Testament.

What Constantine did do that was different was to change the policy of the Roman Empire that had been in force from 64 to 313, a period of almost two hundred and fifty years. He put an end to the persecution of the Christian church, or a large part of it, and took the church into partnership with him in running the Empire.

What induced Constantine to take this apparently radical step and reverse the policy of the Roman Empire toward the Christians? For one thing, the church was growing and becoming influential in the Empire. At the beginning, most believers came from the poor and the slave population, but in time the faith began to reach into the Roman aristocracy and some even in the royal family believed. Constantine's own mother was a Christian.

Second, partly due to the dissemination of Christian teaching, the old pagan religion was losing its hold on the people of the Empire. In any case, the dedication of the Christians to their faith was far more intense than that of pagans to theirs. If that dedication to Christ could be applied to the political situation, Constantine thought, it might hold the Empire together.

The Empire was in danger of breaking up. It was huge and unwieldy. And the "barbarians" were putting increasing pressure on the borders to the north and west. The armies of a united Rome easily held off potential invaders and increased the dimensions of the Empire. But when Rome was divided internally, the barbarians broke through the lines and entered the Empire. The Roman Empire was particularly vulnerable during times of transition from one Emperor to another.

There were twenty-three emperors from the time when Severus died in 211 A.D. until Diocletian became Emperor in 284. All but three died violent deaths at the hands of rebellious troops or by order of a rival for the throne who deposed him.[6] Imagine seventy-three years of practically non-stop power struggles, intrigue, bribery and civil wars! While the Romans were fighting among themselves during those devastating transitions, the "barbarians" broke into the Empire. When the power issue was settled the Romans repulsed the invaders, but the provinces had been devastated during the internal struggles. Many barbarians remained inside the Empire. They were good soldiers—some of them became Roman soldiers and officers—but their loyalties and sympathies were not those of traditional Roman citizens.

Meanwhile, the affluent Roman citizens were content to enjoy the good life and let others defend the empire. The pursuit of pleasure led to the breakdown of traditional morality and weakened family ties.

Conquest brought in an abundance of slaves. Slavery contributed to the increasing wealth of the wealthy, but it was devastating to many ordinary Roman citizens. Slave labor was cheap. Free Romans could not compete in the market place where their produce was undersold by the products of slave labor. Many had lost their family farms and either joined the army or became part of a growing urban mob of ruined citizens bitter over having been cut off from the material blessings of the Empire.[7] Revolutions broke out among such mobs and threatened the unity of the Empire.[8]

Constantine looked longingly on the growing network of Christian churches throughout the Roman world. In spite of persecution and hardship, the church was united. He thought he could use the Christian church and its faith in Jesus Christ to take the place of paganism as the religious glue to hold the disintegrating Roman Empire together. He found Christian bishops who were willing to cooperate with him in exchange for positions of honor and influence in the Empire, the cessation of persecution, tax relief, and other favors. The deal was struck. Constantine succeeded to the throne, and involved the cooperating bishops in the affairs of the Empire. But things didn't turn out as he expected.

The church did not bring unity to the Empire. Instead, involving the church in the politics of the Empire created divisions in the church. It happened right from the beginning. The Donatists of North Africa refused to join the new and unprecedented alliance with the Roman Empire. When Constantine and the new imperial church tried to compel them, the Donatists chose martyrdom, the historic and biblical strategy of the Christian church from its beginning. The new imperial church, in league with the Empire, became a persecuting institution. It began by persecuting dissenting Christians, but soon extended its persecution to pagans as well.

No less a figure than Augustine of Hippo in North Africa (St. Augustine) argued that it was permissible for the Catholic Church to persecute those Christians who refused to join its ranks, acknowledge its claims, and follow its revolutionary new policies. (Of course, Augustine never admitted in a clearly-worded statement that the policies he defended were revolutionary and new. But prior to Constantine the church suffered persecution and did not inflict it on others, so no Christian writer prior to Augustine had ever made such a case). This argument was used against the Donatists in North Africa.[9]

The issue there began with the appointment by Constantine of a bishop, Caecilian, who was said to have renounced his faith in Christ during the last great persecution. The "election" of the bishop was irregular, without the consent of a majority of the bishops of North Africa. Donatus and those who agreed with him would not submit to such a man as Caecilian. Furthermore, they resented the cavalier fashion in which Constantine had rigged the election of a man of doubtful character to the most important post in North Africa, Carthage, because he was willing to cooperate with the Emperor and implement his policies. Constantine passed over men of faith and courage who had risked their lives for the name of Jesus during the recent persecution. The Constantinian church supported this intrusion of the Emperor into the affairs of the church, as well as the use of the coercive power of the Empire to enforce its policies and persecute the Donatist assemblies.

There is, of course, nothing in the New Testament that says anything about Christians persecuting anybody. The New Testament has a great deal to say about persecution. But the entire emphasis of the New Testament is that Christians are the persecuted ones. There is not a single exception, not a single line to justify Christians persecuting anybody for any reason. Of course, prior to Constantine Christians were not in a position to be able to persecute anybody. They were a despised and hated minority. But they were what they were by choice and in agreement with New Testament revelation. It was a choice believers made in response to the teachings of Jesus and the apostles.

Christians chose to stand with Jesus, a man who was condemned and crucified by the established authorities. They were told to expect the same treatment, and that "'A servant is not greater than his master.' If they persecuted Me, they will also persecute you."[10] And, "We must through many tribulations enter the kingdom of God."[11] And so, truth and integrity became casualties of the union of church and state, through the invention of an argument with no basis at all in the New Testament, and in the suppression of opposing opinion by force.

The Donatist argument in the case above has to be gleaned from what was written about the Donatists by their ecclesiastical and imperial enemies. It was not that the ancient world lacked the technology to preserve these documents. I have a set of books containing the writings of the church fathers. Among them are eight large volumes of some six hundred pages each with closely spaced type from the period, most of it written by Augustine. Yet, not one volume written by a Donatist spokesman has been preserved. We know they wrote books of their own because Augustine referred to them. But all we know about them is what Augustine was pleased to tell in the process of refuting them. Their own documents were lost or destroyed. It was not accidental; it was the policy of the Roman Empire and of the Constantinian church. Evidently there was something in those writings that frightened Constantine and his church. They probably contained a convincing case and documented evidence that the Constantinian church had deviated sharply from apostolic teaching. But enough remains, even in the writings of Augustine, to make it clear to a careful observer that fundamental changes had taken place in the church, changes that to a large extent shook the church off its apostolic foundation.

The Donatist split was the first of many. Later when the Empire split in two East and West, the church also split. The division was explained in terms of doctrine, but the doctrinal point amounted to theological hair-splitting; it would not have divided the church unless there were political reasons that divided the Empire and caused a corresponding rift within the politicized church.

With the breakup of the Empire into nation states that waged war against one another, Christians began killing one another in the interest of whatever worldly passions fueled those disputes. The same thing has continued up to our own times. A tragic example in U.S. history is the Civil War, in which American churches split along the Mason-Dixon Line into separate Northern and Southern organizations, not on the basis of doctrine or structure, but of politics and economics. And Americans, most of them professing Christians, slaughtered one another in astonishing numbers.

One denomination that handled the slavery issue with Christian integrity was the Society of Friends, the "Quakers." They were an exception to the rule. Quakers discussed the question and decided slavery was wrong. But they agreed to keep silent until every Quaker who owned slaves had set them free. Then they spoke out. Whether they were in the South or the North, their message was the same. Their entire society took a righteous stand and did not split over the issue of slavery. Quakers in the South, however, suffered for their convictions, and some were driven out of the South by persecution.[12]

Half a century later in 1914 World War I broke out; all Europe was "Christian." The Germans claimed that God was with them in their struggle for national aggrandizement. But the English, the French, the Italians, the Russians, the Austrians, the Hungarians and the Americans also claimed to worship the same God and the same Christ who commanded His people to demonstrate their discipleship by loving one another. Inflamed by nationalist ambitions and hatreds, these "Christian" soldiers shot and killed one another and stabbed one another to death with bayonets in hand-to-hand combat.

The second World War broke out in Europe a generation later. A pop song with a cheerful melody and snappy beat carried the ironic message of Christendom: "Praise the Lord and pass the ammunition!" This is the heritage of Constantine. As sociologist C. Wright Mills wrote, "...the Christian record is rather clear. From the time of Constantine...Christians have killed Christians and have been blessed for doing so by other Christians."[13] It was a tragic and terrible departure from the early church which consistently disapproved of any participation by Christians in military operations. The specter of Christians killing one another in the service of a worldly state, I'm sure was beyond the power of New Testament Christians even to conceive.

The church was in partnership with the state after Constantine. That meant quite naturally that her interest shifted from the age to come, to the present world. From the time of Constantine on the church had a vested interest in the present evil world. It soft-peddled and modified the message of the return of the Lord Jesus, the doom of this present world, and the coming of a better world, which in the early days was a burning issue, a key part of the Gospel. The church's loyalty was now divided between the present and the future. In practice, the church increasingly neglected the future in favor of the interests of the present.

In short, the fourth century witnessed a revolution in the history of the church and of Christian doctrine. But it was a silent revolution. It was not announced and has never been celebrated. In fact, every effort possible was made to cover up the radical change and to make it appear that the church after Constantine was the same church it had been before Constantine.

How that happened and why is a fascinating and important story. We shall now consider the cover-up.

10

The Silent Revolution

The church, Paul tells us, is composed of believing Jews and gentiles who are built on the foundation of the apostles and prophets.[1] The Old Testament prophets foretold the coming of the Messiah, and the New Testament apostles identified Jesus as the Messiah, the One who will fulfill the Old Testament prophecies. The Old Testament prophets had left their writings behind. They required to be complemented by the witness of the New Testament apostles, revealed to them by God, that Jesus is the Christ, the Son of the living God.[2] Jesus wrote no books but the apostles did. Their writings were a kind of charter, revealed to the first apostles by the Holy Spirit and establishing the church in the sight of God. By the fourth century the documents that were to make up the New Testament were in circulation among the churches. The contents of the New Testament were not yet fixed but there was broad general agreement about the apostolic authority of most of them.

But the Constantinian church of the fourth and fifth centuries needed to justify changes that had no apostolic foundation, changes that contradicted Jesus and the original apostles. Specifically, they had to justify the new and unprecedented alliance of the church with the world and the state. The leaders therefore had to soft-peddle the revolutionary changes that had just been introduced into the church by Constantine and the cooperating bishops. Their task was a formidable one. They had to prove that there was continuity from the apostles to the time then present, in spite of the teaching of the apostles in the New Covenant Scriptures to the contrary. In other words, the jarring discontinuity had to be masked, and the impression given that nothing had changed, when in fact a revolution had taken place. That is, the revolution had to be hushed up.

It has always been a kind of open secret. Early church history is divided into three sections: Ante-Nicene, Nicene, and Post-Nicene, before during and after the Nicene Council. In a move unprecedented in the history of the church, Emperor Constantine convened a general council of the church. It was held in Nicea. Nobody doubts that the church-state alliance at the time of Constantine constituted a major turning point in church history. The task of the new imperial church was to make it appear to be a normal development of Apostolic Christianity, instead of the revolutionary departure from Apostolic Christianity that it was.

The new church-state alliance had great resources at its disposal. It had the Emperor of Rome and the wealth and power of the Roman Empire. It had a virtual monopoly on the communications media of the day. Most of the pulpits of the Christian churches were under the control of the Emperor and the bishops who were allied with him. The Constantinian alliance controlled the libraries and the means of publishing and preserving books and employed some of the most talented and influential churchmen of that generation, including the church historian, Eusebius. His writings on the history of the church became the standard work on the period from the end of New Testament times to the age of Constantine. The new imperial church also employed the brilliant and prolific author, Augustine, the bishop of Hippo, in North Africa. His writings provided the theological rationale for the new church-state alliance and all that was involved in it, including the theory of the "just war" and the unprecedented innovations that came with Constantine. According to Augustine, Christians could now participate with a clear conscience in violence and bloodshed on behalf of the Roman Empire. Indeed, military service, which had been prohibited to Christians prior to Constantine,[3] now became the solemn duty of able-bodied Christian men, the clergy alone exempted.[4]

During the second and third centuries the church was already rumbling with tremors of change that anticipated the huge seismic shift at the time of Constantine. For one thing, an old name disguised the emergence of a new office. In the New Testament churches, bishop (overseer) and presbyter (elder) were equivalent terms.[5] They were local elders who supervised the churches. They were what we would call laymen. Beginning in the second century the word bishop gradually became inflated.[6] It came to mean the professional and preeminent leader of the church in a city, as the office grew on the model of the Roman political hierarchy rather than that of the New Testament.[7] It happened this way.

Facing the threat of false doctrines, the church launched a three-pronged attack.

First, church leaders distilled a brief statement of faith called the Apostle's Creed. The creed defined the essentials of the faith in contradistinction to the heresies and put them in a series of easy-to-remember sentences that even the unlettered could learn.

Second, church leaders referred to the written documents of the apostles themselves (or those who were close to the apostles and accurately transcribed their teachings). In time there was a collection of documents widely regarded by the churches as genuine and apostolic. Eventually that collection of documents came to be known as the New Testament.[8]

Third, to interpret and apply those documents to contemporary situations there were a few prominent bishops who claimed to be the successors of the apostles. Their apostolic authority was recognized by bishops from smaller cities in their respective regions.

Bishops of big-city churches claimed apostolic authority. In fact, they were resident elders rather than itinerant preachers and church planters as were the New Testament apostles. Notable examples were the bishops of Jerusalem, Rome, and Antioch. The theory was developing that there should be one supreme bishop, corresponding to the Emperor in Roman politics. Such a bishop would be empowered to render the final decision in disputes. He would be, as it were, the court of last resort for the church. Even before Constantine, prominent Bishops were in competition with one another for the top job.

This kind of competition was already present in New Testament times. The apostle Paul chided the Corinthians for exalting themselves and making themselves rich and comfortable, in contrast to the apostles who were suffering for the faith. Paul wrote:

> You are already full! You are already rich!
> You have reigned as kings without us—and indeed
> I could wish you did reign, that we also might
> reign with you! For I think that God has displayed
> us, the apostles, last, as men condemned to death;
> for we have been made a spectacle to the world,
> both to angels and to men. We are fools for
> Christ's sake, but you are wise in Christ! We are

weak, but you are strong! You are distinguished, but we are dishonored! To the present hour we both hunger and thirst, and we are poorly clothed, and beaten, and homeless. And we labor, working with our own hands. Being reviled, we bless; being persecuted, we endure; being defamed, we entreat. We have been made as the filth of the world, the offscouring of all things until now.[9]

The apostle's rebuke and warning evidently went unheeded, for the tendencies he rebuked eventually prevailed. Local bishops yearned to reign as kings, and when the opportunity came to do so, many of them grasped it. The New Testament scriptures remained as a witness to the integrity of the early church, its doctrines and practices, but the scriptural message was muffled and all but lost for centuries.

In his book *THE REFORMERS AND THEIR STEPCHILDREN*, Leonard Verduin, a Protestant scholar from the reformed tradition, wrote about the consequences of the church-state alliance at the time of Constantine. Verduin calls it the fall of the church and likens it to the fall of man when Adam and Eve sinned and plunged mankind into grief.

Let us not pass lightly over the implications of the Constantinian change. A "fall" is a serious thing. The change that took place in the days of Constantine shook the ship from stem to stern; nothing in the Church's theology, its organization, its place in the world, escaped the effects of the virus that had entered its bloodstream. Medication would have to be strong and in large doses... Had it not been for the fact that the blue-prints of the authentic Church were still accessible, in the New Testament, there would never have been any clamor for the restitution of it.[10]

In his book, *THE CHURCH AND THE JEWS, The Biblical Relationship*, Dan Gruber addressed the theological methods and arguments by which most of the church was persuaded to cooperate with or at least tolerate in silence the radical change that was taking place in the church.

Gruber, a Jew from Highland Park, Illinois, was a college student in search of the truth in the early 1970s. He heard the

Gospel of Jesus Christ from a member of his family. He believed, was filled with joy in his new found faith, and felt called by the Lord to try to introduce his fellow Jews to their Messiah, Jesus. But there were problems.

Gruber grew up in the years when the horrible truth about the Holocaust was being studied. Writers like William L. Shirer in his book, *The Rise And Fall Of The Third Reich*, [11] pointed out the connection between the holocaust and the teachings of the German Reformer and leader of the Protestant Reformation, Martin Luther. Luther may have been more vehement in his anti-Semitism than some other Christian theologians, but he was typical and in no way exceptional.

As a Jew with a call to preach Messiah to his fellow Jews, Gruber needed to know why there was a strong anti-Jewish element in traditional Christian theology. He didn't find in the Bible the kind of anti-Jewish prejudice that he found in traditional Christian theology. Both the Christian and Jewish scriptures were frank enough about the failures and sins of the Jewish people, but both documents held out hope for the eventual restoration of the Jewish people.

For instance, Jesus belonged to the tribe of Judah and was therefore a Jew. He was the Messiah, a descendant of the great King David of Israel and the chosen heir to David's throne. He made His claim to that throne in the city of Jerusalem, the Capital city of David's kingdom. [12]

His first disciples—all Jews—asked the resurrected Jesus if He was going to restore the kingdom to Israel at that time. The traditionalist Christian explanation of the passage would represent Jesus as denying that there would ever be a restoration of the kingdom to Israel; that it was a mistake to believe in a kingdom on earth; that Jesus was a heavenly king of a "spiritual" kingdom, and the disciples should have understood that. But Jesus never said any such thing.

He did not fault the disciples for thinking that the kingdom would be restored to Israel. The question had to do with *when* it would happen, not *if* it would happen. And Jesus answered the question as it was asked. He told the disciples that it was not for them to know the times; the Father had kept that matter under His own authority. In the meantime, Jesus had a job for the disciples to do.

If there was something wrong with the disciples' expectation, that would have been the time for Jesus to say so. He did not say so. He did not suggest or imply or hint that the disciples were wrong to expect the kingdom to be restored to Israel. The restoration of the kingdom of David was a key part of the Messianic hope of devout Israelites. The disciples were convinced they had found their Messiah in Jesus. It was inevitable that they should expect the Messiah to confirm the hope proclaimed by the Old Testament prophets. The New Testament affirms repeatedly that Jesus came to fulfill the hopes and promises of the Old Testament.

The apostle Paul acknowledged that blindness had come on many Israelites, but in the same context he also wrote that when the fullness of the Gentiles has been brought to salvation, "all Israel will be saved."[13] Traditional Christian theology, however, typically ignored the Jewish roots of Jesus, wrote off the Jewish people without hope of restoration, and said little or nothing about the fulfillment of the hope of Israel or the restoration of the kingdom to Israel under their Messiah, His thousand year reign of justice and truth on the earth, or His restoration of Jerusalem as the capital city of the coming kingdom. Traditional Christianity despised the Jews and in its theology rejected them and replaced them with the Christian church.

This anti-Jewish position was challenged in the nineteenth and twentieth centuries by a revival of pre-millennial theology, but the traditional stance of the church was anti-Semitic, and it provided a theological rationale for centuries of persecution of Jews, including Hitler's attempt to annihilate the whole Jewish population of Europe. But why?

Gruber studied Christian theology and church history to find out. His studies led to some amazing discoveries. In his research, the Lord led him to the fourth century, the era of Constantine, and the Council of Nicea in 325 A.D. The council institutionalized the new partnership between the church and the Roman Empire. Gruber commented, "With this dramatic political shift came an equally dramatic theological shift."[14]

One reason why Constantine convened the Council of Nicea was to establish a uniform date throughout the Empire for the celebration of the resurrection of Jesus. Since the resurrection occurred at the time of the Jewish Passover, the churches in the East used the biblical reckoning in the Old Testament to determine the time of the resurrection. In the West another system was developed so that the resurrection would always be celebrated on the first day of the week, the day of the resurrection of Jesus.

Constantine with his passion for uniformity decided the issue in a strange way. He concluded that the system used in the West should be adopted throughout the Empire. The reason? Because the Jews were such perverse people that one could be sure that whatever they believed and practiced must be wrong.

Constantine did not create an anti-Jewish sentiment. That was already present both in the church and in the empire. But Constantine's logic institutionalized an anti-Jewish prejudice in official church policy. And ironically, the issue the Emperor chose was one in which the Jews happened to be correct and biblical. Then Constantine asserted that whatever a church council decides is certainly the will of God. His declaration therefore set the precedent that a church council can overrule the Bible. Perhaps the issue itself wasn't so important. Maybe it didn't matter to God on what day the resurrection should be celebrated. But the reason given and the precedent set by the decision were profoundly important. Their influence remains to this day.

Gruber learned that the church historian, Eusebius, played a key role in bringing about the theological shift that occurred in the fourth century. An admirer and biographer of the Emperor and official church historian in the employ of the Roman Empire under Constantine, Eusebius was a revisionist historian. Today we would perhaps characterize such a person as a propagandist rather than a historian. As to his approach to Scripture, he was influenced by Origen, a prominent interpreter of the scriptures in Caesarea where Eusebius grew up.

Origen was the third century Bible commentator who applied the allegorical method in interpreting Scripture. His motive for doing so was to find the common ground which he believed existed between the Bible and Greek philosophy. Origen believed that every text of Scripture had a hidden allegorical meaning. Moreover, he considered the allegorical sense the highest and the "spiritual" interpretation. The literal meaning he considered of lesser importance, unspiritual and Jewish.

There are times when an allegory is appropriate. The parables of Jesus are little allegories in which, for instance, a farmer sowing seeds stands for a preacher spreading the word of God. The apostle Paul found an allegory in the Old Testament account of Abraham's ne by Sarah, the free woman, and the other by Hagar, a arah's maid. Hagar and her son represent the covenant of ...at brings bondage. Sarah and her son represent the covenant of promise that brings freedom through faith. The slave and her offspring are cast out, indicating that there is no future for the covenant of law. It does not bring salvation but condemnation. Jerusalem at that time was in bondage under law as a result of having rejected the means of escape from that bondage—Jesus, the mediator of the New Covenant of promise—and was therefore rejected by God.[15]

For Origen and those who followed him, the allegorical interpretation of scripture, including the rejection of the Jews, became a kind of paradigm for all biblical interpretation. The only occasions when Origen departed from this preference for the allegorical, Gruber pointed out wryly, is when the Scripture pronounces God's judgment and wrath against the Jews. There Origen accepted the plain literal meaning of the words. The blessings promised to a restored Israel, however, Origen interpreted allegorically and applied to the church.

Sometimes allegories are true. And sometimes Plato came close to saying what the New Testament says. But there are significant differences which Origen took pains to obscure. In spite of his brilliance, Origen didn't convince everybody. He had to flee from Alexandria because there he was regarded as a heretic. Nevertheless, his influence was great, and in some quarters it was dominating, including the region around Caesarea where Eusebius grew up.

Eusebius used Origen's method to bring the prophetic Scriptures into line with the new union of church and state. In the interest of church-state cooperation, Eusebius avoided or explained away the Scriptures that spoke of an apocalyptic struggle between the church and the world (and the state that represented and administered the world). The result was that the orthodoxy of the New Testament church became the heresy of the Constantinian church. And the heresy of the New Testament church became the orthodoxy of the Constantinian church.

For instance, Justin Martyr spoke for the church before Constantine. He lived from about 110 to 165 A.D. He responded to a question by a Jew named Trypho.

Do you really admit [asked Trypho] that this place, Jerusalem, shall be rebuilt; and do you expect your people to be gathered together, and made joyful with Christ and the patriarchs, and the prophets, both the men of our nation, and other proselytes who joined them before your Christ came?...

Justin's answer is a statement of what Christians at that time believed to be false teaching and what they held to be true:

...[I]f you have fallen in with some who are called Christians, but who do not admit this [truth], and venture to blaspheme the God of Abraham, and the God of Isaac, and the God of Jacob; who say there is no resurrection of the dead, and that their souls, when they die, are taken to heaven; do not imagine that they are Christians....But I and others, who are right-minded Christians on all points, are assured that there will be a resurrection of the dead, and a thousand years in Jerusalem, which will then be built, adorned, and enlarged [as] the prophets Ezekiel and Isaiah and others declare.[16]

Justin, speaking for those in the early church who held to the teaching of the apostles, believed in the resurrection of the dead and a literal thousand year kingdom of God on earth with its capital at Jerusalem. He took the Old Testament prophecies in their literal sense as the basis of his belief. In the fourth century Eusebius turned apostolic teaching upside-down. He saw the elevation of Constantine as the fulfillment of the biblical promises of the kingdom of God on earth in what came to be called the Holy Roman Empire. So Eusebius denied the common-sense meaning of the Old Testament prophecies, denied that there would be a literal kingdom of God on earth with its capital in Jerusalem and ruled in person by Jesus, the Messiah of Israel. And Eusebius falsely represented his innovative concept as apostolic truth.

Furthermore, Eusebius knew what he was doing. He was familiar with the writings of Justin Martyr. In his church history he referred to Justin but ignored the relevant statement quoted above when Justin wrote about the millennium. Eusebius was well aware of the millennial faith of the early church. In his history, Eusebius told about Papias who was taught by those who were friends of the apostles. Eusebius admitted that Papias believed in the millennial kingdom on earth, but dismissed the millennial convictions of Papias as a dim-witted misunderstanding of the apostolic teachings, "not perceiving that the things said by them were spoken mystically in figures."[17] Eusebius mentioned Irenaeus and other writers who held millennial conviction, but said that they got their ideas from Papias rather than the apostles. Gruber wrote,

> Eusebius firmly believed, in the fourth century, that the Church was the 'new Israel,' replacing the Jews. He firmly believed that there was no distinct future for the Jews in the plan of God. Whenever he discusses the issue of a physical millennium, he treats it as an heretical view ('Millennium' comes from the Latin *mille annum*, a thousand years). Following Origen, Eusebius rejected the normal meaning of the Scriptures that promise a restoration to the Jewish people. Or he ignored these Scriptures altogether... Eusebius was intentionally inaccurate. He had his own agenda... Eusebius ignored the sources that showed the apostolic tradition to be different from what he thought it should be. He was intent on creating an apostolic tradition that was different from what the apostles had actually believed and taught.[18]

One casualty in this new deal was the church's hope in the age to come. As a result, the church neglected its God-given job of representing the future kingdom of God. This failure to represent the hope of the gospel is not just ancient history; it has had continuing results down to our own times.

In his book *The Secular City* written in the mid 1960s, Harvey Cox wrote about the culmination of this centuries-long process.

> Secularization occurs when man turns his attention away from worlds beyond and toward this world and this time (saeculum = 'this present age').

> The forces of secularization have no serious interest in persecuting religion. Secularization simply bypasses and undercuts religion and goes on to other things. It has relativized religious world views and thus rendered them innocuous.

106

Religion has been privatized. It has been accepted as the peculiar prerogative and point of view of a particular person or group. Secularization has accomplished what fire and chain could not: it has convinced the believer that he *could* be wrong, and persuaded the devotee that there are more important things than dying for the faith. The gods of traditional religions live on as private fetishes or the patrons of congenial groups, but they play no significant role in the public life of the secular metropolis.[19]

Another casualty of the deal with Constantine was the church's prophetic voice. The church had a prophetic ministry to the Roman world and its government when the church was independent of the state. Such speaking of truth to power was no longer acceptable after the church had made its peace with the Empire and many of her bishops were on the Emperor's payroll. Could it really be said that the Roman Empire was doomed when the Emperor did great favors for the church and its leaders? Those who did say such things were silenced by high authorities in the church or branded as heretics. If they spoke out in spite of warnings, they were persecuted or martyred by the state at the direction of the imperial church. Dan Gruber concluded:

Constantine and Eusebius institutionalized many serious errors. They made changes that were to plunge the Church and the world into a literal thousand years of darkness. They laid a different foundation than Jesus and His apostles had laid. A new era in the history of the Church had begun. In actuality, a new Church began...[20] In many ways, Constantine laid a new foundation for the Church. To this day, the Church bears his image. That is what he intended.[21]

Dr. Ramsay MacMullen, Dunham Professor of Classics and History at Yale University, has studied and written extensively about the whole era during which Christendom came into being and Christianity "triumphed" in the Roman Empire. He was interviewed by Ken Meyers for a volume of the Mars Hill Audio Journal, and asked about the attempt by Christian historians to "pretty up" a process that is not altogether flattering to the church. MacMullen's response is instructive. He said that the primary responsibility of any research community is to tell the truth. He found it "troublesome" and a target for his correction that the truth was not candidly told in regard to this era. "It goes beyond the imperative for research," said Dr. MacMullen, "it is a breach of the Golden Rule."[22]

The church "triumphed' in the Roman Empire. Persecution of Christians who belonged to the new church-state union ceased, and the church entered into partnership with Constantine in administering the Roman Empire. But from the point of view of biblical truth and church history, it was a strange sort of triumph. This triumph did not usher in the kingdom of justice and peace on earth as promised in Scripture. Jesus did not return in power and great glory to rule and reign over the kingdoms of the earth from Jerusalem. The resurrection of the dead did not occur. The final judgment did not take place. The nations did not cease waging wars, and men did not beat their swords into plowshares and their spears into pruning hooks, as Scripture foretold would happen when the kingdom of God was established on the earth in power and glory. All of these things were prophesied by the apostles of the New Testament and the prophets of the Old Testament.

What did begin in the early fourth century was a revolution in the relationship of a large part of the church to the state. It required a secret adjustment of the church's teaching about the last days and the second coming of Jesus Christ to the earth. For the New Testament does have something to say about the cessation of persecution and when it will take place.

Paul wrote to the persecuted Christians in Thessalonica and encouraged them with this word of hope:

> ...it is a righteous thing with God to repay with tribulation those who trouble you, and to give you who are troubled rest with us when the Lord Jesus is revealed from heaven with his mighty angels, in flaming fire taking vengeance on those who do not know God, and on those who do not obey the gospel of our Lord Jesus Christ. These shall be punished with everlasting destruction from the presence of the Lord and from the glory of His power, when He comes, in that Day, to be glorified in His saints and to be admired among all those who believe, because our testimony among you was believed.[23]

The passage is a typical apocalyptic message of great conflict. It teaches that here and now in this present age the church suffers severe persecution. But the tables will one day be turned. The saints will be glorified in that day. The glorious Lord will be admired in them. The question is, when does that take place?

According to the New Testament, persecution of believers will cease when Jesus is revealed from heaven at His second coming with the overwhelming power of His heavenly army of angels. And John, in the Revelation, makes the point that "every eye shall see Him, even those who pierced Him."[24] This is not some secret revelation given only to a few specially enlightened scholars; every eye shall see him. Even his enemies shall see him.

Persecution of Christians ceased in the early fourth century (except for those Christians who were persecuted by the new church-state alliance). But persecution didn't cease by means of the second coming of Jesus Christ in great power and glory. And so the apocalyptic message of both the New and Old Covenant Scriptures had to be toned down and modified. The writings of the apostles were well known by this time. There was no way for the scholars and editors of the Constantinian church to delete the apocalyptic books or to remove the apocalyptic texts. They were woven into the fabric of the New Covenant revelation in writings that were well known and widely circulated among the churches. Prior to Constantine they had been the accepted belief of the church, a prominent and distinctive part of the gospel. They remained after Constantine as a silent witness to be revived from time to time by groups that were declared to be heretical after the fourth century. Meanwhile, in the Constantinian church, the apocalyptic message was neglected or interpreted to mean something other than what it said.

But there is one passage in the New Testament which explains what happened at the time of Constantine. And that passage fits the Constantinian church like the tights on a ballet dancer. We shall consider that passage in the following chapters.

11

The Parable of the Wheat and the Tares

In the parable of the wheat and the tares Jesus gave us a panoramic view of church history, before any of it happened. All the volumes written on the history of the church simply fill in the details on this amazing outline. Already it has covered nearly 2,000 years with uncanny accuracy.

The Lord portrayed the whole of the present age up to its end and the beginning of the next, as a growing season, from planting to harvest. The planting is the preaching of the Gospel at the first appearing of Jesus Christ. The harvest is the end of the age at the time of the Lord's second coming to rule in power and glory.

This parable is the church's key to being prepared for the unprecedented crisis at the end of the age, a crisis that has been mounting for centuries. Nothing is more important to the church of Jesus Christ in the present age. For this is her story, her history: past, present, and future. In it we find an explanation of the greatest single problem that has plagued the church for centuries, how God will solve that problem, and how we can cooperate with Him in the last revival before the second coming.

THE PARABLE

The Kingdom of heaven is like a man who sowed good seed in his field; but while men slept, his enemy came and sowed tares among the wheat and went his way. But when the grain had sprouted and produced a crop, then the tares also appeared.

So the servants of the owner came and said to him, 'Sir, did you not sow good seed in your field? How then does it have tares?'

He said to them, 'An enemy has done this.'

The servants said to him, 'Do you want us then to go and gather them up?'

But he said, 'No, lest while you gather up the tares you also uproot the wheat with them. Let both grow together until the harvest, and at the time of harvest I will say to the reapers, 'First gather together the tares and bind them in bundles to burn them, but gather the wheat into my barn....'

He who sows the good seed is the Son of Man. The field is the world, the good seeds are the sons of the kingdom, but the tares are the sons of the wicked one. The enemy who sowed them is the devil, the harvest is the end of the age, and the reapers are the angels.

Therefore as the tares are gathered and burned in the fire, so it will be at the end of this age. The Son of Man will send out His angels, and they will gather out of His kingdom all things that offend, and those who practice lawlessness, and will cast them into the furnace of fire. There will be wailing and gnashing of teeth. Then the righteous will shine forth as the sun in the kingdom of their Father. He who has ears to hear, let him hear![1]

THE MEANING

The Lord represented himself in the parable as a farmer. One hot sunny Spring morning three farm hands hurried across the broad field to meet him as he strode through the bordering grass to begin the day's work. Breathless and alarmed, all three of them were talking at once, gesturing toward the field, turning to look at the new green growth and then back to the farmer.

"Didn't you sow good seeds in your field?"

"Of course," said the land owner.

"It's full of tares!" they said.

The farmer went out to investigate. Sure enough, the entire field was full of weeds growing right alongside of the wheat. It was not the normal amount of weeds randomly growing here and there from seeds hidden in the clods. These had been sown deliberately.

Someone had entered the farmer's field at night when everybody was asleep. The intruder had brought a burlap bag full of weed seeds and scattered them everywhere.

"An enemy has done this," said the farmer.

It was sabotage—an act deliberately designed to spoil the landowner's work, frustrate his purposes, ruin his crop, embarrass him, and drive him out of business.

The field was full of weeds. They would be using up the space that the growing wheat would need, consuming the nutrients of the soil and the precious moisture that ought to be feeding the wheat.

In this parable Jesus told his disciples to expect a disaster in the course of church history. I believe the parable deals with the church. I say that even though the Lord said that the field is the world, and the word *world* is frequently used in the New Testament to mean the evil system ruled by the devil. Often when it is used in that way the world stands in contradistinction to the church. But that is not the only way the word is used in New Testament scripture. It is used to signify mankind, as in John 3:16, "God so loved the world that He gave His only begotten Son..." *World* is also used as the equivalent of the earth. The meaning in a given passage should be determined by the context. Jesus used the word for the setting of the parable, the dwelling place of mankind, the place where the gospel is preached.

The point is, in the parable the field does not represent the evil system that stands in opposition to the church. If it did, there would be no reason for the servants of the Lord to be shocked and surprised to find the field full of weeds. Why expect anything else in the evil world? Jesus called the devil the prince of this world; both He and His disciples expected the world to be full of the sons of the devil. But in the parable the servants of the Lord were grieved and disappointed to find tares in the field. The field therefore represents that part of the world that had been redeemed from the devil's grasp. That is evidently why, in explaining the parable, Jesus refers to it as "His field" and "His kingdom." Jesus contemplates the church. To discover the church full of the sons of the devil is indeed a cause for alarm and puzzlement. That was in fact the reaction of the servants of the Lord to the fall of the church in the time of Constantine and his successors.

If you read it carefully, church history in the fourth century tells precisely the same story as the parable of the wheat and the tares.

After trying unsuccessfully to stamp out the church with persecution, the devil tried another strategy. He couldn't beat the church and so he joined it, filling its ranks with his own people.

A Revolution in Church History

The reign of Constantine marked a revolutionary change in the professing Christian church that has continued with modifications down to the present. Persecution stopped. There was a professing Christian on the throne, seated in the imperial palace itself. It seemed at first like a great victory for the faith. But it wasn't long before those with eyes to see began to realize that this new alliance of the church with the empire was a disaster in disguise. For one thing, the church began to fill up with members who lacked the commitment of the early believers.

It is not that there were no sinners and hypocrites in the church prior to Constantine, there were. But they were like the normal crop of weeds growing in a field. They were random, relatively few, and manageable. With the new policy there were so many whose faith was so doubtful that it was no longer possible to uphold the old standards or to maintain an effective discipline or unity. The reasons for that are not hard to discern.

In the days before Constantine the threat of persecution and martyrdom and the social, economic and political disadvantages that came with being a Christian discouraged people from joining the church, unless they were ready to lay down their lives for Christ and the hope of the Gospel. The church was largely poor; the majority came from the lower classes and many were slaves. Leadership in the church marked a man and made him a special target for persecution and martyrdom. But beginning with Constantine, all these barriers to pride and worldly ambition were suddenly swept away as if with a tidal wave.

Baptisms were administered *en masse*, and included whole armies of Roman troops eager to please their Commander-in-Chief who had publicly identified himself with the Christian church.[2]

Malachi Martin, a Roman Catholic scholar and author, illustrated the radical change that took place in the church in his account of two Bishops of Rome, one preceding Constantine and one following.[3] The first, Pontian, was put to death by Roman guards while doing slave labor in a salt mine. Sylvester, the first bishop of Rome in the new imperial church, died of natural causes in his own comfortable bed. He had been a wealthy, influential man, honored and protected by the political and military might of the Empire.

The "peace" that came with the conversion of Constantine was bewildering to Christians who remembered how things used to be. They remembered a church so absorbed in preparing for the coming age of peace and glory that its members despised the present world and even their own lives. Suddenly, it was safe to be a Christian in this present evil world. And the church, or at least its key bishops, had a vested interest in the present world.

For those who passed through the transition as believers, it was astonishing, incredible. There was nothing in the history of the church to prepare them for it, nothing in their sacred writings to explain it. Many had expected and prepared themselves for martyrdom. Now the former enemy was supposed to be regarded as a friend. Some welcomed the new alliance and thought it was a God-given opportunity to spread the Gospel throughout the world. The prophets and reformers among them, observing the decay of devotion, the fading hope, the worldliness of so many church members, became convinced it was a fraud.

To the reformers among them the new situation did not seem like the triumph of the church, but something else, they hardly knew what. It was as if their enemies were now inside the gates, brought in by the prominent leaders of the church in a kind of Trojan horse.

According to the parable of the wheat and the tares, it was heavy damage inflicted on the church by the devil. And from this time on there was an incessant cry for reform and for a return to the purity and integrity of the early days of the church. It was a cry for what came to be known in the course of church history as reform and revival.

12

The Lesser Of Two Evils

The servants were agitated. "Do you want us to go and pull up the tares?"

"No," he said. And the servants looked back in surprise. "Lest while you gather up the tares you also uproot the wheat with them. Let both grow together until the harvest..."

He chose to let the wheat and the weeds grow together until the harvest. His logic is this: with all the damage that the weeds would do, they would not finally destroy the wheat. The weeds would weaken the wheat and make an ugly looking field. But they would not kill the wheat. The landowner in the parable expected the wheat and tares to survive until the harvest if they were allowed to remain in the soil. Pulling up the weeds, on the other hand, would uproot some wheat along with the weeds.

What the landowner said was that if men were to try to fix things they would do more harm than good. This problem, therefore, will not be solved until God Himself solves it in His own time and way.

The solution chosen by the farmer in the parable is not a very satisfying one. He had to choose the lesser of two evils. The disappointments of the Constantinian church are painful and often heartbreaking. It is the fall of the church and very much like what happened to Adam and Eve in the Garden of Eden. God offers hope, but the consequences are serious. And it will be a long, long time before the problem will be solved. The reaction of the servants in the parable represents with uncanny accuracy the reaction of the prophets and reformers in the course of church history.

One curious example of the frustration on the part of the servants of the Lord has been preserved in stone as a tourist attraction in Qalaat Semaan, Syria. It is a pillar on which Simeon

Stylites (d. 459) sat for forty-two years. I suppose he is the patron-saint of all champions of forlorn causes. His pillar-sitting was a protest against a church that had become worldly, self-indulgent, and filled with pseudo-saints. His strange exercise in austerity was a sort of self-inflicted persecution at a time when real persecution of most Christians had largely ceased in the Roman Empire.[1] Nevertheless, people came from great distances to hear his wisdom. He was one of many witnesses who attracted the seriously devout and reminded all Christians of how far the church had fallen.

St. Antony and Monasticism

Monasticism was born from a similar frustration with the Constantinian church and an impulse for reform. The word *monk* comes from a word meaning alone. Monks were originally hermits who withdrew from the fellowship of a compromised church and lived in solitude. Later, the meaning of the word changed with changing practices to include cenobites, who lived together in religious communities. Christian monks were reformers who tried by their teaching and especially by their examples to revive a devotion to the Lord Jesus characteristic of the early Christians, a devotion that was so compromised from the fourth century on, that it was all but lost.

The monastic movement began with St. Antony (251-356) in Egypt and grew rapidly in the wake of Constantine's reign in the fourth and fifth centuries. Antony began his Christian life by giving away his inherited wealth in response to the gospel story of the rich young ruler. He did what the biblical character was unwilling to do. Antony lived outside of town, ate little, slept little, worked with his hands to provide a meager living for himself, and gave the rest away to the poor. During one of the last persecutions, he went to Alexandria to minister to Christians who had been condemned to prison or to slavery in the mines. He was hoping to be a martyr, but it was not to be. When persecution ceased, Antony imposed greater austerities on himself: fastings, wearing an uncomfortable garment of skin, no longer bathing. He attracted the attention of many Christians who were troubled by the state of the established church.

Antony lived through the silent revolution in church history. He reached manhood and began his experiments in monastic life in the generation preceding Constantine's reign. In the generation following Constantine's rise to imperial power, Antony lived to see the monastic principles and practices he adopted spread widely throughout the Empire.[2]

Did monasticism fulfill the Lord's will as given through the parable? That is, did it hold up the high standard of New Testament commitment without ruthlessly trying to root out unbelievers and hypocrites?

The monks usually cooperated with the established church. The various orders tried to model the purity and sacrificial commitment of the early church, without exactly condemning the worldly church that was unable to measure up to New Testament standards. They tried hard to preserve the memory of a pure church in the face of a church mired in unbelievers and unbelief like a truck up to its axles in mud.

The monks stayed close enough to the church to help if and when they could, but far enough away to keep out of the deep muck. It was tough duty. In a situation in which believers and unbelievers coexist in the same church, there aren't a lot of flag-waving, band-playing successes. Among the contributions of the monastic orders is this: they painstakingly copied out the Scriptures. They could not restore the church to the integrity of the New Testament original. And soon they discovered tares in their own corner of the field. But they at least kept the memory of those early days alive by making and preserving copies of the Bible. They did what they could.

The Donatists of North Africa

Donatus was a North African, part black, part Semitic. He was a bishop from a small town called Casae Nigrae. Donatus was convinced that the church's alliance with the Roman Emperor was bogus, that nothing had changed, that the Empire was not and could not be converted. He was sure the Lord Jesus would return soon, and that He was coming for a pure and spotless church. Donatus was appalled by the compromise the church made by uniting with the Empire.[3] Donatus is remembered as a heretic, but not because he taught false doctrine. His quarrel with the Constantinian church was not a doctrinal issue, but a practical one.

Faced with the threat of death in the most recent persecution, some Christians had renounced their faith in Jesus Christ. With Constantine's rise to power and the cessation of persecution, many who had denied the faith wanted to return to the church. The main body of the church, including the bishop of Rome, was inclined to be forgiving if there were sincere repentance and sorrow for their lapse on the part of those who had defected. Donatus was not convinced that those who had renounced their faith could be restored.

Before the issue was resolved Emperor Constantine, Sylvester, Bishop of Rome, and a couple of other European bishops appointed Caecilian as the new Bishop of Carthage in North Africa where Donatus lived. Caecilian had renounced his faith during the persecution of Emperor Diocletian. The issue in this case was not only whether a defector could return and be received as a penitent sinner back into the fellowship of the church. There was something else, something far more serious. The issue was whether or not a former defector should be put in a place of leadership in the church.

Carthage was no ordinary place of leadership. It was one of the most important centers in the ancient world. Appointment to such a post should be a reward for faithful service in a lesser post. It seemed to Donatus to add insult to injury to pass over faithful men who had endured torture—including the loss of eyes and limbs—for the sake of Jesus, and then appoint to a key post a man who under threat of persecution had renounced his faith to save his own skin. What kind of message did this act send to the churches and in particular to the young men chosen by the Lord for leadership in the church? It seemed plain to Donatus, and to many others with him, that it didn't matter to the imperial church whether one was faithful to Jesus or not, just so long as one was willing to cooperate with the Emperor.

Donatus has been portrayed by his ecclesiastical enemies as a hard-hearted man without compassion for human weakness. Since all of his writings were destroyed by Constantine and his associates in the imperial church, we can't be sure about the convictions of Donatus on that issue. But we do know that that was not the point over which he broke fellowship.

The issue over which he separated from the Constantinian church was an issue that concerned leadership and promotion. He had a valid biblical point. Jesus said that the man who had proven himself faithful in the small sphere of responsibility with which he had been entrusted, was the man who would be trusted with greater authority and responsibility. Constantine and Sylvester violated that principle. For political considerations, they appointed a man to a place of high authority who had not been faithful in a place of lesser authority. Charity may incline us to agree that he should have been forgiven and received back into the church upon his sincere confession and repentance. But he ought not to have been promoted to a place of high authority.

That was why Donatus broke with the new church-state alliance. "What does the Emperor have to do with the church?" he demanded. When the imperial church sent soldiers from Constantine's army and attempted to force the dissenting churches to join the church-state alliance, the Donatists did what Christians had been doing from the beginning. They refused to act contrary to the will of God and suffered persecution and martyrdom. For the Donatists, persecution and martyrdom were signs of genuine faith. Jesus had said something similar in the Sermon on the Mount.[4]

But the policy of persecuting dissenters was to Donatus a sign of false faith. In the New Testament the persecutors are the enemies of God. The Donatists, therefore, not only separated from the imperial church, but insisted that those who joined their fellowship from the Constantinian church be rebaptized. In doing so, the Donatists invalidated the baptism of the imperial church. Because of the Donatists' policy of re-baptism, the imperial church labeled them heretics rather than simply schismatics.

They continued for three hundred years under the name of Donatists.[5] Although they were harassed and persecuted and their books were burned by the imperial church, the convictions of the Donatists have survived to this day. This includes the policy of requiring baptism when someone came to their communion from the main-line churches, although they may have been "baptized" previously by those churches.

There were people identified as "neo-Donatists" at the time of the Protestant Reformation more than a thousand years later. They were known as anabaptists, or rebaptizers, and were persecuted by Catholics and Protestants alike. The "neo-Donatists" were not, however, proclaimers of false and bizarre doctrines. Their faith was typically consistent with the New Testament and has been preserved today in such groups as the Mennonites, Amish, and Hutterites, the communal anabaptists

The Arians

The Arians, on the other hand, held a doctrine that was justly regarded as in error. The Arians were named for a man named Arius, a teacher who denied the deity of Jesus. Arius had a large following and his teachings were widely disseminated. One of the reasons why Constantine called the Council of Nicea was to deal with the controversy over the teachings of Arius. Constantine called the council because, as he said, he considered disagreements in the church a more serious threat to the Empire than war. It was an amazing statement. He was declaring that the state had a greater interest in promoting the uniformity of church doctrine and practice than in defending the borders of the Empire against a military invasion.

In other words, Constantine addressed these issues of church doctrine and practice as if they were political issues that he was competent to deal with, and in much the same way that he dealt with the other affairs of state. His interest clearly was in the unity of the church, which he considered essential to the unity of the Empire. The bishops and regular clergy were brought together at the emperor's invitation and at his expense. They were under pressure from the Emperor to resolve this dispute and to do it quickly. The ensuing debate was intense and bitter.

The council decided for the deity of Jesus, a decision that was theologically accurate. But instead of bringing peace and unity to the church, the council further divided the church. The intrusion of a political figure into the affairs of the church, and the use of political methods—including the use of force and intimidation to establish the truth of the Gospel—was a complete misreading of the New Testament.

If the Arians were wrong in their teaching, the "orthodox" were wrong in their procedure and methodology. And here is the problem with Constantine and his legacy that is still with us: it divided the church because it divided the truth. I personally do not believe that the Constantinian church was totally devoid of God's grace. The doctrine it upheld concerning the deity of Jesus Christ is, I believe, an accurate reading of the New Testament revelation. But the attempt to establish its view of orthodoxy by the power of the state and to impose it by force, was a terrible mistake. Furthermore, it didn't work, not in North Africa, not at Nicea, not in the Spanish Inquisition, not in Geneva or Germany or Scotland or England during the Protestant Reformation or anywhere else. The use of force to establish "orthodoxy" disfigured the church horribly by turning it into a persecutor, by forsaking the path of humility and suffering for Christ and the gospel.

The Constantininan church is responsible for the official establishment of hypocrisy, for it displayed the cross as a symbol but in practice and policy it avoided the cross. And forcing a decision on a spiritual issue made a true resolution of the problem impossible.

The Arians can be faulted for doctrinal error but not for refusing to be coerced into theological conformity for the sake of political goals in the present, evil world. It is possible that if Constantine had not forced the issue with a church council and the implied threat of imperial force, the issue might in time have been resolved peacefully. Arianism survives to this day in such groups as the Jehovah's Witnesses.

The Donatists were not wrong in the point they felt called by God to make. They were being faithful to the words of Jesus Christ and the apostles. In making their confession and sealing it with their blood, they were witnesses to the truth. We can honor their faith and courage and the measure of grace they retained. The Donatists were accused of being divisive because they separated from the imperial church. But how could they have stayed within the church, believing as they did, without violating their consciences and compromising New Testament truth?

There is evidence to suggest that a great many of them accepted suffering and death without retaliating against their persecutors. In other words, they were martyrs. The Vatican II document on religious liberty in effect exonerated them. After almost seventeen centuries the Catholic Church has in principle, it seems, admitted that its fourth century representatives were wrong.

The monastic movement carried a measure of truth as well. The monks represented a costly commitment to Jesus, even though it was often an ersatz commitment, a kind of spiritual shadow-boxing. Their disciplines have been called the new martyrdom, or the bloodless martyrdom, or a martyrdom of the conscience,[6] but whatever they were, they were not the same as the real martyrdom and persecution of the pre-Constantinian era.

Constantine divided the church and by dividing it, weakened it. The image of a sabotaged wheat field tells the tragic story poignantly. The wheat may survive even when the field is full of weeds, but it does not thrive. And a field full of weeds and stunted wheat is not a pretty sight. Men have built fences in the Lord's field, but there has been wheat and weeds on both sides of every fence. That's how it has been from the fourth century up to our own times. That's how the Lord said it would remain until the time of the end, the time of the final harvest. I believe the time of harvest is at hand, and we are about to witness the last revival and the separation of the tares from the wheat.

13

End Time Resolution

The farmer and his hands stood in the field looking at it the way victims of a Ku Klux Klan visit survey the gutted remains of their home. Yesterday it was their treasured, comfortable dwelling. Today it is devastated. Someone threw a fire bomb through the window. It will be a long time before it will be home to them again—a very long time. Worse than a hurricane or a flood, this was a deliberate act. It is not only the damage they can see; the deed was also a threat. The enemy who could do such a thing would do it again. Or worse; what he did to their home he would just as soon do to those who dwelt in it.

So the characters in the parable were sad and angry and apprehensive. But they were not in despair. The farmer had a plan. He spoke with quiet determination and confidence. His servants listened. His voice was strong but soothing. And as He spoke, hope arose in their hearts.

"Let them grow together until the harvest," said the landowner to his servants. "And when harvest time comes I will send out the reapers. I'll tell them, 'now go on out into the field. The first job you have to do is gather up the tares and bind them in bundles. When the time is right we'll burn them. And then, when you have finished that, go out again and gather the wheat into my barn.'"

The harvesters, the Lord explained later to His disciples, are the angels. The harvest time stands for the end of the age.

Angels are usually invisible to human beings. Normally, their work is hidden from our eyes, except in special instances when God reveals to chosen people what the angels are doing. For instance, Daniel was seeking understanding of what would happen to his people in the latter days, the distant future from Daniel's time. He was taken behind the scenes, as it were, and shown what was going on in the heavenly realm. Daniel saw a glorious heavenly being, "a certain man...whose face was like lightning and his eyes like torches of fire." This angel or perhaps the Son of God Himself, appeared and explained the long delay in bringing Daniel the answer to his prayer. The glorious being said that he was hindered from coming for twenty-one days by "the prince of the kingdom of Persia." Finally the glorious one was helped by "Michael, one of the chief princes."

A heavenly being strengthened Daniel so that he could receive the message, for this experience had overloaded his human circuits and weakened him. Michael, the archangel whose assignment had special reference to Israel, apparently relieved the glorious "man" in his battle with the prince of Persia, so that he could come to Daniel and give him the information he requested. The "man" said he must return to the fight. He explained that after he (the glorious "man") goes, the Prince of Greece will come, and "no one upholds me against these, except Michael your prince."[1]

It is an amazing revelation. Beings whose natural habitat is heaven are engaged in a conflict involving "the prince of Persia" and soon "the prince of Greece." Evidently, what goes on in the heavenly realm affects earthly history, including the rise and fall of empires, and Israel's future. Daniel, a human being, was made aware of this heavenly conflict and was somehow involved in it through his prayers to God.

The New Testament expands on this revelation. For instance, in the Revelation John saw things happening in heaven which caused cataclysmic events to occur on earth.[2] Angels are involved in the affairs of the kingdom of God, and will be present in force at the final triumph of the kingdom of God and of His Messiah, the Son of Man. In that day both the Messiah and His army of holy angels will be visible. Scripture says explicitly that "every eye will see Him" at his second coming when He will return in power and glory to judge and rule.[3] Matthew tells us that after the tribulation of those days the Son of man will send His angels to gather together His elect.[4] That corresponds to the parable when the angels gather the wheat.

But something happens *first*, that is, *before* the gathering of the elect; that will be the gathering of the tares, or false believers, into bundles to be burned. This is also the work of angels. But it happens first, before the gathering of the elect at the revelation of the Lord; before He and His angels become visible. I understand this work of the angels prior to that glorious revelation to be an invisible work, typical of the secret, behind-the-scenes work of angels in this age.

In other words, although it is a phenomenon of the end times, it occurs in what we call ordinary history before God makes a public, universal and visible revelation of His Son, the Messiah. This doesn't, of course, rule out the appearance of angels to selected individuals, for this has always happened throughout the whole course of history. These appearances may in fact be more frequent—and I suspect they will—as we reach the end of the age. The point is simply that until the moment of Christ's appearing with His angels, both He and they remain invisible, except to a few especially chosen people, and even to them only at particular and unusual times.

What is it that occurs at the end of the age, but prior to the revelation of the Messiah, that separates false believers from true believers? The answer to that question is the apostasy, the rebellion against God and Christ, and the rise of the anti-Christ. The chief characteristic of the end times is deception, a deception so strong that Jesus says it would "deceive, if possible, even the elect."[5] The source of the deception is false prophets and false Christs.

Are the angels behind this, too? The prophet Michaiah gives an interesting revelation before king Ahab. He pictures a scene in heaven in which the Almighty, like a king with his counselors, asks the angelic company before Him, how they would persuade Ahab to go into a battle in which he will be slain. Various suggestions are offered. Finally one of the spirits steps forward and offers to deceive Ahab by being a lying spirit in the mouth of all his prophets. The Lord appoints him and he succeeds in luring the king into the fatal trap.[6] Something like that is predicted for the time of the end.

The classic passage relating to the apostasy at the end of the age, is 2 Thessalonians 2. It is complementary to the parable of the wheat and the weeds. Prior to the coming of the Lord Jesus to gather His elect comes the falling away and the revelation of the man of sin. This is how the unbelievers are gathered out of the Lord's kingdom. It is a time when anti-Christian evil seems to be invincible, overwhelming, and powerfully attractive.

Now, brethren, concerning the coming of our
Lord Jesus Christ and our gathering together to
Him, we ask you, not to be soon shaken in mind
or troubled, either by spirit or by word or by letter,

as if from us, as though the day of Christ had come. Let no one deceive you by any means; for that Day will not come unless the falling away comes first, and the man of sin is revealed, the son of perdition, who opposes and exalts himself above all that is called God or that is worshiped, so that he sits as God in the temple of God, showing himself that he is God.[7]

Out of the general rebellion against God and Christ already in progress and well advanced, comes one who embodies the rebellion in its most intense form and articulates it with astonishing boldness, clarity, and appeal. He is endued with a deceptive "charism," a dark but apparently invincible wisdom, and a seemingly miraculous power.

His effect on the masses is electric. They are caught up in a great enthusiasm that carries everything before it. It is a movement that spreads with superhuman speed and power.

It is indeed the work of angels, fallen angels, I suppose. It is reminiscent of the NAZI movement in Germany when the spellbinder, Adolph Hitler, carried all Germany with him by his passionate oratory and led the German people in a disastrous adventure in world conquest. He will be like Hitler, but far more dangerous: wiser, more powerful, more deceptive, more ruthless, more appealing. And he will succeed where Hitler failed. He will unite the whole world in his revolt against God and Christ. He will appear to be irresistible. His method will be deception.

For the mystery of lawlessness is already at work; only He who now restrains will do so until He is taken out of the way. And then the lawless one will be revealed, whom the Lord will consume with the breath of His mouth and destroy with the brightness of His coming. The coming of the lawless one is according to the working of Satan, with all power, signs, and lying wonders, and with all unrighteous deception among those who perish, because they did not receive the love of the truth, that they might be saved. And for this reason God will send them strong delusion, that they should believe the lie, that they all may be condemned who did not believe the truth but had pleasure in unrighteousness.[8]

We are dealing here with people who had some knowledge of the truth, but had no love for it. Rather, they found their pleasure in unrighteousness. And since they had no love for truth, God sends them a strong delusion, so that they will believe a lie. And it is not a subtle lie. It is an incredibly bold defiance of God, a renunciation of all traditional religion and morality. It defies and ridicules all that is called God or worshiped. And it will be accompanied by miracles, as if to confirm the blasphemous message. The anti-christ will declare war on all who continue to believe in any traditional God, but especially those who believe in Jesus. There is a great, world-wide persecution.

This delusion is the twine and bailing wire that, in the terms of the parable of the wheat and the tares, bind the unbelievers (weeds, tares) into bundles to be burned. The lie will release people who do not truly believe in Jesus from all pretense of a Christian commitment, and will bind them into new commitments that are openly and brazenly anti-Christian, and anti-God. They will be prepared for burning in the fire of God's judgment. For there is no other possible fate for those who join this rebellious movement, except destruction. It is their own choice. They will follow their own hearts and they will believe the lie.

The wicked, blasphemous empire will be cut short by the sudden appearance of the Messiah in the clouds of heaven with His army of holy angels. The anti-Messiah will be immediately silenced and undone by the word of God in the mouth of the Messiah, Jesus. This will be the dramatic culmination of the apostasy at the moment when the last trumpet will be sounded by the arch-angel. The Messiah, the Son of man will appear in the heavens. The dead in Christ will be raised. The living believers will be transformed and glorified without actually passing through physical death. They will all be gathered together to Jesus Christ in the air and accompany Him to earth in triumph, to reign with Him forever.[9]

But this climax is preceded by a long, historical process leading up to the revelation of the Son of man. That process is a gradual apostasy that has been gaining momentum in spite of temporary setbacks and apparent reverses until evil at last comes out into the open in an apparent triumph over all godliness. Its special target will be those who believe in Jesus Christ.

What happens during the apostasy will reverse the Constantinian era when the church experienced an apparent triumph in the Roman Empire in the early fourth century. Just as that deceptive "triumph" brought multitudes of unconverted pseudo-Christians into the church, this opposite event at the end of the age will draw unbelievers out of the church in the times directly ahead. As the ascension of Constantine to imperial power in 312 of the present era ended the persecution of most Christians in the Roman Empire, so this opposite event, the apostasy, will unleash a new and universal persecution against the church of Jesus the Messiah in the last times.

> Then they will deliver you up to tribulation and kill you, and you will be hated by all nations for My name's sake. And then many will be offended, will betray one another, and will hate one another. Then many false prophets will rise up and deceive many. And because lawlessness will abound, the love of many will grow cold. But he who endures to the end shall be saved. And this gospel of the kingdom will be preached in all the world as a witness to all the nations, and then the end will come.[10]

This final and terrible persecution, worse than anything ever seen before in history, will be the ultimate test of faith. Many will be offended, will renounce their faith and betray one another to the authorities. Confessing Jesus Christ will once again be a capital crime, and the prosecution of believers will be both zealous and intense. "But he who endures to the end shall be saved."[11]

There will be those who maintain their faith in spite of the enormous pressures of those times. They will confess their faith although to do so will put their lives in immediate danger. Those who endure the persecution of the last times will proclaim the gospel of the kingdom of God with integrity, for they will be illustrating by their lives the word of God they preach and for which they are suffering and laying down their lives. "And this gospel of the kingdom will be preached in all the world as a witness to all the nations, and then the end will come.[12] In the midst of the crisis and persecution of the last days something wonderful is happening to the church. While a profound darkness is covering the earth the glory of the Lord is rising on His church.

The great sociologist, P.A. Sorokin, wrote during the middle of the twentieth century about the crises and calamities of our age. His studies were based on his experience and observation during the revolution in his native Russia, and the two world wars that occurred during his lifetime. He identified a law of polarization in crisis times. His analysis and counsel are appropriate for us as we anticipate the ultimate crisis and the last revival.

The bulk of the population will divide increasingly into sinners, libertines, profligates, downright criminals, atheists, and cynicists on the one hand, and into stoics, saints, moral heroes, sublime altruists, intensely religious prophets, martyrs, ascetics, mystics, gnostics, and the like on the other hand. Militant atheism will be countered by religiosity of the greatest intensity, and utter moral depravity by sublime moral heroism.

Such are some of the developments which we must be prepared to meet as observers, actors, and victims of the age of calamities and crisis. Since the trends are already in operation they cannot be prevented or averted. They can be shortened and alleviated, however, by the individual as well as by societies.

The best way for an individual to meet them is by integrating his values and rooting them—not so much in the values of the sensory world—but rather in the moral duty and the transcendental values of the kingdom of God. Persons with such a system of values deeply ingrained will bear any calamity with fortitude. And they will endure it much more easily than persons either entirely lacking any integrated value-system, or having a system rooted chiefly in earthly values, from 'wine, women and song' to wealth, fame and power. Such values crumble under the impact of calamity, and their devotees become complete bankrupts, ruined wretches, and helpless derelicts who have nothing to live for and nothing to fall back upon for support. Persons with a transcendental system of values and a deep sense of moral duty are the possessors of the values which no man and no catastrophe can take from them. Under all circumstances they can maintain their peace of mind, their conviction of human dignity, their self-respect, and their sense of duty. With these inviolate, they can weather any trial, no matter how severe.

This, the best way out of the crisis, was marvelously formulated a long time ago. [He proceeded to quote from the sermon on the Mount, Matthew 6:25-34.][13]

I believe the final crisis in an age of crises and calamities, the one Scripture calls by the names of apocalypse and apostasy, is now at hand. The gradual, centuries-long process that Harvey Cox called secularization has eroded away the fear of God that until our times still acted as a barrier to the evil tendencies of human nature. Our western world has cast off the restraints of religion and morality. It's a more honest situation with less hypocrisy, but far more dangerous. There is, after all, something worse than hypocrisy. There is an open and arrogant rejection of God and Christ.

Our civilization and its rulers now defy God and assert their liberation from His rule. Such defiance provokes God to anger. I believe there is evidence that our western civilization—the civilization that by its commercial and industrial power has remade the whole world in its image—has passed the point of no return.

14

The Point Of No Return

Judge Robert Bork published a provocative book in 1996 with the apocalyptic title, *Slouching Towards Gomorrah*. The title comes from the poem "The Second Coming," written in 1919 by William Butler Yeats that refers to the rise of the antichrist. Bork fastened on the 1960s as a turning point in American history, and his title suggests that the apocalyptic age was born with the baby-boomers.

Robert Bork, you will remember, was the jurist nominated for the Supreme Court by President Ronald Reagan in the 1980s. Bork was a brilliant jurist, eminently qualified, perhaps the best judge in the United States. But his opposition to the Roe v. Wade decision legalizing abortion was well known. And for that reason the modern liberal establishment raised a furor against his appointment. He was rejected by the U.S. Senate—was "borked" as the saying has it (his name became a verb meaning to shout down, discredit, reject for no valid reason).

Bork's book documents the decline of America and perhaps of Western civilization, since America's influence at this point in history is practically definitive for the West, and enormous in much of the rest of the world as well. He attributed the decline to a generation that was too numerous to assimilate into the existing culture and that created its own, based on the conviction that politics can create a utopia, without the need for God or morality. This is the generation that burned books at Yale Law School, held sit-ins, takeovers, and demonstrations at colleges and universities across the country, shouted obscenities and intimidated faculties and administrations, and even the Democratic National Convention in 1968. That generation is now running the country. They are running it on the principles they hammered out in their youth. He refers to Bill Clinton's continued popularity—in spite of the revelations that would certainly have disqualified a man for public office a generation ago—as a sign that "something about our moral perceptions and reactions has changed profoundly."[1]

Judge Bork's analysis is compelling. From his viewpoint as a jurist and an educator, he saw the same reality that theologian Francis Schaeffer described in his *Christian Manifesto.* Bork observed that the government with its instruments of coercion and power is in the hands of radicals who have changed this nation into something quite different from what it was in the past. And he doesn't see anything presently on the scene with the power or the will to reverse the disastrous course. Bork is pessimistic about the future, but he has not completely given up hope that the United States may yet return to something like what it was before the "barbarians" descended on the land in the 1960s. Like Francis Schaeffer, he sees a kind of window of opportunity for change.[2]

My own sense is that Bork himself represented that window of opportunity. Had he been appointed to the Supreme Court, Judge Bork would have been in a position to implement some of the changes he saw as urgently necessary to save the nation. If Roe v. Wade was indeed the key indicator that Francis Schaeffer believed it was, Bork represented the last chance for the Supreme Court to reverse itself on that decision. Bork categorically rejected the notion that the Constitution contains a right to privacy in the decision to abort a baby. That is why there was such an outcry by the modern liberal establishment against his appointment to the Supreme Court. As a Supreme Court Justice, Robert Bork might have been able to derail the modern liberal juggernaut. Instead, he was rejected. Roe v. Wade remains in place. Abortion continues to be legal. And the window Francis Schaeffer believed was still open in 1981 was closed in 1983 when Bork's nomination was rejected.

Judge Bork has not only contributed a new verb to the American vocabulary, he is a sign to the nation. Instead of being an instrument to uphold the integrity of the Constitution of the United States, Judge Bork has written a book and sounded a prophetic warning of coming judgment and destruction.

Although he used an apocalyptic allusion in his title, Judge Bork's hope is not based on the apocalypse and the second coming of Christ. He thinks a religious revival may be the salvation of the nation, but the only hope he sees is in the return of America to something like it was in the fifties. I believe that a consistently biblical analysis of what has happened in the United States and the world in recent times—culminating in the revolutionary changes of the last generation—leads to a different conclusion: we have reached the time of the end. We have passed the point of no return.

The term "point of no return" can be illustrated by an analogy from trans-oceanic travel. An aircraft reaches a point where its fuel supply will no longer permit it to return to an airport on the continent from which it took off. It is now committed to going forward to its destination on the other side of the ocean. There is no turning back.

It is my conviction that in the 1960s God signaled us that world history has passed the point of no return. We have moved decisively into the close of the age, and are now moving toward the prophesied end. That end includes the final apocalyptic battles and Christ's personal, visible return in power and glory to the earth. That's a bold claim, I know, in view of all the identifications of the end of the world made prematurely through the years by students of biblical prophecy.

B.W. Newton, the nineteenth century English writer on biblical prophecy, observed,

> a river of lengthened course makes many a bend. Sometimes, it may seem to be retracing its backward way to the source whence it began to flow. Yet it is not really so. All the time it is steadily advancing toward the appointed end. So is it in the stream of things. The course is steady, and the end sure, however appearances may vary.[3]

In those words Newton illustrated the tendency of history to take a winding course toward the apocalyptic climax and the fulfillment of the end time prophecies of the Bible.

There are times when the stage of history seems to be set for the return of the Lord, and then there is an apparent reversal. The signs of the end become less definite and clear. Sometimes it appears that the clock of prophecy stops, like the play-clock at a football game during half time and time-outs. In our experience, time goes on, but it doesn't count for game-time. That time is suspended until the time-out is over, or the kick-off sets the game-clock ticking again for the last half. There appear to be half-times and time-outs in the process of fulfilling the prophecies of the Bible; that is, there are times when prophecy moves forward and times when it stops. So it is risky to be too confident about identifying the time of the end.

135

Nevertheless, Jesus gave us signs by which we can know we are at the end, when we see them all converge at a point in history. Had He wished to leave us without any certain knowledge of the end, why did He give us the signs? It seems to me that our own history in a unique sense has witnessed all the signs of the end given in the New Testament. And I believe the 1960s saw striking fulfillments of biblical prophecies that appear to me to mark an irreversible change in the course of history. In this chapter I will deal with just two that to my mind settle the question.

The decade of the 1960s was certainly one of the most turbulent in history. It was a decade of assassinations, of the struggle for Civil Rights by the black people of America, the expansion of the Communist Empire in the world, the Viet Nam War, the election of the first Catholic President of the United States, and the convening of the Second Vatican Council of the Roman Catholic Church. It was the time when the drug culture became mainstream, the sexual revolution changed the world's attitude toward morality, and the Beatles and a host of other musical groups led the "baby-boomer" generation during its youth in a movement that was not mere kids' pranks, but a social upheaval with a lasting impact on western civilization.

We had already moved into the nuclear age; for the first time mankind possessed the capability to destroy himself and his civilization. Yes, mankind had always had wars, for instance, but never on the massive scale of the twentieth century wars. Our memories of World War II were still fresh and vivid and we were aware that men did in fact use their astonishing technical knowledge to do terrible things. I lived through those years as a young Christian and a minister with one eye on the news and the other on the Bible. I concluded from my study of biblical prophecy that the 1960s marked the point of no return. Let me explain.

The most significant event in centuries with regard to biblical prophecy occurred in 1967. I watched it on television. The newly re-established state of Israel conquered the old city of Jerusalem. I had been watching Jerusalem for that very thing, the old city where the temple had stood 1900 years before, the city of David of which Jews all over the world said wistfully and dreamily at every Passover meal during all those centuries, "next year in Jerusalem." Next year never came. Until June 1967 no Jew had access to the old city of Jerusalem. The recovery by a Jewish state of the capital city of David is so terribly significant because that act fulfilled a key prophecy of Jesus regarding the time of the end.

The prophecy concerns the Jewish people and is recorded in Luke 21:24. It contains just two sentences: "And they will fall by the edge of the sword, and be led away captive into all nations. And Jerusalem will be trampled by Gentiles until the times of the Gentiles are fulfilled."

When Jesus spoke those words they seemed improbable if not impossible. The Jews were in their land, and although they were ruled by the Romans, they still enjoyed a measure of self-government. Temple worship went on daily. The Sanhedrin met regularly. Jews lived in Jerusalem, inhabited the city that once dominated the Middle East, and dreamed of the day when the Messiah would come and restore the glories of the Monarchy as it was during the reigns of David and Solomon.

But the Messiah came, and the majority of the Jewish people and their leaders—hence the Judean state—rejected Him. Jesus spoke this lament:

> O Jerusalem, Jerusalem, the one who kills the prophets and stones those who are sent to her! How often I wanted to gather your children together, as a hen gathers her brood under her wings, but you were not willing! See! Your house is left to you desolate; and assuredly, I say to you, you shall not see Me until the time when you say, 'Blessed is He who comes in the name of the LORD![4]

Again He wept over the city, saying:

> If you had known, even you, especially in this your day, the things that make for your peace! But now they are hidden from your eyes. For days will come upon you when your enemies will build an embankment around you, surround you and close you in on every side, and level you, and your children within you, to the ground; and they will not leave in you one stone upon another, because you did not know the time of your visitation.[5]

Jesus then predicted the scattering of the Jews throughout the world and the trampling of the city of Jerusalem by non-Jewish nations until the times of the Gentiles was fulfilled. The word

Gentiles means *nations*. The first to drive the Jews out of their city and trample Jerusalem were the Romans. The Jews rebelled against Rome in 70 A.D. The Romans captured Jerusalem, destroyed the temple, killed multitudes of Jews and sold others into slavery by the thousands and ten thousands, until the markets were glutted with them. The remaining Jews rebelled once more in 132 under the false Messiah, Bar Kokhba. In 135 Bar Kokhba and thousands of his followers died in a Roman siege. The Romans, after they had put down that uprising, changed the name of the country from Judea to Palestine (for the Philistines), drove the Jews out of the land and made it unlawful for any Jew to set foot in Jerusalem. The city was trampled by non-Jews, precisely as Jesus had predicted. The Jewish people were scattered throughout the world and those who believed in Jesus as the Messiah carried the Gospel to all the nations, beginning from Jerusalem. The Jewish people wandered among the nations of the earth, without a state or a homeland until the middle of the twentieth century.

The modern state of Israel was established after the terrible persecution of the Jews by Hitler and NAZI Germany (1933-1945). In the wake of that persecution the state of Israel was established in May 1948. The Jewish people began returning to the Promised Land from all over the world. The great majority were not religious. But they knew enough about the historic faith to realize that they were fulfilling the predictions their prophets had made in the name of the God of Israel centuries earlier. And, as the prophets had also written, the land began to blossom and be fruitful in the possession and care of the Jewish people.

Beginning with 1948 the Jews had their own state in the land that had once been Judea, but they did not yet possess the ancient city of Jerusalem. It was still held by the kingdom of Jordan. And Israel was surrounded and vastly outnumbered by its Arab enemies.

In June 1967 Israel's Arab enemies had made their preparations for war. Led by Egypt's President Nasser, the Arab coalition massed its troops and armaments, forced the United Nations to withdraw their peace-keeping forces, and boasted that they would drive the Jews into the sea. Instead, Israeli warplanes destroyed Egypt's air force before it got off the ground. Israel's land forces seized vast areas of strategic enemy territory and tons of war materiel in a campaign that was reminiscent of Hitler's blitz-krieg (lightning war). It was over in less than a week, and is remembered as the Six-Day War, an astonishing Israeli victory. When the dust settled and the smoke cleared, a Jewish state was in possession of the ancient city of Jerusalem for the first time in nineteen centuries.

I remember watching the TV reports of Israeli soldiers weeping at the historic Wailing Wall, the only remains of the temple structure razed by the Romans in 70 A.D. I knew the significance of what I watched unfolding before my eyes. I had purchased a book in 1958 that dealt with this issue. It was written in 1950 by Wilbur M. Smith and entitled, *World Crises and the Prophetic Scriptures*. In it Smith dealt at length with the prophecy of the times of the gentiles, a prophecy he said had been ignored by the church fathers, by the Protestant Reformers and by most commentators. Smith wrote that the clearest interpretation he had seen was by Bishop Ryle, in his *Notes on the Gospel of Luke*, which he quoted, and I reproduce below along with Smith's observations.

> A fixed period is here foretold, during which Jerusalem was to be given over into the hands of Gentile rulers, and the Jews were to have no dominion over their ancient city. A fixed period is likewise foretold which was to be the time of the Gentiles' visitation, the time during which they were to enjoy privileges, and occupy a position something like that of Israel in ancient days...Both periods are one day to end. Jerusalem is to be once more restored to its ancient inhabitants. The Gentiles, because of their hardness and unbelief, are to be stripped of their privileges and endure just judgments of God...Yet a few years, and "the times of the Gentiles will be fulfilled." Their day of visitation will be past and gone. Their misused privileges will be taken away. The judgments of God shall fall on them. They shall be cast aside as vessels in which God has no pleasure. Their dominion shall crumble away, and their vaunted institutions shall fall to pieces. The Jews shall be restored. The Lord Jesus shall come again in power and great glory. The kingdoms of this world shall become the kingdoms of our God and of His Christ, and the 'times of the Gentiles' shall come to an end.

> I am not an alarmist [Smith wrote in 1950]...but it seems to me that almost any day or

night this prophecy of our Lord could be fulfilled. Already there are more Jews living in Jerusalem than there were Jews living in the whole of Palestine at the dawn of this century. Furthermore, there is a government of a newborn nation in the modern city of Jerusalem—Israel. One hundred feet of no-man's land, some barbed wire fences, and a few machine guns manned by a mere handful of Arabs—these are all that keep the Jews from fully occupying this city and setting up their government there...

May it not be true that, when the "times of the Gentiles" have come to an end, not only will Israel be in possession of her Holy City, but calamities may break forth among the nations of the earth, the very wrath of God, which may be the end of much of the liberty in the preaching of the gospel, and almost the termination of these days of grace?[6]

I watched the news on television of the events of the Six-Day War; it occurred to me that we now knew the terminal points of that prophecy. The times of the Gentiles began with the destruction of Jerusalem and the temple in 70 A.D. and ended with the recapture of the city of Jerusalem by the state of Israel in 1967 A.D., a period of almost 1900 years.

I believe this event was a sign that a great historic change has taken place. The capture of the ancient city of Jerusalem in 1967 was a flashing warning signal that God was beginning to restore the kingdom to Israel and bring the times of the gentiles to an end. It pointed dramatically to God's intention to move ahead with the restoration of the Davidic kingdom. The Davidic kingdom is the kingdom that began with David and will be established forever by the Messiah, the Son of David, who is also the Son of God. The kingdom spoken of is the kingdom of God that Jesus proclaimed. It is the kingdom of Israel whose capital is Jerusalem.

The capture of Jerusalem by the Jewish state of Israel also means that the time of the proclamation of the Gospel to the nations of the world is nearing completion. And that is the sign that the end of the age is at hand.[7] The Messiah will soon return in power and great glory and "the kingdoms of the world will become the kingdom of our Lord and of His Christ."[8]

The restoration of the kingdom of Israel under the Messiah is associated in Scripture with a great world crisis. It comes in connection with an international revolt prophesied in Psalm two against God and His Anointed (Christ, Messiah) by the kings, rulers and judges of the earth.[9]

That brings me to the second sign that occurred in the 1960s pointing to the our own times as the time of the end. I am referring to the death of Christian civilization. It was one of the big news stories of the 1960s. Do you remember?

15

The Death Of Christian Civilization

The death of Christian civilization came into general view on the most sensational cover in the history of TIME Magazine.[1] In red letters on a black field TIME asked the question "IS GOD DEAD?" Theologian Thomas J. J. Altizer and others claimed it was true. "God has died," Altizer wrote, "in our time, in our history."

The death of God was first proclaimed by the German philosopher, Friedrich Nietzsche (1844-1900) more than a century ago. In a work called *Joyful Wisdom*, Nietzsche wrote about a madman who lit a lantern on a bright morning and rushed into the market place crying, "I seek God! I seek God!"

The madman was regarded with some amusement by the people, most of whom didn't believe in God. They asked him if God had taken a cruise or was perhaps on vacation or out for a stroll.

> 'Where is God gone?' he called out. 'I mean to tell you! We have killed him—you and I. We are all his murderers. But how have we done it? How were we able to drink up the sea? Who gave us the sponge to wipe away the whole horizon? What did we do when we loosened this earth from its sun?... Do we not stray, as through infinite nothingness?... Does not night come on continually, darker and darker? Shall we not have to light lanterns in the morning? Do we not hear the noise of the grave-diggers, who are burying God? Do we not smell the divine putrefaction? For even Gods putrefy. God is dead! God remains dead! And we have killed him! How shall we

console ourselves, the most murderous of all murderers? The holiest and mightiest that the world has hitherto possessed, has bled to death under our knife—who will wipe the blood from us? With what water could we cleanse ourselves? What lustrums? What sacred games shall we have to devise? Is not the magnitude of this deed too great for us? Shall we not ourselves have to become Gods, merely to seem worthy of it? There never was a greater event—and on account of it, all who are born after us belong to a higher history than any history hitherto.'

Here the madman was silent, and looked again at his hearers. They also were silent, and looked at him in surprise. At last he threw his lantern on the ground, so that it broke in pieces and was extinguished.

'I came too early,' he then said. 'I am not yet at the right time. This prodigious event is still on its way, and is travelling—it has not yet reached men's ears. Lightning and thunder need time, the light of the stars needs time, deeds need time, even after they are done, to be seen and heard. This deed is as yet farther from them than the farthest star—and yet they have done it!' [The madman then entered different churches to announce God's death and to intone His funeral dirge.]

When he was led out and called to account, he always gave the reply: 'What are these churches now, if they are not the tombs and monuments of God?'[2]

Nietzsche foretold the coming of the antichrist, as one who welcomed the man of sin. Nietzsche denounced Christianity as "the one great curse, the one great innermost corruption, the one great instinct of revenge, for which no means is poisonous, stealthy, subterranean, *small* enough—I call it the one immortal blemish of mankind."[3]

Nietzsche became the madman of his prophetic vision. He spent the last decade of his life 1890-1900 hopelessly insane. Like Balaam in Old Testament times, Nietzsche was a false prophet, not because what he saw and proclaimed was false, but because his motives were wrong and his heart was impure. The revolt against God by our world and its leaders at the time of the end was also proclaimed by David, by Daniel, by the apostle Paul, and John in the Revelation. Nietzsche saw it accurately. But in his heart he was in sympathy with the rebellion. He spoke for the devil, not for God.

Nietzsche saw what few could see in his own time. The death of God really meant the death of Christian civilization. Nietzsche observed that the great majority of people no longer had a serious faith in God. Christianity was no longer the base of western civilization. In a real sense, it never was.

The Christian ethic cannot be socially and politically incorporated and applied in this present age. It can only live where the Holy Spirit has planted the love of God in the hearts of those who believe in Jesus and have been converted. The attempt to impose Christian values on the whole of society by law and governmental coercion, never really worked. Where Christianity was established as a state religion, the possession by the church of wealth and the political influence to order and direct state coercion resulted inevitably in a distortion of the faith. Christian civilization never satisfied those who truly believed in Christ, and it was oppressive for those who didn't believe.

On the other hand, there remained a measure of grace and truth. For those who truly wanted to know the truth, it was accessible. For those who were willing to bear the cross, it was still true, as Jesus said, "he who seeks, finds."

The emphasis on the mercy and grace of God to man produced a tradition of good works, including the many-faceted ministry of healing and compassion that has eased the sufferings and hardships of mankind. Christendom achieved some remarkable successes. The faith provided the inspiration for many magnificent works of art in painting, sculpture, architecture, literature and music. The belief in God who created the world, not capriciously but with wisdom and order, laid the foundation for the discoveries and applications of modern science and technology. The emphasis on the Bible as the word of God, particularly in Protestantism, resulted in the widespread progress of literacy and education. The Christian interest in the poor and oppressed brought about the abolition of slavery, legislation for the protection of women and children, the poor, minorities and workers. The prophetic tradition of Judeo-Christian revelation made it possible to impose limits on government and overcome tyranny. The world has been willing to enjoy the fruits of Christian civilization but has cut itself off from the roots of faith.

There were good reasons for wanting the death of Christian civilization; there were also bad reasons. For a truly converted believer it was impossible to be satisfied with the hypocrisy and inconsistency of the "Christian" world. Christians yearned for a society that was truly holy. Many devout believers sought to model such a society. They resented the coercive policies of the established church which enforced conformity and persecuted dissenting Christians. Non-Christians and anti-Christians resented the restraints not only of the mores and customs but also of laws against their lusts and desires. They wanted—many of them passionately—a society in which they could do whatever they wished to do, however selfish and evil, without restraint or punishment. These unconverted people seized on the hypocrisy of Christian civilization as a lever with which to discredit the churches and undermine the influence of Christian faith on society and government.

Most people in Nietzsche's generation in the latter half of the nineteenth century were practical atheists. They had religious opinions, but not faith, for their lives were not informed by the faith they professed. Nietzsche pointed this out and urged them to throw off the pretense and live as consistent pagans. But they were unable to understand Nietzsche's message about the death of God and Christian civilization. They continued to cling to the myth of Christendom and to a superficial and hypocritical Christian faith.

But in the 1960s a generation arose that was ready to listen to Nietzsche's madman. The "death" of God was announced to the world in the mid-1960s from professedly Christian theological schools by professedly Christian theologians in the United States of America. The world listened and many believed. The fact is, the madman's prophecy was already being fulfilled. The Marxist revolutions in Russia, Eastern Europe, and China were serious attempts to build a civilization on the denial of God. But the revolt against God was no less real in the United States, a nation many regarded as the last bastion of Christian civilization. In a sense the death of God was an American phenomenon.

In the last generation, beginning with the 1960s, there has been an attempt here in the United States to build a civilization without faith in God, particularly without the Christian God. Like Christianity, this kind of atheism is more than a philosophy; it is a way of life. It is not usually called atheism, but it is an intentional replacement of Christian faith. Nietzsche hailed it as a renewal of paganism. Today we call it "humanism."

What is humanism but the murder of God? God has been rejected from public life, made irrelevant to the great decisions by which the society lives. And man has taken His place. As Nietzsche said, "God is dead...And we have killed him! Shall we not ourselves have to become Gods, merely to seem worthy [of a deed of this magnitude]?"

That is the effort the United States has been engaged in for more than a generation. The revolt against God that was first philosophical and academic, broke into social and cultural life with the coming of the twentieth century. It became the law of the land in the 1960s.

In 1962 and 1963 Bible reading and prayer in public schools were declared unconstitutional by the United States Supreme Court. A decade later the moral implications of the death of God were legislated by the Supreme Court in the Roe v. Wade decision. It was now "legal" to kill innocent human beings, created in the image of God, so long as the killing was done while they were still in the womb. The lesson is clear. If God is dead, there is no point in obeying His laws any longer, even as basic a law as the sixth commandment against murder. Men and women are determined to make their own laws to suit their own convenience and to permit them to indulge their own lusts. Justice will be whatever men decide it is, just as the Constitution now means whatever the Justices of the Supreme Court decide it means, never mind the meaning of words or the intentions of those who wrote the Constitution.

From God's point of view, this is lawlessness. It doesn't mean there are no laws. It means that the laws are in violation of God's laws and contrary to His justice. Like Judea and an apostate Judaism in the first century, the leaders of an apostate Christendom have taken counsel together to throw off the cords and break the bonds of God and murder God's Messiah.

This substitution of man for God, and the creation of a new code of law and ethics is known in biblical terms as the apostasy. The Greek word for it is *apostasia*. It means a revolt against God and His law. This revolt appears in the New Testament in 2 Thessalonians 2. It is occasioned by a spirit of antichristian lawlessness, a climate of public opinion which is an invitation to the antichrist. The antichrist is a man who embodies the lawless spirit

147

of the age, articulates it with power and a deceptive appeal, and leads the lawless population into an open revolt against God and Christ. This revolt will be allowed free reign for a short time in the last days under the world-wide leadership of the lawless man or the antichrist.

It is this lawless one, this antichrist, that Christ will destroy with the brightness of His coming.[4] Christ's return is the climax of the unparalleled apocalyptic conflict of the end times, a never-to-be-forgotten showdown between God and Satan, good and evil, Christ and antichrist in which God will show His power in triumphing over all evil.

Scripture gives this explanation of the terrible judgment against the people of those days.

> The coming of the lawless one is according to the working of Satan, with all power, signs and lying wonders, and with all unrighteous deception among those who perish, because they did not receive the love of the truth, that they might be saved. And for this reason God will send them strong delusion, that they should believe the lie, that they all may be condemned who did not believe the truth but had pleasure in unrighteousness.[5]

The rebellion is here already and will soon become the law of the land in every nation of the earth. But there is a people who will not join the rebellion. Their faith in Jesus Christ did not depend on the institutions and laws of Christendom in the first place. And when Christendom is destroyed their faith in the living God will remain intact. They will continue to believe in God and Jesus Christ in an age that has become officially and overtly godless. They will hold to God's law in a lawless generation. They believe in the Bible. For them the New Testament is God's final word. To them God is alive, His grace is their salvation and his laws remain in force. They do not march to the beat of the humanist, antichristian drum. They hear the voice of the Good Shepherd and follow Him, even to death.

The majority explains them as an historical anachronism, and considers them a dangerous influence, a monkey wrench in the works of the humanist machine. For they continue to proclaim the

Gospel. And what is worse, they are determined to live or die according to the gospel.

What will be done about these people who won't be part of the new order, who won't play by the new rules? They will be treated the way the devil has always treated God's people. They will be tempted by the world's pleasures and honors. They will be threatened by its punishment and alienation. And if that doesn't work?

Ask Nietzsche's madman.

For the Christians, bearers of "the one great curse, the one innermost corruption, the one immortal blemish of mankind, no means is poisonous, stealthy, subterranean, *small* enough." A civilization which did not blanch at murdering God will certainly not hesitate to murder His people. If innocent human beings in the womb can be declared non-persons and put to death because they are inconvenient and interfere with the plans and ambitions of the people of this "brave new world", a revived paganism will not scruple against doing a similar thing to Christians.

Scripture agrees. "Then they will deliver you up to tribulation and kill you, and you will be hated by all nations for My name's sake."[6] The stage has been set, philosophically, socially and now politically and legally, for the apocalyptic showdown between good and evil, God and the devil, Christ and the antichrist, predicted in Scripture for the end of the age.

It has already begun. It will go on with increasing speed and fury until the end.

The good news—the gospel—is that God and His Messiah win in the end. Good will finally triumph decisively and permanently over evil, "...he who endures to the end will be saved. And this gospel of the kingdom will be preached in all the world as a witness to all the nations, and then the end will come."[7]

This is the crisis I believe the church must face in the years directly ahead. It is a crisis which has been building for centuries. The Lord has been preparing His church for that crisis during all those centuries by means of revivals.

16

Protestantism:
Revival, Reform, And Revolution

"The Reformation of the sixteenth century," wrote church historian Philip Schaff in 1888, "...marks the end of the Middle Ages and the beginning of modern times."[1] It was a turbulent time in Europe. Powerful new nation-states were rising to challenge the feudal system. A middle class of business and professional men arose to challenge the aristocracy. Explorers discovered new lands and trade routes. Scholars came from the East with the classical works of art and literature of ancient Greece and Rome, shaking traditional ideas and prejudices. The recently invented printing press spread the exciting news quickly and efficiently. It was a time of startling changes, from the static medieval society to the dynamic modern society.[2] And the Protestant Reformation was the engine that drove that change.[3]

Church reform was not a new idea. But now it had powerful new resources: kings of emerging nation states who resented the influence of the Pope in their national affairs and businessmen and independent farmers opposed the drain of currency from their own towns and cities to Rome and the papacy. They were gaining wealth and they yearned to rise to places of influence that in the medieval system were held on hereditary rights by the nobility and with the sanction of the established church. There were economic, social, political, and intellectual reasons for the success of the Reformation. But, as James Burns wrote, "the Reformation was supremely a revival... it marked, for a vast multitude, the recovery of faith. it was a rebirth in the world of primitive and evangelic Christianity, and lighted myriads of human hearts with the flame of spiritual joy."[4]

Revival is a cherished theme among evangelical Protestants. Revival is a spiritual awakening, like a conversion experience, in which God becomes real and the most important reality in a person's life. A revival occurs when many people are awakened at the same time. The Protestant Reformation was like that. It influenced an entire civilization.

Protestantism was born of an intense longing among the seriously devout in many places, a burning and urgent search for something real in their religion. Many, like Martin Luther himself, sought desperately for a relationship with God that the rituals, creeds, disciplines and services of the religious establishment symbolized but typically did not deliver in living experience. The prayers of the faithful became an anguished cry that would not be put off. The Reformation was the answer to that prayer, the self-revelation of God to the deep need and earnest search of many believers. They heard the word of God and believed.

Martin Luther experienced a spiritual awakening. He was terrified of God's wrath and afraid of hell. He joined the Augustinian order in search of peace, and his earnestness is unquestioned. But he found no peace. His spiritual counselor, Staupitz, became frustrated trying to instruct the tormented brother Martin, who never seemed to be able to grasp a sense of forgiveness. Finally, he pushed the young Luther to prepare to teach the Bible at the University of Wittenburg. Evidently, Staupitz felt that as Luther studied the Bible for the purpose of comforting others, he would find comfort for himself.

As Luther studied the Scriptures his heart came to rest gradually and quietly in the sufferings and death of Jesus Christ, who became one of us, even to the point of feeling forsaken by God, as Luther had so often felt.

> He who was without sin... so identified himself with us as to participate in our alienation. In the utter desolation of the forsaken Christ, God was able to reconcile the world to himself...What God first worked in Christ, that he must work also in us. If he who had done no wrong was forsaken on the cross, we who are truly alienated from God must suffer a deep hurt. We are not for that reason to upbraid, since the hurt is for our healing.[5]

This vision of the Christ was different from the avenging judge who troubled Luther's sensitive conscience. Jesus was no less the Judge, but the apprehension by faith of the One who suffered for man and with him, revealed the merciful and gracious side of the Lord to the young monk, and brought him peace. It also made sense of Luther's inward pain.

The Reformation grew out of the profound dissatisfaction with the state of the established church in the late middle ages. Hypocrisy and corruption were nothing new in the church. The dissatisfaction of serious believers had been a constant factor from the early fourth century. In the late middle ages the cry for reform became incessant and implacable, like the beating of war drums in the night. There was a general outcry against the corruption and greed of the Catholic Church which had gone beyond tolerable limits. There was a growing impatience with a religious institution that claimed exclusive rights to dispense or withhold salvation, in spite of the obvious and admitted insincerity, ignorance and corruption of the clergy at every level, and the general ignorance and indifference of the laity. There was a ground swell of resentment against a religious establishment that either intimidated and tamed the reformers who rose up within it or destroyed them and squelched the reform movements that they inspired.

The Franciscans are an example of a reform movement that was tamed. Even during his lifetime Francis was broken-hearted over the compromises that had occurred within his order. John Hus of Bohemia was branded a heretic and burned at the stake. Savonarola was denounced, excommunicated, discredited, tortured, hanged and burned.

The Protestant Reformation began in the college town of Wittenburg in Germany with an obscure Augustinian monk, a professor of theology desperately in search of personal peace with God. He sincerely followed the counsels of the established church, but they brought him no help. At last he found his long-sought-for peace by believing the promises of God in Scripture. Aflame with zeal and the joy of his new-found salvation, Martin Luther began to share his insights into the Bible, and to challenge some of the teachings and practices of the established church.

Luther's passionate faith coincided with the general discontent of the times. The Renaissance was calling attention to ancient documents recently rediscovered. Among them was the Bible. And with the Bible, reformers could uncover the falsehoods and errors that had crept into the church over the centuries.[6] The Reformation began when Luther used the New Testament to expose the corrupt fund-raising scheme of selling indulgences, by which the Pope financed the expensive construction of St. Peter's basilica in Rome. A lot of that money came out of the pockets of poor German folk. The pitch was that in exchange for money contributed to the papacy, the length of time in purgatory could be reduced for oneself and one's relatives. Luther challenged that scheme from the New Testament, writing out ninety-five theses for debate and nailing them to the door of the church in Wittenburg on October 31, 1517.[7]

Thanks to the recently invented printing press, Luther's sermons and books were printed and distributed throughout Germany and beyond. Translated into the languages of Christendom and printed, they spread rapidly throughout Europe and created a sensation. Here at last was somebody who dared to speak the truth that many people were thinking, but lacked the knowledge or the courage to put into words. Luther not only exposed the corruption of the religious establishment, but he showed people the way to God though faith in Jesus Christ. For many, dry rituals and perfunctory prayers were replaced by personal faith and the excitement of an experience of God through believing in the word of God that had been preserved in the Bible. Based on the teachings and historical record of the New Testament, the revival gave promise of returning the church to the purity and passion of its beginnings.

Luther began within the monastic movement as an Augustinian monk. Initially, he sought to reform the church from within the religious establishment.[8] But he ran into an official stone wall in the Catholic hierarchy. On his part, Luther would neither be intimidated nor tamed. Convinced of the rightness of his cause, the reformer decided to risk everything to make his point. The Pope sent a decree of excommunication, and burned Luther's books. Luther, in turn, burned the papal constitutions, the Canon Law, the works of scholastic theology, and the bull of excommunication.[9] It was high drama and the people got the point. They may not have understood the theological issues, but they knew what had happened. The break was made. A little later Luther, the monk, renounced his vow of celibacy and married a nun, who of course, had also renounced hers. The message was clear. The break was irreparable.

The high water mark of the Protestant Reformation came at the Diet of Worms, an august assembly convened by the young Emperor, Charles V, with the Electors of the Empire, its wise men and princes, and some prelates of the Catholic Church. They had political, economic and religious issues on their agenda, but the most important business had to do with Martin Luther. The papal representatives were asking the Emperor to enforce the excommunication legally throughout Germany, deal with Luther, and commit all of his books to the flames. They did not want Luther to speak at the Diet at all. The Pope had already ruled. The Emperor's clear Christian duty, they insisted, was to support the decision of the papacy.[10]

Charles V was a Roman Catholic. But there were other things the Emperor had to consider, political matters that pointed to moderation. Charles decided to let Luther appear before the assembly, but not to allow him to make a lengthy defense of his teachings.[11]

Luther was popular throughout Germany and his journey to Worms was like a triumphal march. Crowds greeted him in the towns and cities along the way.[12] They cheered this man who exposed the corruption in the church and dared to challenge the Pope himself. The people and the nobility were yearning to be free from the oppression of a corrupt church.

There was a restlessness in Europe. Not all of it was born of the Holy Spirit. But it was a religious society and the secular impulses were masked in religious symbolism. Luther was a reformer and a servant of Jesus Christ. But he was also a revolutionary with earthly and political ambitions, and different people followed him for different reasons. Those very different motivations were not sharply differentiated in the sixteenth century. They were not all that clear in the minds of the reformers themselves. But at this critical moment, if his understanding was unclear, Luther's heart was pure.

It was pure because his life was at risk. Yes, he had been promised safe passage. But so had John Hus before him.[13] It had not been honored in Hus's case, and Luther knew very well that it might not be honored in his case, either. He had discussed the matter with Philip Melancthon before he left, and told Melancthon to carry on the work of the reformation without him in case he didn't return.

Luther knew he was probably walking into the jaws of death. He had prepared himself for martyrdom. He was going to Worms to give his witness for Jesus Christ and the word of God. And he knew he might never get out alive. At that critical juncture, it didn't matter to him. Later in his life he looked back to that moment and remembered being filled with a desperate boldness, a wonderful confidence that came from the Holy Spirit.[14] His life didn't matter; his witness to Jesus Christ and the word of God did. In the face of death a man discovers what is really important to him and what he really believes.

He stood before that august assembly of powerful and learned men. He was shown a pile of the books he had written. He was asked only two questions: Are these your books? And Will you renounce the things you have written?

Luther asked for time to consider what to answer to those questions. He knew that eternity hung in the balance. His request was granted. Luther had expected to be given an opportunity to address the delegates. He was only going to have the chance to answer two questions. But the two questions sharpened his focus. He had to say in a few words what the key issue of the Reformation was. That night as he prayed he saw the issues clearly and formulated his answer. That answer stated with clarity and unforgettable power what was essential to and true about the Protestant Reformation.

In response to the first question, his answer was yes. They were his books. As to the second question, his answer was clear and to the point. "If I am convinced from Scripture or from clear reasoning from Scripture that I am wrong, I will recant, and I will be the first to throw my books into the fire. But if not—for Popes and councils have been mistaken and have contradicted one another—I cannot recant. My conscience is captive to the word of God, and it is never safe to act against conscience. Here I stand. God help me."[15]

It was the shining moment of the Protestant Reformation. Then it was that Martin Luther made his good confession.[16] There at Worms he put his life on the line for the sake of the truth. This was the speech of a prophet who spoke for Jesus Christ, and a reformer who represented the church and its restoration to New Testament integrity. For he spoke as a man condemned to death in this world, whose hope in that moment was in a better world to come and he stood in the power of that coming world. The issue was the Word of God as recorded and preserved in writing.

156

Luther didn't see it all. But he laid down the principle for all the reforms and revivals that would follow. It was the Scripture—not as interpreted by Origen and Eusebius in a hidden and allegorical sense that could be understood only by a few learned initiates into the secrets and mysteries—but in its plain grammatical and historical sense that the fishermen and farmers and carpenters and tax collectors could understand and believe and obey, with the help of the Holy Spirit. After all, the New Testament Scriptures were written by fishermen and farmers and carpenters and tax collectors who believed in Jesus and were moved upon by the Holy Spirit.

Luther bore witness to the church's constitution, the Bible and the faith once delivered to the saints by the Son of God and those who heard Him and saw Him. And he dared to defy the pretensions of a fallen and profoundly compromised church to the exclusive right and the infallible power to "interpret" that constitution.

Yes, when a man stands before God, depending solely on the Holy Spirit, and with his life at risk bears witness to Jesus Christ as revealed in Scripture, a man in such a situation has a clearer grasp of the truth than all the learned scholars and councils and high officials in the world.

Martin Luther bore witness to a God who is faithful to His covenant, who in spite of all the opposition of men—be they judges and princes, the wise and the wealthy, the high and the mighty—and in spite of angels, principalities, powers and the devil himself, has set His Son on His throne in Zion.[17] He saw God as a mighty fortress. Within its walls of salvation he feared neither man nor devil. His counsel, which he first took himself and then gave to all believers was, "Let goods and kindred go, this mortal life also. The body they may kill. God's truth abideth still; His kingdom is forever!"[18]

Luther stood against the church, and yet he gave his witness on behalf of the church—not indeed as it was then constituted, in its fallen and divided state, but as it would be when the reform that Luther had started was finished. It was a long-range vision. In that moment he did not see what the end of the reformation would be. But he saw the principle on which the reform would proceed. The church would be reformed according to the word of God contained in the Bible and in particular, according to the New Testament. That was the vision God gave Martin Luther to see and declare in a few words in that moment of truth. As it turned out, Luther and the other reformers did not dare to apply the New Testament consistently to their reforms. But the mistakes and sins that came afterwards did not nullify the truth he spoke at that moment.

Luther was rescued by the political system and by the Elector, Frederick. And he spoke after that from a place of relative safety under the protection of that system and as its representative. It was a system he helped to create as an alternative to the Roman Catholic system. He spoke as a revolutionary who opposed the Catholic Church, because he aspired to replace the Catholic Church with a reformed church of his own design and to exercise the authority and power the Catholic Church had exercised.

The Reformation was a complex movement. If at its heart it produced a personal faith in the word of God among sincere believers, at its outer fringes it had a political, economic and social agenda. The Reformation was persuasive on many levels. It not only converted sinners to faith in Jesus, it also provided an opportunity for princes and kings and businessmen to throw off the oppressive yoke of an imperial church. There was a secular motivation that drew to the reform movement people who had no real commitment to Jesus Christ and the kingdom of God. They were willing for a while to climb aboard the Protestant bandwagon, because it was the only thing moving at the time.

This secular motivation was Protestant in the sense that it was anti-Catholic, and it helped to make of Protestantism a religious establishment in its own right. It was not the intention of the Protestant Reformers to eliminate the religious establishment that had misrepresented and distorted the New Testament revelation for more than twelve hundred years; it was their intention to replace the Catholic establishment with a Protestant establishment. They succeeded in part. But they succeeded by making some of the same compromises and committing some of the same sins the Catholics had made before them. It was Constantinianism all over again.

The Protestant establishment made war with the Catholic establishment. It began with a war of words and it came to literal wars, bloodshed and carnage. It was a standoff. The only way the leaders could end the bloodshed and restore peace was to agree that warring states would become officially either Catholic or Protestant according to the faith of the prince. So, for instance, France and Spain became Catholic because their sovereigns were Catholic while England and Scotland became Protestant. But whether Catholic or Protestant, the union of church and state stood.

In Scotland John Knox, who led the Protestant reform there, cried out to God in a prayer modeled on Old Testament Scripture, "Give me Scotland or I die!" We know what happened and how it happened. Knox preached. Many were converted. But he also recruited the nobility to his cause in a political movement that waged a civil war. Knox and his military coalition took Scotland by the sword. And that is how Scotland became Protestant.

England, following King Henry VIII, also became Protestant. Henry's interest in the Reformation was conditioned by his determination to divorce his wife who could not give him a male heir to the throne, and marry another woman who could. The Pope would not allow the divorce and remarriage, so Henry used the Reformation as a pretext for breaking with the Papacy and creating his own English national church with himself as the head of that church. Then he could do what he wanted to do. The motivation was political. Henry had no real interest in church reform for its own sake.

But in the new Protestant establishment in England, there were those who wanted a thoroughgoing reform of the church. They were called Puritans, for their determination to purify the church of all the unbiblical doctrines and traditions that had accumulated through the centuries. They wanted to return the church to the purity and simplicity of the faith as it was first delivered to the saints. But they carried with them the same inconsistency as the original Protestant Reformers. They set out to convert people to Christ by preaching the gospel to them. But they took it for granted that the state would endorse and protect their institutions and personnel as they did God's work. They wanted to purify the state church, but they didn't want to purify the church of the unscriptural influence of the state or give up the protection, support and other favors of the state.

The Puritans were influential in England, but they were unable to accomplish their goals. Frustrated by the resistance to their reforms within the Anglican establishment, many Puritans left England for the new world. In America, the Puritans had the freedom to put their reforms into practice. But they did everything they could to deny that freedom to anybody else. Their method was revival, an evangelical proclamation of the gospel in the power of the Holy Spirit as taught in the New Testament. But the Puritans could not go beyond the limits set by the Protestant reformers. They erected a religious establishment in New England supported and protected by the state. They persecuted "heretics." They were involved in a contradiction: they believed in the proclamation of the gospel that required a free choice; and they believed in the coercive power of the state which restricted one's free choice. On the one hand, they preached the gospel from the New Testament. And the gospel taught believers to expect to be persecuted by the state. On the other hand, they controlled the machinery of the state and persecuted non-conformists.[19] Even when they lost control of the state to the Unitarians and other secularists, the Puritans and their evangelical brothers did all they could to maintain a dominant influence on American society and culture and never gave up their dreams of being dominant politically.

The Puritan dream survives to this day in the notion of a Christian America, and the expectation that the laws and policies of the state ought to reflect the laws of God and the agenda of the church. The dream also survives in the disappointment Christians still feel when the decisions of the state and society do not reflect the will of God as they understand it or the agenda of their church. It survives, too, in the efforts and expenditures of Christians to influence the politics of the nation.

Nevertheless, the evangelical revivals have made an important contribution to the restoration of New Testament Christianity and of the New Testament church. Revivals have a lot in common with one another, but they are never identical. There are new issues that arise with every outpouring of the Holy Spirit. It is as if the Holy Spirit has illuminated first one aspect of the Scripture and then another and with each successive revival has restored one thing and then another to the church.

In the sixteenth century Luther discovered the judicial aspect of salvation, the pardon and justification received by faith. The Puritans in the seventeenth century stressed the dynamic side of faith: regeneration or the new birth. The Methodists in the eighteenth century emphasized holiness. The Moravians recovered the missionary impulse in the revival movement associated with them in the eighteenth century. The missionary mandate took hold in the nineteenth century revivals.

In the nineteenth century a new movement was born in England among believers who wanted to find out what the Bible taught about the end times. Until that time most Christians believed that the return of the Lord was a thousand years away at least. The millennium—a revival lasting a thousand years, or maybe just a very long time—would come first. But as these earnest brethren searched the Scriptures, they rediscovered the hope of the early church that Jesus will come back before the millennial kingdom rather than after it. His coming will inaugurate the thousand year kingdom of God on the earth. They began to preach that the Lord could return soon. The recovery of a premillennial scheme of interpreting biblical prophecy has spread through the evangelical church and has become a major doctrine in our times.

The place of the Jews in God's redemptive plan has likewise been recovered, and the expectation of their conversion. The fact is, more Jews have believed in Jesus as their Messiah in last three decades of the twentieth century than at any other time since the first century.

The twentieth century could almost be called the century of the Holy Spirit. The major revivals have all emphasized the return of the supernatural, the doctrine and experience of the Holy Spirit, miracles and the charismatic gifts, including the gifts to the church of pastors, teachers, evangelists, prophets and finally apostles. The New Testament doctrine of the church has come to center stage.

If, as Schaff asserted, the Protestant Reformation ushered in the modern world, what lies ahead now that historians are writing about the "Post Modern" era of history? Some have called it the "Post Protestant" era. Clearly some shift has occurred in the heavens affecting whole civilizations, one that seems beyond the scope of traditional Protestantism to handle. In any case, Protestantism is not leading the parade. That does not mean that the insights of the Protestant Reformation will be abandoned; they remain a large and significant part of the restoration of New Testament faith. But there was an aspect of reform that the Protestants refused to address.

The Protestant Reformation was a doctrinal and theological reform. Its focus was on the doctrines of salvation. The Protestant reformers didn't do much about church reform as such, and they were as resistant to addressing the church-state issue as were the Catholics. Protestants flirted with that crucial issue at the beginning, but soon dropped it like a hot potato. For Catholics and the Eastern "Orthodox," the New Testament relationship of the church to the state was not seriously discussed. To implement a New Testament reform would have required a radical revision of their whole theology and the dismantling of their whole structure. It was unthinkable in the sixteenth century.

The people who actually addressed the issue of church reform from the New Testament point of view and did something about it were the despised Anabaptists, the "stepchildren" of the Reformation. Today at the beginning of the twenty-first century, and at the end of the modern world the Protestants helped to create, the final stage of the reform is at hand in a new world that is increasingly hostile to Christians of whatever sort. Contemporary Christians are beginning to experience the tensions with state and society that believers in the New Testament era took for granted.

In the history of revivals, it was the Anabaptists who pioneered a church reform along New Testament lines. In the next two chapters we will consider the contributions of the Anabaptists to the restoration of the New Testament church, the cross, and martyrdom.

17

The Anabaptists:
Pioneers On The Way Of The Cross

Until the twentieth century, the history of the Anabaptists was almost exclusively a tale told by their enemies. For the most part, the only information readily available about them were the rumors, reports, and propaganda spread by the people who hated them. It was a literature produced in order to justify harassing and killing Anabaptists. Their own records were suppressed or destroyed, or hidden away by the Anabaptists themselves to protect them from destruction. The official record was taken pretty much at face value. There wasn't much interest in reopening a case that the main line churches, both Catholic and Protestant, had judged and closed.[1] But changes were taking place that raised anew the questions the Anabaptists raised, and led to a reassessment of their answers.

The nineteenth century was a restless one, with vast movements of populations—immigrations to the new world, movements from the farms to towns and cities with the rise of industry, the relative ease of trade and travel with the coming of the railroads. Science asserted its independence from religious dogma, and some of its practical successes enhanced its prestige over religion. A secular spirit took over the mainstream culture, and Christians found themselves a minority and on the defensive in lands that had once been the home of Christian civilization.

The effect on the Roman Catholic Church was most dramatic. It was the Catholic Church that had invented the rationale for the partnership of church and state after it embraced Constantine in the fourth century. It was driven to re-examine the alliance that had formed and marked it during its journey. Latourette wrote,

> In countries which had been the main strongholds
> of the Roman Catholic faith thousands of

monastic houses were dissolved and their properties confiscated, and the education of youth was in part taken out of the hands of the Church. In several marriage was put under the control of the state, and in France Church and state were formally separated. The Popes were deprived of the territories upon which they had depended to make them politically independent. The Popes set themselves resolutely against these currents, and, condemning them, sought to stem them. Thus the distinction between the Church and the world was made sharper than at any time since the conversion of Constantine.[2]

Church and state were separating, sometimes by Christians themselves out of concern for religious liberty for all and resistance to state control. This tended to be the case in Protestant countries. Sometimes the separation of church and state came by a secular revolt against the church and its influence. It tended to happen that way in Catholic countries. But one way or the other, Christians found themselves a minority in a de-Christianized society.[3] On the other hand, there was a remarkable expansion of the church outside the boundaries of the old Christendom. "For the first time in its history Christianity made actual its inherent genius and became world-wide. In this it surpassed the achievement of every other religion. Christians were...a small fraction of the population. Yet by 1914 nearly every culture felt to a greater or less extent the influence of Christianity."[4]

That's not far from the New Testament situation; early believers saw themselves as aliens and strangers in the world, even in their own homeland. The church was a minority everywhere, but it showed a remarkable vigor and carried the gospel to the ends of the earth.

The twentieth century intensified the struggle of church and state. The rise of Communism in Russia precipitated a violent rejection of Constantinianism by the state. The Russian Orthodox Church had accommodated itself to the Czars. But the Communist revolution overthrew the monarchy and attacked the church as an accomplice to the crimes of the political regime. Religion itself was characterized by the Marxists as "the opiate of the people," a kind of mind drug employed by the ruling elite to keep the masses submissive to tyranny and compliant to those who exploited them.

Religious education of children was outlawed. Anti-religious propaganda was encouraged. Between 1917 (when the communists took over the nation) and 1940 an estimated 90% of the Orthodox church buildings had been converted to secular uses, the number of bishops had declined by 75%, the number of deacons by 80% and the number of priests by 90%.[5] Itinerant preaching by Baptists, evangelicals and Pentecostals was forbidden, and those who persisted were sentenced to hard labor in the North and in Siberia.[6] The communist empire spread rapidly throughout the world, and even where it was stopped, it was a threat that could not be ignored.

The rise of Hitler in Germany raised similar urgent questions in Western Europe about the viability of the church-state union. Hitler's policy toward the church was to put it on a leash and train it to serve his political will like a performing dog. He tolerated what he called a "positive Christianity" which amounted to a church of the German Empire in which Aryan blood and German soil were more important than the blood of Christ or the will of God. When church leaders resisted the Nazification of the church, Hitler bared his teeth. Pastor Martin Niemoller, though a German hero in World War I, was put in prison and then in a concentration camp for speaking out against National Socialism. Although vindicated of the charge of treason in a court of law, the Pastor was arrested and placed under "protective custody." Niemoller remained in Dachau as Hitler's personal prisoner until Hitler was dead and the war was over.[7]

Public opinion in Germany was not yet ready for a "final solution" for Christians; they made up ninety seven percent of Germany's population when Hitler came to power. It is pretty clear, however, that had he continued in power in Germany, Hitler would have compromised most of the church to the point of irrelevance. Those Christians who resisted him would have been discredited and demonized by his propaganda, marginalized, and finally destroyed as were the Jews.

It wasn't only the state that attacked Constantinianism. Soren Kierkegaard, the nineteenth century Danish writer, had launched a withering attack on Christendom and the state church in Denmark in the mid-nineteenth century.[8] He was ignored or ridiculed in his own time, but by the 1930s and particularly during and after World War II, his works were studied and given serious attention inside and outside of the church. Despite his criticism of the church, Kierkegaard himself, from the point of his conversion in 1848, wrote from a position of faith in Jesus Christ. He wrote, I believe, as a prophet of God.

Another factor challenging the church-state union was the success of the free churches. The United States was a prime example. Originally colonized by people who came to this country when it was "a howling wilderness" to escape religious persecution, America was the scene where the struggle for religious liberty won perhaps its greatest successes. Americans considered freedom of worship the first and most basic freedom. The first item in the bill of rights in the United States Constitution prohibited the federal government to establish a religion, that is, a state church with a legal monopoly and tax support, or to prohibit or hinder the free exercise of religion.

The federal government was officially neutral in regard to the different religious institutions in its domain. Soon the individual states adopted the same position. The churches in the United States survived very well on a voluntary basis and without state support. Free churches did well even in countries like England that had a national religious establishment. After trying to suppress dissenters, England finally decided to tolerate them and allow them to propagate their faith without state interference.

These are some of the influences that contributed in our time to the awakening of interest in the Anabaptists and their understanding of the church. For the Anabaptists rejected the whole notion of a politicized church. They represented an ancient conviction dating back to before the fourth century, a conviction rooted in the New Testament itself. They understood the church as authorized directly by Jesus Christ, and dependent upon Him, rather than the rulers and authorities of this present sinful world. Anabaptists saw the church as a company of believers dependent on God, loyal to Jesus Christ, and separate from the rest of the people of the world; separate, not in the sense of being isolated from the rest of mankind, but of being holy, set apart for God. Dedicated to Jesus Christ, the church as they understood it was called to represent the coming King and to bear witness on His behalf to the people of the world.

The Anabaptists can trace their origins to the sixteenth century. But they are part of a much older tradition. The Anabaptists were part of an underground already on the scene when the Protestant Reformation began. Leonard Verduin, in his book, *The Reformers and Their Stepchildren*, makes the point that none of the names applied to the Anabaptists in the sixteenth century were new. They were "old, very old." The Reformation precipitated "a resurgence of those tendencies and opinions that had for centuries already existed over against the medieval order; it was connected with ancient circles in which, in spite of the persecutions, a body of ancient opinions and convictions was still alive," wrote Verduin. "The dissent against the medieval order was in 1517 already a millenium old and extremely widespread."[9]

Initially the Anabaptists greeted the Protestant Reformation with enthusiasm. But they were concerned about issues the Protestants were unwilling to deal with—notably, the church-state issue—and when the Reformers backed away from those issues the Anabaptists withdrew from the Protestants and instituted their own reform at great cost.

The issues to which they bore witness concerned the nature of the church and its relationship to the surrounding world. Catholics understood the church to be essentially the same as the Empire. From the time of Emperor Theodosius, the imperial church had a legal claim to everybody born in the Roman Empire. Hence, being born in the Roman Empire was tantamount to being born a Christian and baptism of infants was virtually universal throughout the Empire.

The Anabaptists said no; baptism was for those who heard and believed the gospel, and voluntarily accepted it, making a personal and intentional commitment to Jesus Christ. Baptism administered apart from hearing, understanding and believing the Gospel, and making confession of Jesus Christ as Lord, was no baptism at all. That is how the Anabaptists read the New Testament. They took the New Testament at face value and put it into practice the way the early church had. When somebody came to them and believed, they baptized the believer, even if he or she had been "baptized" as an infant, that is, before having believed and confessed their faith.

Anabaptists denied being rebaptizers, for they denied, on New Testament grounds, the validity of baptism apart from faith and confession of that faith by the believer. An infant was not in a position to hear and understand the gospel, to accept it by faith, and to make a confession of that faith. So infant baptism to them was no baptism at all. But infant baptism was the universal practice of Christendom. To oppose it was to tread on the sacred ground of a whole civilization. The practice of believer's baptism was an act that invalidated "Christian" civilization, defied a tradition that had stood at least since the fourth century, was endorsed by the official "church," and defended by the state. The Anabaptists rejected state support, denied any tradition which contradicted the New Testament, and declared that the official church had lost touch with its New Testament roots. It is no wonder that the Anabaptists were persecuted.

The church, then, from an Anabaptist point of view, was composed of those—and only those—who had believed and been baptized. The church, in their view, stood over against the rest of the society and in contradistinction to it. The issue of baptism made that difference as clear as daylight—shockingly clear.

One can argue with their position. One can say that because of the conversion of the Emperor, because of the Christianization of society, because of church traditions, it is possible or even necessary to change some things. One can argue—and many did—that in effect, church councils and decisions by the official church and its various authorities superseded the New Testament. One can point out that the tradition of infant baptism pre-dates Constantine. But there is no denying that the Anabaptists were reading the New Testament accurately in regard to the relationship of the church to the world. They had a point. They backed it solidly with New Testament Scripture. And for this conviction Anabaptists experienced persecution as did the New Testament believers. The Anabaptists were put to death as heretics. Their belief and practice of believer's baptism in itself was all that was necessary to call down on them the sentence of death.

The Protestant Reformers understood the point the Anabaptists were making. Their reform, like the Anabaptists', was based on the Scriptures, largely on New Testament Scriptures. They too were unwilling to admit that church councils, the decisions of Popes or the accumulated traditions of the established church could overthrow or modify the New Testament. But the Protestant reformers were unwilling to renounce the Constantinian legacy of state support and protection. The Protestants stood firm on the New Testament in their doctrine of salvation. They waffled when it came to the doctrine of the church.

We shall hear from the Anabaptist's own documents about their beginnings and the point at which they separated from the Protestant Reformation, and why. And we shall also hear from a scholar from within the Protestant Reformed tradition, Leonard Verduin, whose book, *The Reformers and Their Stepchildren*, reflects the changing attitude of many believers in the standard brand churches toward the Anabaptists. The issue is important to our times.

Verduin, writing in the 1950s and 1960s, admitted that "the Radicals of the Reformation times receive more sympathetic treatment than they are wont to get, especially in the Reformed tradition." He gives two reasons for this sympathetic treatment.

> One is that the time seems to have come to reverse the derogatory treatment to which these Stepchildren of the Reformation have been traditionally subjected. One can speak very well of them indeed before he becomes guilty of a bias as pronounced as that of those who have so long spoken evil of them; one can let these Stepchildren play the role of the hero and he will be at least as near to historic truth as is the tradition that has so long assigned to them the role of the rogue.
>
> A second reason for the sympathetic treatment given these Radicals of the Reformation is that history has to a large extent demonstrated that they were in a large way right. Little by little, step by step, item by item, Protestantism has, at least in the New World, come to endorse the very emphases for which these men pioneered. The free Church, the Church by voluntary association, the missionary Church, and a host of other features for which the Stepchildren agonized, have become part and parcel of the Protestant vision—so much so that men are often surprised to learn that it was not always thus. It is not too much to say that in the New World, as well as among the so-called younger Churches, the vision of the men of the Second Front has, to a large extent, fought through to victory...There are voices even in the Catholic Church in the New World asserting that the Catholic Church is nowhere else in possession of the state of health in which it finds itself here. The heritage of the 'heretic' seems therefore to be salubrious. For that reason also we have dealt kindly with it.[10]

The hour has struck when the story lived and told by the Anabaptists must be heard and heeded by the whole church. They blazed a trail that all faithful Christians will have to follow in these last times in which we now live.

18

An Anabaptist Revival And Reform

The scene was Zurich, Switzerland. The Protestant Reformation was going forward there under the leadership of Ulrich Zwingli. Until the twentieth century, Zwingli's side of the struggle was all that was commonly known about it. In our times, the Anabaptist side of that story has become known. It is recorded in the Chronicle of the Hutterian Brethren. There the Anabaptists speak for themselves. I will quote them at length.[1]

It began in Switzerland, where God brought about an awakening. First of all a meeting took place between Ulrich Zwingli, Conrad Grebel (a member of the nobility), and Felix Mantz. All three were men of learning with a thorough knowledge of German, Latin, Greek, and Hebrew. They started to discuss matters of faith and realized that infant baptism is unnecessary and, moreover, is not baptism at all.

Two of them, Conrad and Felix, believed that people should be truly baptized in the Christian order appointed by the Lord, because Christ himself says, 'Whoever believes and is baptized will be saved.' Ulrich Zwingli (who shrank from the cross, disgrace, and persecution that Christ suffered) refused to agree—he said it would cause an uproar. But Conrad and Felix said that was no reason to disobey the clear command of God.

At this point a man came from Chur, a priest named GEORG FROM THE HOUSE OF JAKOB, later known as Georg Blaurock,...a priest...He, too, had first approached Zwingli and discussed questions of faith with him at length, but he got nowhere. Then he was told that there were other men more on fire than Zwingli. He inquired eagerly about them and met with them, that is, with Conrad Grebel and Felix Mantz, to talk about questions of faith. They came to unity about these questions. In the fear of God they agreed that from God's Word one must first learn true faith, expressed in deeds of love, and on confession of this faith receive true Christian baptism as a covenant of a good conscience with God, serving him from then on with a holy Christian life and remaining steadfast to the end, even in times of tribulation.

One day [January 21, 1525] when they were meeting, fear came over them and struck their hearts. They fell on their knees before the Almighty God in heaven and called upon him who knows all hearts. They prayed that God grant it to them to do his divine will and that he might have mercy on them. Neither flesh and blood nor human wisdom compelled them. They were well aware of what they would have to suffer for this.

After the prayer, Georg Blaurock stood up and asked Conrad Grebel in the name of God to baptize him with true Christian baptism on his faith and recognition of the truth. With this request he knelt down, and Conrad baptized him, since at that time there was no appointed servant of the Word. Then the others turned to Georg in their turn, asking him to baptize them, which he did. And so, in great fear of God, together they surrendered themselves to the Lord. They confirmed one another for the service of the gospel and began to teach the faith and to keep it. This was the beginning of separation from the world and its evil ways.

Soon after this, more people joined them, like Balthasar Hubmaier of Friedberg and Ludwig Haetzer, and other scholars of German, Latin, Greek, and Hebrew, well acquainted with the

Scriptures, as well as priests and preachers and other people. Soon they all gave witness with their blood.

Felix Mantz was drowned at Zurich for the sake of the true faith and baptism, thus giving his life in steadfast witness to the truth.

Later, Wolfgang Uliman was condemned to death and burned at Waldsee, also in Switzerland. His ten companions, including his own brothers, were executed with him. Valiantly and resolutely they gave their lives as a witness that their faith and baptism were founded on divine truth.

Melchior Vet, Georg Blaurock's traveling companion, was burned at Ettach for the sake of his faith.

So the movement spread through persecution and great tribulation. The church increased daily, and the number of the Lord's people grew quickly. This the enemy of divine truth could not endure, so he used Zwingli as a tool. Zwingli began to write and preach with fanaticism that baptism of adult believers was false and should not be tolerated. This was contrary to his earlier confession, when he himself had taught that not one clear word from God justified infant baptism. But now, because he wanted to please men and the world rather than God, he opposed true Christian baptism. He persuaded the authorities to use the imperial law to behead as Anabaptists those who were truly dedicated to God, those who out of conviction had made the bond of good conscience with him.

If Catholics trace their history by reference to Popes, doctors, councils and the founders of religious orders, and if Protestants trace their history through reformers, preachers, evangelists and revivalists, then the Anabaptists trace their history through their confessors and martyrs.

Leonard Verduin took a novel approach in explaining the basic beliefs and practices of the typical Anabaptist. He employed the terms of derision used against these believers, terms forged by their enemies to make them look stupid, evil, or dangerous, and traced these terms back to the core belief the Anabaptists actually held, which led their enemies to use that particular epithet. Here I will try to summarize briefly a work that is well worth reading in its entirety.

Donatists, or *Neo-Donatists*. "The stage on which the sixteenth century conflict was enacted," wrote Leonard Verduin, "was set in the fourth, as informed observers in Reformation times saw very clearly." The heart of the battle between the Protestants and the Anabaptists which Verduin calls the "second front," (the first, of course, being the conflict between the Protestants and the Catholics) had to do with their different evaluation of the change that took place at the time of Constantine. The Anabaptists raised again in the sixteenth century the question Donatus raised in the fourth, "What has the Emperor got to do with the church?" The Anabaptists believed in the separation of church and state at a time when the term *church and state* was unknown and the distinction had been long forgotten. Church and state were mixed up together like a couple of scrambled eggs, and it took the persistent faith and witness of the Anabaptists and more than four centuries to unscramble them.[2]

Stabler is a term of abuse used on and about the Anabaptists. It refers to their habit of carrying a staff. Anabaptist teachers typically carried a staff instead of a sword as a sign of their rejection of force and coercion in matters of faith. There was some disagreement among them at first about whether or not to use the sword. It was resolved in a couple of ways. There was a group of Anabaptists in Munster that decided to take up the sword. They tried to establish the kingdom of God on the earth by military force. They were opposed by Menno Simons, from whom the Mennonites got their name. Menno was a Catholic Priest who became convinced of the truth taught by the Anabaptists and who became troubled in his conscience when he observed their courage in the face of persecution and martyrdom. After a long internal struggle, Menno left the Catholic Church and joined the Anabaptists, thereby putting his own life at risk. He preached and wrote in support of Anabaptist beliefs over against the beliefs of the state church. He spoke out with equal vigor against what he perceived to be the error of the Munsterite Anabaptists and their use of the weapons of war. Menno's teaching reflected the message and the method of the New Testament; it prevailed among the Anabaptists. The Munsterite experiment with the use of force ended in a military defeat. That ended the Anabaptists' flirtation with force.

Their enemies seized on the Munster event for propaganda purposes and exploited that mistake as if it were typical of all Anabaptists. It never was. As Estep pointed out, the mistake at Munster must be interpreted in the light of the Anabaptist movement, not the Anabaptist movement in the light of Munster. The attention given to the Munster incident is out of all proportion to its real importance. The debacle there represented a small minority of Anabaptists; its influence on the movement as a whole was small and brief.[3]

The Anabaptists believed in serving Jesus Christ by following His example and suffering persecution for His sake, not by persecuting others. They were willing to die for Christ; they were unwilling to kill for Him, for they were convinced that would be to serve the devil, not Jesus Christ.[4]

Catharer means cleansed, and points to the emphasis the Anabaptists made on living a clean and pure life. This emphasis was made in contrast to the inclusive church which could not maintain consistently high standards of conduct because its membership included everyone in the community, most of whom lacked a vital, life-changing commitment to God.[5]

Sacramentschwarmer was another term of opprobrium and insult used against the Anabaptists. It means anti-sacramental, and there is some truth to it. The Anabaptists reacted (Verduin suggested it may have been an overreaction) to the misuse of the sacraments by the established religions in which ceremony tended to take the place of experience and religious forms tended to be without power and reality in the lives of the devotees. The Anabaptists saw medieval sacramentalism as a throwback to paganism and to the sacral state that maintained by priestly manipulation a public and superficial religious unity. That kind of unity worked, after a fashion, for pre-Christian paganism. It was manifestly a falsification of New Testament Christianity in which the church is called out of the world and the believer is a stranger and pilgrim in the present evil world.

The Anabaptists stressed the word of God and the power of the Holy Spirit and deliberately de-emphasized the sacraments. Anabaptists looked for genuine conversions and holy lives rather than attendance at religious ceremonies as the sign of the true church. They objected to the magical notion that the wafer was actually transformed into the flesh of Jesus, and they rejected the idea that a worldly church and its official clergy could manipulate the grace of God by controlling the communion wafer.[6]

Winckler. The word means corner and signifies a kind of hiding place. The idea is that the Anabaptists met in secret and were unauthorized by the ruling authorities. Ministers who preached without authorization from the ruling powers—a civil and religious mix—were the equivalent of someone today practicing medicine without a license. It was a capital offense in medieval Europe because it constituted a threat to the cohesion of the sacral society, the society united by a common government and religion. The Anabaptists, by their own understanding of Christian faith, were not part of that common religion and so were outlaws in medieval society. In New Testament terms, they were strangers, aliens and pilgrims in the present evil world. The fact that the present evil world was nominally Christian did not make an essential difference to the Anabaptists. In their thinking, the established church was a fallen church, compromised, and had become a part of the evil world. The Anabaptists believed that Jesus Christ had called them to separate from the evil world, even if that world called itself "Christian," even if the world called the Anabaptists "heretics" for doing so.

In some places the "heretics" had a large popular following. The larger their following, the greater was the threat they posed to the established order, and the harsher the methods that were used against them.[7]

Wiedertaufer was the smear word used by the establishment to refer to the Anabaptists' beliefs and practices of baptism. The established churches defended infant baptism by making baptism the equivalent of circumcision in the Old Testament. There are similarities. Both are rites of entrance. Both represent the grace of God and look forward to nurture and instruction. But Old Testament circumcision and New Testament baptism were different things. The Old Testament type and shadow are incomplete and inadequate to express the new reality.

The Anabaptists were accused of being divisive. From the standpoint of a church that is inclusive of everybody in the society, they were divisive—for the same reason that Jesus and the New Testament church caused division in Judea in New Testament times. For although baptism signifies the unity of the church, it also signifies the separation of the church from the world. In the Old Testament there was no clear distinction made as yet between the people of Israel and the true believers, the holy remnant. The prophets made references to that all important distinction, but it was not until John the Baptist and Jesus that the distinction was given dramatic expression in baptism.

For the Anabaptists, baptism was connected with conversion, with a radical break with sin, with the entrance into a holy life. It was part of the response of the believer to the gospel of Jesus Christ. It was not just a ceremony performed on one person by the will of another. The believer was consciously, willingly, and intentionally involved. And according to the Anabaptists, in contrast to the Protestant reformers, it signified not only pardon for sin, but also the beginning of a new life lived in the power of the Holy Spirit. The believer willingly cooperated with God in doing good works. That was the faith of the Anabaptists. It is also the teaching of the New Testament.[8]

Kommunisten. The Anabaptists were called communists because they practiced community of goods. The followers of Jacob Hutter lived communally and held material possessions in common. This was not the case with all Anabaptists. But they all believed that material things were entrusted to them by God, not as if they were absolute owners but rather stewards of goods belonging to God. They were responsible as stewards to share their excess with those who were in need. However, the Anabaptists were unwilling to be exploited by people who wanted to use the system to avoid working or to take advantage of the industry of others. The Anabaptists shunned such people. That was as far as their church discipline could go. They did not persecute anybody, and they did not imprison, torture or kill dissenters.

Anabaptists were falsely accused of holding wives in common, a throwback to the pre-Constantine accusations by the pagans against the early Christians. And they were also falsely accused of wanting to destroy the civil government. These were old prejudices that Anabaptists denied. But so convinced were their enemies that the Anabaptists were guilty of those things that they tortured the Anabaptists in order to try to obtain a confession of what they were sure was true. Neither pleas nor proofs could satisfy their accusers.[9]

"Certain it is," wrote Verduin, "that, whatever was novel in the economic vision of early Christianity, this was again lost in and with the Constantinian change. The economic conscience, if indeed

177

there was one in medieval society, can hardly be said to have derived from the New Testament writings."[10]

Rottengeister. A rott is a clique, a faction, and Rottengeister are those who make factions. The Anabaptists were seen as agitators. Their vision of the church tended to create a composite society; that is, a society with alternatives in matters of faith, rather than a sacral society which is united by a common faith. Both the politics and the religion of sacral societies are legal monopolies enforced by the sword. Our word for such societies is totalitarian. Dissent is not tolerated, it is punished.

The Anabaptists were dissenters. They were considered disloyal, for they challenged what was held to be sacred in the society in which they lived. Anabaptists, like the pre-Constantinian Christians, refused the oath, which was not only designed to secure veracity or truth-telling in a court of law, but also loyalty or fealty to the establishment and its leaders. It carried a strong religious content. The Anabaptists, like the early Christians, refused to take such an oath. Indeed, the oath was designed to catch the Anabaptistst in its web.[11]

The Cross. The Anabaptists, like the Donatists before them, believed that suffering for the faith was a mark of true discipleship. As the New Testament puts it, "all who will live godly in Christ Jesus will suffer persecution."[12] Augustine's response to this was that it is the cause, not the punishment, that makes the martyr. The Protestant reformers used a similar argument against the Anabaptists. Verduin commented:

> One thing that Augustine left unexplained was left unexplained by the Reformers also. It is this. If one withholds from the people whom they called 'Donatists' the passages in the New Testament that speak of Cross-bearing as the mark of the believer, to whom then are they applicable? Least of all can they appropriate them who sit snug and smug behind the arm of flesh, the sword of the civil ruler, in a situation of 'Christian sacralism,' in a situation in which there was nothing even remotely resembling the Cross-experience of the early Christians.[13]

Leufer was another word of reproach applied to the Anabaptists. It means one who walks or runs. It was applied to the

178

Anabaptists because of their mobility. Anabaptists saw the church as a mission society. They moved about with the gospel and they fled from the persecution their preaching provoked.

> Missions in the New Testament sense the medieval world did not know. The prevailing view was that the Great Commission, the command to preach the gospel to all nations, had been executed, finished, in and with the 'larger fulfillment' of which Augustine had spoken so oracularly. As a consequence, the eschatological hope that had lived so fervently in the early Church came to a halt; that far-off event to which the New Testament Church had cast its eyes had been realized; all promises had been fulfilled.[14]

The loss of hope went hand in hand with a loss of mission. For if everybody was already a Christian, to whom would one preach the gospel? "A sense of mission and a practice of mission did continue to manifest itself—in the camp of the 'heretics.'"[15]

So effective were the "heretics" that the medieval church determined to use their own methods in combatting them—to fight fire with fire, as it were. The Dominicans were established for that very purpose. They were known as the order of preachers. Under the leadership of a Dominican friar, perhaps the best preacher the Dominicans ever produced, the Catholics experienced a revival of their own, a revival full of significance for the church today.

19

A Catholic Revival

When Columbus was planning his historic voyage of discovery, the focal point of Western civilization was Florence, Italy. The Italian Renaissance was at flood tide. The Capital of the Eastern half of the Roman Empire, Constantinople, had fallen at last to the Muslim Turks. The scholars from that great center of Christian civilization in the East fled to the West carrying with them the treasures of art and literature of ancient Greece and Rome. These treasures had escaped the Barbarian invasions that had virtually destroyed the cultural heritage of the Western half of the Empire. Finally, Constantinople's time had come. Priceless documents and works of art from antiquity had been arriving in the West since the Turks first threatened Constantinople. Now that it had fallen, the flight to the West had speeded up. The refugees, conservators of classical wisdom and art, found a royal welcome in Florence.[1]

Lorenzo de Medici

The city was administered by Lorenzo de Medici, known as the Magnificent. Lorenzo was an heir to the fortunes of the Medici international banking firm. The Medicis were commoners rather than nobility. But they were extraordinarily gifted and fabulously wealthy. Lorenzo was an able financier, a capable politician, a gifted diplomat. Above all, Lorenzo was a man of culture, learning, and charm, a scholar and poet in his own right, and a generous patron of the arts at a time when the arts and literature were to Western civilization what science and technology are today. And Lorenzo, by his wealth, his patronage of the arts and scholarship, his administrative skills, had made Florence the wealthiest city in Europe and the cultural capital of the western world. It was her golden age.

The Medicis were among the earliest examples and perhaps the most striking in all history, of that feature of the end times as revealed in the Biblical book of the Revelation. God says to "Mystery Babylon," the dominant power of the last days, "your merchants were the great men of the earth."[2] For the Medicis stood among the great men of the earth, and they were merchants (bankers) and not aristocrats, kings, warriors, philosophers, priests or prophets. The judgment of the Scripture on that ultimate mercantile civilization is stern: "for by your sorcery all the nations were deceived. And in her was found the blood of prophets and saints, and of all who were slain on the earth." And so it was in Florence in the late fifteenth century. For there in the midst of a revival of paganism there arose a prophet whose message was apocalyptic, steeped in the images and judgments of the book of Revelation.

The revival associated with Savonarola was a preview of the apocalyptic struggle of the last days in a way that the Protestant Reformation never was. The Florentine revival was characterized by the emergence of the gift of prophecy; the Protestant Reformation never was. And it is chiefly known for the martyrdom of its godly leader. Both Protestantism and Catholicism have produced their martyrs, but both of them typically and in their eyes, normally and properly, enjoyed the protection of the state. Savonarola began that way, but as he was led on by God, he relinquished the power and protection of the state and ended up following his Lord and Master, Jesus, to martyrdom. In this way, too, Savonarola's reform and revival anticipate the apocalyptic struggle of the last days as the Protestant Reformation did not, and has therefore a relevance to our times and to the coming ultimate revival that the Protestant Reformation does not.

The sorcery of a mercantile civilization is rooted in mammon, the power of money. It has the power to deceive the nations and to lure them into rebellion against God. The deception is that mammon promises the good things of the earth, and seems to offer them in a peaceful way. For if kings and warriors triumph by violence and bloodshed, merchants seem to thrive on peace and order. And, as in the case of the Medicis, they foster a high degree of civilization and culture. The deception is that culture is looked upon as more important than salvation, usually as a substitute for salvation or at least as a distraction from the paramount and urgent need for salvation.

Florence offered all of that in a preeminently attractive package. For the Renaissance was not simply a copy of the greatness of ancient Greece and Rome; Florence augmented that grandeur with an authentic grandeur of its own. The grandest parties and celebrations, the most brilliant learning, incomparable sculpture and painting, the most sophisticated conversation, the most elegant and sublime architecture graced the city by the Arno in the waning years of the fifteenth century. Not since the Athens of Pericles, said Pierre Van Passen, had there been such a concentration of talent, wealth, and the accumulated wisdom of the ages at one place and time.[3] And this achievement was due largely to one family: the Medicis.

It was indeed a renaissance, a rebirth of the classic art and literature of ancient Rome and Greece. There was a new emphasis on man and his capacities for greatness, the kind of thought that occupied the ancient Greeks and Romans. It was called humanism, and it found expression in the sculpture of Michaelangelo, for instance, in the statue of the young David, as Francis Schaeffer has pointed out.[4] It is man conceived as bigger than life, magnificent, independent and free, but unreal. There never was a man like Michangelo's statue. It is humanist hype, no more real than the comic strip *Superman*. It is doubly ironic that the figure is a biblical character who was a man of faith. For the figure does not point to God, as the real David did, but to man. It was typical of the confusion of the times, a time of transition from the medieval to the modern world, from a religious to a secular society.

> Michaelangelo's style changed as he grew older, and it is a matter of historical record how and why he changed. Like the rest of Florence in his time he was deeply moved by the preaching of a Dominican Friar with amazing gifts of preaching and prophecy and a comprehensive knowledge of the Holy Scriptures. Michelangelo heard Savonarola's sermons. He owned a copy of the Friar's printed sermons which he read and pondered for as long as he lived. It has been said that Michelangelo's "greatest single composition of the Last Judgment in the Sistine Chapel is essentially a Savonarolian sermon in color."[5]

Michelangelo was evidently converted to Christ from the humanist paganism of the Renaissance. Boticelli's paintings reflect a similar conversion to Christ as a result of his exposure to Savonarola's preaching.[6] There were many who were likewise converted through Savonarola's ministry. But Savonarola was a counter force to the Renaissance; the main thrust of the Renaissance was humanist and anti-Christian, as the clash between Savonarola's reform and the Florentine Renaissance makes clear.

A beast was emerging from the sea of humanity that will soon challenge God Himself for control of the earth. The fifteenth century was its infancy. The lion whose roar strikes terror, the leopard who can track you down and kill you, or the bear whose claw can tear off your head or your arm with a single swipe, can be cute and lovable as a cub. And this cub was charming. It had not yet begun to roar, breathe fire, and trample everything in its path. It wasn't yet possible to number its heads and horns. It was still frolicking in the sunshine, almost innocent in its joy at being alive.

In the heart of the Renaissance, however, was the vision of mankind without God, of human civilization proudly declaring its independence from God and Christ, its freedom from the restraints of His law. But in the Florence of Lorenzo the Magnificent the Renaissance was still in a measure innocent, not yet suspecting that freedom from God is slavery to the devil. Nevertheless, it met in Savonarola a formidable challenge.

Fra Girolamo Savonarola represented the reform and renewal of the Christian church. He carried within him a vision of a purified Christianity, and he gave expression to it with a rare gifting and intelligence that was in no way inferior to the greatest of the Renaissance talents. But above his natural ability was a supernatural grace that brought the powers of the world-to-come to bear on the highly significant era of the Renaissance and the magnificent city of Florence in the 1490s.

The book of Genesis records that Rebekah, Isaac's wife, was pregnant with twins. She was distressed because the two children struggled within her womb. She inquired of the LORD, and He said to her, "Two nations are in your womb, Two peoples shall be separated from your body; One people shall be stronger than the other, and the older shall serve the younger."[7] So it was in Florence and indeed all of Italy and Europe, but it came to Florence first and in its most intense expression. In her womb two manner of people were struggling.

Both were human—for the humanist instinct was not in itself evil. It was the urge for life, the struggle for freedom from oppression, the passion for liberty and for the realization of man's dreams and hopes. The oppression, the restraint was a religious one. But it was a religion that had become corrupted and did not really represent God. The human passion for life and liberty struggled against that religious oppression. But it took two different and conflicting directions in the two very different children struggling in the womb. In the one was the determination to throw off all restraint and to find fulfillment in man himself apart from God. The freedom for which the second child struggled was not freedom from God, but freedom to seek God in truth and in Spirit, to throw off all that misrepresents God, distorts His truth and exploits His people. It was the passion for reform, the determined urge to reflect with accuracy and in the beauty of holiness, the true character of God.

God chose Florence as the womb in which this struggle would begin. There in Florence for the first time were two different and opposing revivals. There were brought together the two different and hostile tendencies that continue to move men to this day, that constitute, in fact, man's ultimate conflict. There in the womb of Florence, not yet differentiated clearly, but already struggling with each other, were a renewed paganism and a renewed Christianity. There and then was a recurrence of the apocalyptic struggle that will characterize the last days, represented by twin movements with very different tendencies and destinies. The first and older of these twin movements was the pagan Renaissance. The second was the Christian reformation.

Lorenzo de Medici represented the Renaissance. As a ruler he was "one of the most remarkable men who ever held the rule of a state; a leader in an age which abounded with great men."[8] Lorenzo brought Florence to a pinnacle of commercial and cultural success and prosperity, brought peace to the competing city-states of Italy, and made Florence the most influential city in the world. And he did it without creating a police state or a standing army. He was firmly in charge, but he did not flaunt his power. Lorenzo allowed the Florentines a small measure of liberty and worked hard to maintain the illusion of real liberty. He was generous, using vast sums from his own fortune for the common good as he saw it. He was unfailingly courteous to both the high and low born.

Because of his collision with Savonarola, Lorenzo came to a knowledge of and respect for God. In this respect, he was like Nebuchadnezzar, the king of Babylon, who was the head of an evil system destined for destruction. And yet, the king was changed by his encounters with the God of Israel, the God of Daniel, the king's trusted minister and a servant of the true God whom the king tried in vain to challenge.[9] So it was with Lorenzo. He represented an evil system, but the God of Savonarola intruded into his life. Lorenzo became a believer in spite of himself and of the neo-pagan world he worked so hard to build. Girolamo Savonarola, a Dominican Friar, represented the godly twin who bore the features and the beating heart of reform and revival in that Florentine womb.

Girolamo Savonarola

Savonarola was born in1452 in Ferrara, where his grandfather was court physician to the Duke of the house of Este and a lecturer in medicine at the famous University of Ferrara. Girolamo's father intended a career in medicine for his son, and so it was only natural for his grandfather, Ser Michele Savonarola, to undertake the lad's education. Ser Michele was eminently qualified for his work as tutor. Girolamo read and wrote Latin fluently at the age of ten. He picked up a lively interest and ability in medicine from his grandfather.

But the true passion of the old man's life was his Christian faith. He was a devout student of the Bible, and he communicated his passion to young Girolamo. In study sessions, ser Michelle and his grandson would save the Scriptures for last and savor them, often discussing biblical themes and stories far into the night and sometimes until the break of dawn. Ser Michele wrote a textbook on gynecology, but his most cherished writing was a theological work on the prophetic ministry, a study of the life and work of John the Baptist. It contributed in a material way to the formation of the mind and to the prophetic calling of young Girolamo.[10]

As a preacher in Florence years later Girolamo would quote from his grandfather's writings. For instance, Fra Girolamo read this from his notebook, his grandfather's words:

> Neither the popes nor their vicars have the right to teach anything contrary to the things instituted by God...I say this for those who pretend to find an excuse for their unworthy conduct in what they are pleased to call the broader view of life and doctrine...God's law is strict: 'strait is the gate and narrow is the way that leadeth unto life and few there be who find it...'[11]

The straight-laced convictions that the godly old doctor passed on to his grandson were in stark contrast to most of life in Ferrara. A university city, Ferrara felt the impact of the Renaissance almost as intensely as Florence did. A revival of paganism was flourishing there with its center in the palace of the Duke. As court physician, Ser Michele Savonarola was well aware of it; of course, he did not approve. The ducal palace was the scene of some of the wildest and most extravagant partying in Italy. The typical entertainment consisted in the reenactment of the pagan tales of gods and heroes. Like our modern American movies, they featured violence, nudity and explicit sensuality of both the heterosexual and homosexual varieties.[12] The most discreet performances would probably get an R rating today. Most of it was blatant pornography.

In 1471 the Savonarolas witnessed the violent and cruel side of paganism in a civil war between two members of the Este family and their factions.[13] The issue concerned who was to succeed to the ducal throne. The two factions indulged in unbridled atrocities of rape and killing. The bodies of two hundred leading citizens from the losing side were stripped, mutilated, and nailed to the eaves of the palace where they hung for ten days rotting in the sun. Girolamo Savonarola, a student at the university by this time, walked past the palace and witnessed this barbarity on his way to class.

When it was over the victors dropped their victims from a chute into a dungeon under the palace where they were left to die and decay in the darkness and stench. Their groans and cries could be heard from the street above. Meanwhile, the victorious faction celebrated with the new Duke, Ercole I, in the banqueting hall upstairs.

After the civil war the new Duke Ercole I took a bride. His wedding to Eleonora of Aragon was the most lavish event Italy had ever seen. Officiating was Cardinal Pietro Riario. The featured entertainment was *The Triumph of Venus*. In the procession of local clergy and visiting prelates from Rome came the nude statues of Greek gods and goddesses with a statue of Venus lifted up over the crowd. She was followed by a statue of the virgin Mary. Girolamo was present among the guests with the other university students. The whole show disgusted him—the extravagance, the lewdness, the mixture of pagan and Christian symbols—evidently with the approval of the Pope, for the papacy was well represented.

187

While the procession was still moving, Girolamo fled the scene with his fists clenched and his eyes reflecting the fire of his anger. His departure created a stir in that august assembly. His angry display in the presence of the Duke and his bride, the nobility and the high ranking churchmen put Girolamo's medical career in jeopardy.

Back home in the study that had been his grandfather's, Girolamo wrote a poem, entitled, "The Ruin of the World."

> All values are reversed. All goodness and virtue have disappeared. Nowhere is there a shining light. No one in all the land is ashamed of his sin. The man who lives by robbery and rapine, and feeds on other men's blood, who despoils the widows and orphans entrusted to his care, who hastens the utter downfall of the poor, he who gains most by fraud and violence, he it is who is deemed gentle and noble of soul. He it is who stands to gain the highest prize. Rome, which should rule the world and impose silence on the evil, has herself slipped into the cesspool. St. Peter is thrown down. His scepter has fallen into the hands of evildoers. Luxury and pillage abound on all sides. One cannot see how long heaven will put up with the injustices rampant in the universe.

His father hoped to salvage Girolamo's future. "What Girolamo needs is polish," he told his wife. "A young man of such phenomenal intellectual capacity must succeed..." His mother was thoughtful for a moment, then responded, "In order to be a courtier Girolamo should have less nobility of spirit and more charm... He is as stiff-necked as the Old Testament Jews, as uncompromising as the prophets. And then Girolamo has a higher mission to fulfill than any other man now living in this world. He knows it not himself, though I think he is beginning to hear the call." Her eyes misted and she whispered, "His mission is a terrible one."[14]

An interval of peace and earthly hope followed. Savonarola fell in love with the illegitimate daughter of an exiled nobleman from Florence, who was living in Ferrara. Girolamo played his lute and serenaded the young lady. She responded with a courteous smile. They walked together a few times under the watchful eye of a chaperone. At last he found the courage to speak to her of his love. He was devastated by her answer.

"Do you think," she replied haughtily, "that the daughter of the noble Strozzi family would consent to an alliance with one so lowly and menial as a Savonarola...?"[15]

After this Girolamo took long, solitary walks, struggling with his thoughts. On one of those walks he came to a chapel in Faenza where an Augustinian monk was preaching from the book of Genesis about the call of Abram. God told the patriarch to leave his city and his father's house and go to a land He would show him. Through the monk's preaching, God spoke to Girolamo Savonarola. Like Abram, he left his native city and his father's house. He took only the clothes he was wearing and the Bible his grandfather had given him, and walked to Bologna where he joined a Dominican community.[16]

During his seven years in Bologna, Savonarola gave himself to work, worship and prayer. He worked in the kitchen and served as a sort of medical technician, helping to treat the sick and ministering to the elderly brothers. He was recognized for his devotion. A writing of Savonarola from this period in his life is a poem entitled, *The Ruin of the Church*, in which he expressed his passion for church reform. He saw the church as a chaste virgin, but disheveled, mistreated and sad.

He asked her, "Where are the precious stones, the white robes of purity, the burning lamps of faith, the sweet chants of devotion of former days?"

The virgin took him by the hand and lead him to a cavern. "When I beheld proud ambition invade Rome and contaminate all things, I fled here for refuge. Here, where I spend my life in tears." She showed him her wounds.

"Who has dethroned you, marred your peace, and brought you to so lamentable a state?" he asked angrily.

The virgin replied, "a false, proud harlot."[17]

Again the young Savonarola burned with indignation. He wanted to strike down the spreading evil that had wounded the church and driven her out to wander in the dens and caves of the earth. He foresaw war, famine and pestilence striking Italy.

Savonarola became an itinerant preacher in the towns and cities around Bologna. At first his plain-spoken style did not impress his audiences. But one day—it appears to have been a sudden rather than a gradual change—he found his message and the power of God to deliver it. James Burns wrote, "At last he had found his message; at last those enormous powers, lying so long dormant, blazed into fierce and inextinguishable flame. In the Apocalypse, amid the flaming images of the prophet-evangelist, his imagination awoke, his message came to him, the fire of the prophet descended upon him."[18]

He was chosen to represent his order at a conference in Reggio devoted, probably, to church reform. Savonarola spoke with wisdom and passion in the gathering of theologians, scholars, princes and monks. One of the most learned men of the times, Count Pico Della Mirandola, heard Savonarola speak and was impressed. He became the Friar's friend. On returning to Florence Pico urged Lorenzo de Medici to bring Savonarola to St. Mark's Dominican convent in Florence. Eventually he did.

Savonarola walked from Bologna to Florence. He had taken neither food nor drink for his journey. He was exhausted and parched with thirst. Under the burning noonday sun he collapsed and was unable to rise. The Friar thought the end had come for him. He awoke in an inn. A stranger had found him, lifted him onto his mule and brought him to the tavern. His benefactor paid for the Friar's food, drink and lodging for the night, and when Savonarola awoke the next morning he felt ready to continue his journey. The man accompanied him on his way until Florence's graceful towers came into view in the twilight.

"'Go now into Florence,' said the man, 'and do the work God has called you to do in this city.' With these words the stranger vanished. Savonarola regretted all his life that he had not asked the good Samaritan's name."[19]

20

Truth And Power In Florence

At St. Mark's in Florence, Savonarola was assigned the task of instructing the novices. His teachings attracted others, members of the regular clergy, instructors form the Platonic academy, Pico Della Mirandola and others of the Florentine intelligencia. Soon there wasn't room in St. Mark's lecture hall for all who wanted to attend. He moved his classes outside into the rose garden, but soon that too was filled. At last he was invited to speak at the Duomo, the largest cathedral in the city.

Savonarola was teaching from the book of Revelation applying its symbols and portents to contemporary events and predicting other events he said were coming. He foresaw a scourge coming upon Italy for its sins.[1] Instead of congratulating the Florentines on their magnificent culture, he denounced the corruption, the self-indulgence on the part of the rich that resulted in the exploitation of the poor, the breakdown of public morality, the decay of faith, the indulgence in neo-pagan revelry and cruelty, and the abuse of power.

Savonarola wasn't exaggerating. Florence's magnificent cultural facade covered up a filthy and fatally diseased body. The contrast between the wealth of the few and the poverty of the many was jarring to Savonarola's soul. Florence was full of beggars and there was an alarming number of blind people, so many that they formed a kind of union and pooled resources in order to hire guides. Savonarola, the former medical student, was aware that venereal disease accounted for much of the blindness, and behind the sexually transmitted diseases were the corrupt morals of the celebrated neo-pagan society.[2]

Behind the corrupt morals was a corrupt religious establishment desperately in need of reform, and desperately resistant to it.

"Murder and incest, lust and cruelty, haunted alike the palaces of the great and the hovels of the poor. Italy was full of bravos and cut-throats, who, before they struck down their victims from behind in the quiet street, did not think it incongruous first to visit the cathedral and, kneeling down, ask God's protection."[3]

Lorenzo de Medici and his brother were themselves victims of this corruption. Pope Sixtus IV wanted Florence for his nephew. He was a party to the so-called Pazzi conspiracy which involved a plot to murder the two young Medici brothers, seize control of the Signoria, Florence's house of representatives of the city's guilds, and in the anticipated confusion march on Florence and conquer it. The place selected for the assassinations—stage one of the plot—was the Cathedral of Florence. The time was High Mass at the precise moment when the priest raised the host and the worshippers' heads were bowed.

An archbishop and a Cardinal were co-conspirators, along with priests and the members of the Florentine Pazzi family who coveted the power the Medicis wielded. A mercenary soldier assigned to kill Lorenzo refused to add sacrilege to murder, but a couple of priests were willing to take on the assignment. They bungled it. Giuliano, Lorenzo's brother, was killed instantly. But Lorenzo escaped. The attempt to seize the Signoria backfired, and the enraged Florentines executed swift justice against the conspirators, including the archbishop, and successfully resisted the Pope's military attack on the city. In return the Pope excommunicated the whole of Tuscany and pronounced the anathema on those who imposed the penalty on the conspirators and murderers. The Pope's bull identified Lorenzo as "the child of iniquity and the nursling of perdition."

"My only fault," said Lorenzo ironically, "is that I was not murdered."[4]

The reaction of the clergy of Tuscany was unprecedented. "On receipt of the Pope's bull of excommunication the whole body of Tuscan bishops assembled in council in the cathedral of Florence, justified the action of the state, and not only appealed to a General Council against the interdict, but excommunicated the Pope."[5] In the past such an act by a Pope created a crisis in the principality addressed. Pope Innocent III, for example, brought the kings of France and England to heel with his interdict in the twelfth century. But this was the fifteenth century in Florence. The Florentines knew something that nobody else in Christendom knew as yet. The Renaissance scholars uncovered a colossal fraud of seven centuries' duration. They discovered that the documents on which the claim was made by the Roman bishops to preeminence and final authority, were forgeries: the *Donation of Constantine*, the *Donation of Pepin*, and *The Decretals*. All of them contained gross historical errors and inconsistencies, unnoticed during centuries of ignorance and illiteracy, but glaringly obvious now that Florence had fostered a revival of learning. The vicious attack on Florence by an evil Pope provoked an exposé of the long-standing fraud concocted by the Roman curia during the dark ages.

Not only was the attack on Florence and her government by Pope Sixtus IV cruel and criminal, and his interdict against Tuscany unjust, but the very authority by which he presumed to hurl such a lightning bolt of raw, vindictive power was based on a fraud. The Tuscan bishops published the discoveries of recent research by Renaissance scholars, and sent them throughout Christendom. The first to discover the truth, the Florentines were the first to defy a Pope and get away with it. They had undeniable evidence that Tuscany had been defrauded of justice by the Pope. This act of defiance by the Bishops of Tuscany was an ominous sign of more of the same kind of things to come.[6] It sent a cold chill through the Vatican and a visceral fear of what a general council of the Church might do.

Savonarola came to preach, therefore, at a time that was ripe for reform and to a people who were prepared to receive his message. A scholar himself, Lorenzo probably knew better than Savonarola did how vulnerable the papacy and the Catholic Church were to the truths the friar was preaching. But Savonarola's sermons scorched the injustices of the civil government as freely as they did the Church. Without naming names, he laid the blame for Florence's corruption, inequities, and immorality at the doorstep of Lorenzo the Magnificent and his administration. And the friar alarmed the Florentines by prophesying God's judgment on the cities of Italy, particularly Rome and Florence.

> At Lorenzo's instigation, Pico Della Mirandola spoke to the friar suggesting that he moderate his tone and not raise questions about the government of the city. Later Lorenzo sent a delegation of other leading citizens to underscore the points Pico had brought up. They claimed to be coming on their own initiative, and they hinted that if he didn't heed their advice the friar might be

banished from the city. Savonarola's answer is astonishing.

> You are acting on the bidding of another. You have been sent by Lorenzo de Medici. I do not fear your threat of banishment. For although he is the first citizen here and I am a humble Friar, it is he who will go and I will stay, and I will speak what God gives me to say. And this is the first thing I say: go and tell Lorenzo de Medici that he should without delay repent of his sins, for God is no respecter of persons. Even the mightiest must appear before the divine judgment seat. I see disaster coming on these Italian countries and on Florence and Rome especially. There is coming a great change in the affairs of Florence and of all Italy.

Before he was finished, Savonarola prophesied to the astonished delegation the deaths of Lorenzo, the Pope and the King of Naples. These deaths would all occur soon, the Friar announced, and would have serious consequences for the Florentines, for the church and for all of Italy.

When Lorenzo heard the report he decided to speak to the friar personally. The opportunity was before him. Savonarola was elected prior of St. Mark's. It was customary that every new prior pay a courtesy call on the head of the Medici family, the patrons and supporters of the convent. Savonarola, however, neglected to observe the custom; he did not pay the expected courtesy call.

Lorenzo chose to overlook the discourtesy. He attended a service in St. Mark's chapel. At the end of the service he waited in the convent garden. The monks urged Savonarola to go out and speak with Lorenzo, but the friar refused.

"But he brought you to Florence, reverend father," said one of the monks.

"He did not bring me to Florence, God brought me to this city and to God alone I owe an accounting."

At this point one of the novices ran into the prior's cell to inform him that a hundred gold ducats had been left in the offering that day. Savonarola immediately sent the money to the Good Men of St. Martin for distribution among the poor.

"I will neither be intimidated nor bribed by Lorenzo," said Savonarola.

Lorenzo was used to being complimented and flattered; he didn't know what to do about this rude response. He had the raw power to banish the friar, imprison him or kill him outright. He had done such things to other men for lesser offenses than Savonarola committed. But he hesitated, considering the effect of such an act on public opinion, and perhaps the will of God. The friar had a large popular following. To move against him might cause trouble for the Medici dictatorship. He confided to his advisors, "As a rule, I prefer injustice to disorder, but in this case I can neither do the one nor allow the other." If he would not respond to threats, Lorenzo thought, perhaps the preacher could be won over by honors. Savonarola received an invitation to preach in the private chapel at the Magnificent's palace. It was a command performance. The friar was inclined to refuse the invitation, but an old monk convinced him otherwise. "It is your duty to go," he told the prior. "Perhaps Lorenzo is a soul in distress."

Savonarola used the occasion to speak the truth to power. Without mentioning names, he addressed the abuses of the Medici regime, the high taxes, the inflationary policy of debasing the currency, the injustice to the poor. He traced the history of the kings in the Old Testament and showed how godly decisions by the leader brought blessing to the nation, ungodly decisions brought judgment. He spoke in Latin, the language of the scholars, which Lorenzo loved. At the end of the sermon, Lorenzo gave the signal and his people applauded.

Lorenzo congratulated the friar on his Latin and on the soundness of his doctrine. To his own people Lorenzo said, "There goes a brave and honest man." And then he added, "but he must be broken."[7] It would not turn out as Lorenzo expected. To break the friar, Lorenzo enlisted the services of Fra Mariano, an Augustinian monk with a large popular following in the city. A creature of the Renaissance, Fra Mariano quoted the pagan poets and philosophers more than the biblical prophets and apostles. He was an entertainer rather than an exhorter, more a pagan than a Christian.

Fra Mariano was eager to please the Magnificent, but he had his own reasons for wanting to see the Dominican broken. He was jealous of the growing popularity of Savonarola. He attacked Savonarola in a sermon, but Mariano went too far. He made accusations against the Prior of St. Mark's that were not true and that he could not prove. Lorenzo was displeased with Mariano's performance. Savonarola easily refuted his Augustinian rival a few days later. Mariano left Florence soon after his failed attack on Savonarola.[8]

Meanwhile, Lorenzo became sick. Nothing the physicians could do helped. As he lay dying Lorenzo sent for Savonarola. "I know no honest friar but this one," he said. Savonarola did what he could to comfort the man. Lorenzo the Magnificent departed on April 8, 1492 at the age of forty-three.[9] His son, Piero, took his place as ruler of Florence.

Savonarola remained in Florence as he had predicted. He was invited to preach a series of Lenten sermons for the second year in a row at Florence's Cathedral Church. The church was packed. On Good Friday, Savonarola included in his talk a vision he had received while he and his monks were mourning the death of Lorenzo de Medici. He saw two great crosses rise in the sky. The first was a black cross that arose from the city of Rome. It was the cross of God's wrath. When the top reached the sky the heavens became dark, there was thunder and lightning, a hail storm swept all Italy, and a great multitude were killed.

When the sky cleared a second cross appeared. On it was written, "The cross of God's mercy." It came not from Rome but from Jerusalem. The whole world was illumined by the light from above it. As he watched, flowers budded and bloomed in its light. The air was filled with a wonderful perfume, and the sound of hymns came from every direction, as if a host of angels were singing. It was a vision of the Second Coming of Christ.

All Italy was abuzz about the vision. The Friar did not explain it. But two months later Pope Innocent VIII died after a long illness. It was the second death predicted by the Friar of St. Mark's. Innocent VIII was followed in August 1492 by Rodrigo Borgia, who took the title of Alexander VI. During his reign, the wrath of God would strike Rome and a foreshadowing of the kingdom of God (that will one day be established on the earth with its capital in Jerusalem) would come to Florence.[10]

21

Judgment And Revival

The new Pope, Alexander VI, was a canny politician, but a corrupt man whose pontificate would be a sad disappointment to those who hoped that the new Pope would initiate a reform of the Catholic Church. In the end he would do everything in his power to resist reform and undermine a revival in the institution he headed. Yet in the early days of his reign, Alexander made a couple of decisions permitting Savonarola to initiate reforms first at St. Mark's and secondly in Florence that laid the groundwork for a remarkable revival.

First, Alexander reluctantly agreed to disconnect St. Mark's in Florence from the Dominican district of Lombardy. This left Savonarola autonomous in Florence, subject only to the General of the order and the Pope himself.[1] Second, Savonarola took the bold step of removing St. Mark's from the patronage and control of the ruling Medici family. The Friar was troubled because his moral authority suffered from the identification of St. Mark's with the house of Medici. The common people distrusted the Dominicans, who were supported and protected by the ruling family. The Florentines had a saying, "whose bread and cheese I eat, to his tune I dance."[2] Savonarola winced when the saying was applied to him and his convent. The Dominicans were suspected of supporting the Medici tyranny and even of being spies for the regime against the citizens.[3]

As the Prior of St. Mark's, Savonarola was now in a position to do something about the compromising relationship. Savonarola sold certain properties belonging to St. Mark's and returned the price of the sale to Piero, the scion of the house of Medici. The expensive furniture that had been given to the monks over the years was auctioned off and the proceeds given to the poor. The Friar then relinquished the regular financial support of the ruling house of Medici and restored the original rule of St. Dominic, including voluntary poverty, subsisting on offerings from the people, and begging for food when necessary. The monks were forbidden to wear fine clothing and were put to work diligently serving the people, especially the poor.[4]

It was an amazing decision, amounting to a voluntary disestablishment of the Dominican community, a separation of the monastery from its association with the political authority of the city and its dependence on the financial support of the Medici regime. By these acts, the Prior moved to put the convent directly under the authority of Jesus Christ so that it would not be under obligation to any man.[5]

These stern measures and the strict discipline did not discourage new applicants. On the contrary, young men came from all over Italy and beyond to St. Mark's to serve God under Savonarola's inspired leadership.[6] And the finances were abundant. The people gave willingly as they saw the monks diligently and sacrificially serving the needy of Florence. The Prior labored day and night and gave the order that nobody was to be turned away who came to St. Mark's for help. Some days as many as five hundred people came for counseling, for medicines, for food. Many found a living faith in Jesus Christ.

Savonarola could now speak with freedom and integrity against corruption and immorality both in the church and the various ruling houses of Italy. One of his remarks is typical of Savonarola's approach to the reform of the church. He points his hearers to the New Testament church as the standard by which he measured the contemporary church and its ministry. "The clergy take no interest in the salvation of souls," he said. "They speak against pride and worldly ambition, yet are plunged in both up to their eyes. They preach chastity and keep concubines. They prescribe fasting and gorge themselves on choice and expensive food." Then he dealt with the chalices, the gem-studded goblets in which the communion wine was poured.

> Men gaze on these vanities and rejoice in these pomps, and say the Church of Christ was never so flourishing, nor divine worship so well conducted as at present. Likewise (they say) that the Church's first prelates and bishops were inferior to these of our time...The former, it is true,

had fewer gold chalices, for indeed what few they possessed were often broken up to relieve the need of the poor; whereas our prelates for the sake of obtaining chalices, will rob the poor of their sole means of support. The truth is this, in the primitive Church the chalices were of wood but the prelates of gold. In our day the situation is reversed: the chalices are gold, but the prelates are of wood.[7]

Savonarola had another prophetic vision; this time it was a sword. It would come, he said, from the north over the Alps. Alexander VI monitored the friar and his preaching. He knew some of the friar's rebukes applied to himself as Pope as well as to the other clergy. But Alexander VI also realized that Savonarola was respected far and wide as an honest, learned and able man. To his aides who were critical of the friar, Alexander said, "Do you not realize that the greatest scholars of the Florentine Academy, Poliziano, Ficino, and Pico sit at his feet, and that the most consummate artists, Michelangelo, Boticelli, and Bartolomeo are his friends and admirers? We cannot lightly dismiss this man's words..."[8] Alexander was puzzled by the Friar's prophecy of a sword from the North, but he was not alarmed and did not try to stop Savonarola from prophesying.

The third death predicted by Savonarola occurred in the summer of 1494. The King of Naples died. King Ferrente was succeeded by his son, Alfonso II. This ended the peace of Italy and precipitated the fulfillment of Savonarola's prophecy of the sword to chasten Italy and reform the church. For Charles VIII of France chose this opportune moment of King Ferrente's death to enforce an old claim to the throne of Naples. He assembled his army and made plans to march over the Alps and down the whole length of Italy, depose Alfonso and put one of the French princes of the royal blood on the throne in his place.[9]

Charles had worked out a deal with the Duke of Milan, who had ambitions of his own that he thought would be facilitated by the French invasion. He gave the French army free passage through his land. The long history of feuds among the Italian states kept them divided and suspicious of one another, and so made it possible for Charles to invade. Italy was already divided; with a little intrigue and a well-equipped army, Charles thought he could conquer.

The French king almost turned back. It took the persuasion and flattery of Cardinal Della Rovere, Alexander's bitter rival for the papal throne, to convince the vacillating Charles to continue. Cardinal Della Rovere had fled Rome when Alexander VI was elected Pope. He had encouraged the French king in his dreams of conquest and glory in order to force a council, depose Alexander and get himself elected Pope.

The invasion imperiled Florence because of the ineptitude and lack of character of its leader, Piero de Medici. Under his father Lorenzo's leadership, Florence was allied with France. When the French king invaded Italy, Piero reversed the city's policy and broke the alliance. Then as the French army approached Florence Piero panicked. He sneaked out of the city to meet Charles, made degrading concessions, surrendered outlying towns that were strategically located, fortified, and that stood between Florence and the French army. He surrendered three other towns and the harbor of Livorno. The king of France was in possession of the whole region of Tuscany, without having fired a shot!

But that wasn't all. Piero promised the king 200,000 ducats of gold, and three days for him and his army to plunder and rape at will in the city of Florence. In exchange for exposing the city to mortal danger, humiliation and suffering, Piero received the king's guarantee of personal safety, the safety of the other members of the de Medici family and the protection of the family fortune.

Refugees from the front streamed into Florence with the news of Piero de Medici's betrayal. The people exploded in rage. Thirty thousand Florentines marched through the streets striking the Medici emblems from monuments and walls of public buildings and convents endowed by the Medicis. They broke into the Medici bank and found it empty. Evidently Piero had hidden the money somewhere before leaving the city to meet with Charles VIII. Now the crowd was even angrier. They approached the Medici palace intending to burn it to the ground.

Savonarola met them, got their attention, and reasoned with them. Piero was not there, the servants of the palace were as much victims of his treachery as they were, and to destroy the palace and its art treasures would impoverish the whole city. They were persuaded not to do it. Such was the trust and confidence the people had in their friar.

The Signoria, the assembly of leaders of the guilds of the city, reflected the outrage of the citizens. They voted unanimously to depose Piero de Medici. But that wasn't all. They decided that for all time to come he and his successors were unworthy to hold any position of authority and trust in Florence.[10] As for the advancing French army and the immediate threat it posed, the Signoria decided to send a delegation of leading citizens to meet the king and promise him a royal welcome on condition that he enter Florence peacefully. Savonarola was asked to be one of the ambassadors. He agreed to do it, but before he left on his mission the Friar took the precaution of warning the Florentines to send the young women and girls away to a place of safety.

Charles knew of Savonarola by reputation. He was awed in the presence of the man of God. Savonarola warned the king that God would hold him responsible for the behavior of his troops. Charles trembled when the words of the Friar sank in. Charles entered Florence with his army. There was a royal welcome. There were also tensions and some skirmishes. The French overstayed their welcome. Savonarola had another interview with king Charles VIII in which he told him in the name of God to get on with the work to which God had called him and not to trouble the Florentines any further. The French left without sacking the city or violating the women, although the officers who were billeted at the Medici palace stole all the works of art that the Medicis had collected over fifty years. What they didn't steal they destroyed.[11]

The French left Florence. The Medicis had ruled the city for seventy years, but now they, too, were gone. There was nobody left who was experienced in statecraft. Florence was in a state of confusion. People were out of work. Factions arose angry over old grudges and seeking revenge on their neighbors. There was a power vacuum that was as great a threat as any tyrant.

Word came that Piero de Medici was gathering an army of mercenaries with the intention of returning to Florence and taking charge. In the face of confusion within the city and danger without, the Florentines needed a wise and able leader. The only person on the scene with the respect and trust of the people was Savonarola. Reluctantly, but with the sense that he was called by God, the friar stepped into the vacuum.[12]

Savonoarola never held an office and never sought one. But drawing on his knowledge of the Bible, his reading in history and philosophy, the Friar guided the Florentines in establishing a constitutional republic. Week by week, he expounded the principles of just government in which no one man would be allowed absolute power. He applied these principles practically to the Florentine situation. His sermons drew a packed house Sunday after Sunday. Wooden bleachers were built to accommodate the multitudes who waited for hours to get in. His preaching called the Florentines to conversion and faith in Christ. He told them that Jesus Christ was willing to be their king. They shouted their approval.

Savonarola's sermons also included instructions in setting up a government.[13] What Savonarola preached was tested, debated, adjusted, and finally written into the Constitution. It became the law of the land. He reformed the sloppy and inconsistent tax system of the Medicis into a simple and uniform code that prevailed until 1865. And for a time his advice to the city and to the officials of the new government became public policy. He established a popular government on a moral foundation.

Savonarola's ideas took hold in Florence and beyond, and outlived him even to our times and to our own Constitutional Republic. His reforms were just and fair; they were based on the Bible, Christian faith, and the moral law. And the establishment of the Republic was achieved without the shedding of a drop of blood.[14] Basic to Savonarola's thinking was the conviction that a just society required just people.[15]

The revival really begins here with a decision the Friar had to make about the nature of the state and its relation to religion. Savonarola was now in a place to direct the sword of the state. He began to call for stiff penalties for sins, as if true righteousness could be produced by the threat of punishment, or sins could be overcome by coercion. The Friar was admonished and corrected by a brother in his convent, Fra Antonio Benivieni. He asked Fra Girolamo,

> Are you aware, that since you began to hurl your imprecations to left and right men and women run for cover when they see a man in the Dominican habit coming their way? Would they run if our Lord Jesus Christ came into their poor hutches and hovels?

> All Florence approves of the changes you have brought about so far...but it is not by compulsion or physical constraint or by holding a

threat of punishment above their poor heads. The Saviour always began by forgiving sins...Reform there must be, reform of Florence, reform of Italy, reform of the Church, all things must be made over. But I warn you that the kingdom of God cannot be forced. "Not by might, nor by violence, but by my spirit shall it come to pass, saith the Lord."[16]

Fra Girolamo took the admonition to heart. So much so that for weeks Savonarola didn't preach. He remained in his cell, fasted, prayed and wrestled with God. He emerged a changed man, but a man whose health was broken.[17]

After his long session of heart searching and prayer, Savonarola devoted his energies to the young people. He organized special meetings for the children and youth. His first children's sermon brought two thousand youngsters, the second, four thousand. The third meeting packed the cathedral with children and their parents. The friar told the children that "religion was not a brief intermission in their everyday activity; it was life. It had to be lived, nourished, developed, and to be manifest in an all-encompassing reform."

He urged the young people to organize themselves into permanent companies or clubs. He made two of his friars available to each of the young peoples' associations, one to supervise and one to teach. The boys pledged not to use the Lord's name in vain, not to listen to the solicitations of the homosexuals, not to gamble or carry knives, to be kind to animals, to treat their elders and teachers with respect, to go to church on Sundays, to confess once a month, and tactfully and kindly to speak a corrective word to girls and women who wore immodest or indecent clothing.

Savonarola sent his friars to function as youth leaders in the different quarters of the city. Some worked among street gangs to put an end to the fighting. Some youth companies collected offerings for the poor. Youth companies devoted themselves to keeping the shrines and statues on street corners cleaned and polished. The cathedral windows were washed every month. The youth companies set an example for the rest of the people of Florence by keeping the city streets clean. Other companies made banners and flags to be carried in processions and festivals.

In place of the elaborate, expensive and typically immoral celebrations of the Medici era, Savonarola instituted folk dancing in the piazza of St. Mark's. The monks wrote the music and the words to the songs. Thousands of all ages came to participate in the ring dances or to watch them.

A girls' brigade made up of young women from prominent Florentine families visited the houses of prostitution and by prayer and persuasion urged the young women to give up their sinful and self-destructive way of life. They assured the prostitutes that God loved them as much as the wealthiest women in the community. The young Christians met with astonishing success. A district infamous for its immoral trade was deserted. One house after another closed its doors, not by police raids but because young women voluntarily left the profession.

In an Easter parade in 1495, the youth companies marched through the city. Among them, walking under the blue and silver banner of St. Mary Magdalene, dressed in white, were the ex-prostitutes singing praises to Jesus Christ. Tears streamed down the cheeks of many of these young women as crowds lining the streets greeted them with applause and acceptance.

The churches were full, while gambling houses went out of business for lack of customers. Bankers and businessmen returned money amounting to thousands of ducats to people they had cheated. The Florentines gave generously to the poor. During worship meetings women of means would take off their jewelry and deposit it with the clergy or with the friars to be sold, with the proceeds distributed among the poor.

People came to Florence from surrounding towns and cities, and waited for hours to get into the Cathedral to hear Savonarola preach. Others stood outside the packed Duomo. Inside the cathedral the Florentines waited in silence until the friar appeared and when they finally heard him preach they were often overcome with weeping or with joy. Michaelangelo attended Savonarola's meetings and was profoundly moved by the Friar's sermons. The brilliant Pico Della Mirandola took notes. At one point he wrote, "Here I was so overcome with weeping that I could not write."

There were conversions among the young and old, among the plain people and among the upper classes, too. And it was not only St. Mark's and the Duomo where the Friar ministered that experienced revival. All the churches were filled. "The extraordinary movement which [Savonarola] brought about," wrote G.F. Young, "is without a parallel; Florence for a time put on a Puritan garb..."[18]

> The transformation in the social and religious life of the people of Florence has led foreign and Italian historians and sociologists of the most diversified schools of thought and confession to declare that Christ's Kingdom, albeit for a short time, was once a tangible reality in the city on the Arno. Nor was it ushered in or enforced by clerical or secular authority. Tens of thousands of Florentines chose to walk the strait and narrow path voluntarily. Throughout Italy and in foreign lands, men and women, lay and clerical alike, looked up with great reverence to Savonarola.[19]

But there were also those who hated Savonarola. There were, for instance, the Campagnacci, the "good companions." They were militant homosexuals led by Doffo Spini, a wealthy banker who invented gay pride nearly five centuries before the term was coined. Savonarola invited him and his fellow homosexuals to convert themselves. Homosexuality was not outlawed in Florence and homosexuals were neither harassed nor jailed. But Savonarola preached against homosexuality in no uncertain terms. He lamented publicly that sodomy was Florence's besetting sin.[20] He warned young boys and men against homosexuality as against a deadly sin. The Friar restricted their fun and called their perversion by its proper name. And for this the Campagnacci hated him unrelentingly. They put all their energy and ingenuity into destroying him.

There were others, such as the *Arabbiatti* (the enraged). They were the upper class people who wanted to see the return of the Medici regime. They sought a place of power in the new Republic in order to destroy it. When trouble arose for Florence the Arrabbiatti delighted in the opportunity it afforded them to denounce Savonarola.[21] They resented the reforms Savonarola was promoting, and they dreaded the friar's preaching, for he said that those who had an excess of this world's goods should share them with the poor. They were afraid that some kind of equitable division of wealth would be enforced by law as a result of Savonarola's influence in the state.

Savonarola's moral reforms, however, were not forced. They were urged and exhorted, but they were voluntary. The people of Florence, in response to the friar's preaching and the exhausting and sacrificial work of the monks of St. Mark's, chose Jesus Christ as their king, repented of their sins and embraced a life of godliness and practical goodness.[22] Those who supported Savonarola were called the Frateshi, the Friar's people. There was a period of four years or so, from 1494 to 1498, when they were probably a majority in Florence. During that time there was righteousness, peace and joy in the city. Some called it heaven on earth. For a few years the famous Renaissance city became a city of God, a shining expression of the kingdom of heaven on the earth. But the freedom to believe granted by Savonarola and the Republic implied the freedom to disbelieve. And the forces of unbelief, the powers of darkness, were gathering both inside of Florence and outside.

Savonarola had admonished the French king to reform the church. Charles VIII had boasted that he would. One wonders what a reform of the church initiated by a dissolute man like Charles VIII would have looked like. We can guess, but we will never know. It never happened, although for a while it seemed inevitable. Charles had the opportunity, but not the character. And his failure to act decisively cost him dearly. Ultimately, it cost Savonarola his life.

22

Prophet Vs. Pope

When King Charles VIII left Florence, he marched to Rome and entered the city unopposed. The Pope fled the Vatican and shut himself in the Castle of Sant' Angelo. The downfall of Alexander VI now seemed certain. Cardinal Della Rovere, who accompanied the king, was already rejoicing in the reform of the Catholic Church. But the only reform Della Rovere was really interested in was one that would remove Alexander and install him in Alexander's place as Pope. For that to have occurred, a council would have to be called, and that needed the consent of the Pope. It was certainly not Alexander's will to convene a council that would depose him, but it now appeared that the Pope had no alternative. He would be forced by the French to cooperate in his own downfall. If he escaped with his life, he would be fortunate. It was one man against an army. But then a strange thing happened.

While the French army waited outside the castle, a part of the castle wall fell away. The French didn't even need a battering ram. They could have walked right into the fortress and seized the Pope. In the opening, Alexander VI appeared wearing his pontifical robes and his tiara. Six cardinals stood by his side. The Pope said not a word, but lifted the monstrance containing the consecrated bread up in his hands as if in celebration of the Eucharist. The French army dropped to its knees. The king and his staff, the royal princes, all bowed their heads. The Pope disappeared and that was the end of it. But to the dismay of Cardinal Della Rovere, nobody did anything.

Four days later the French army returned, but it was the same thing. The Pope appeared again, this time wearing a simple white cassock and without the papal crown. The French Archbishop warned a company of musketeers, "If you fire on the Holy Father and the relics, you will commit a mortal sin!" That was as close as Charles VIII ever came to reforming the Church. The Pope lifted his hand in blessing and the troops dropped their weapons and bowed down. In addition to his blessing, the Pope gave the king a gold medallion with the enigmatic inscription, "Charles the Emperor." It was a long march for a trinket. Alexander VI single-handedly neutralized the most powerful army in Europe. Such was the awe inspired by the Pope as late as 1494.[1] In a few years the response would be different.

The king of France and his army then marched to Naples. The King of Naples fled and the French king, made up to look like Charlemagne (Charles the Great) entered the city. Charles VIII listened to some flattering speeches honoring him as "Charles the Still Greater," congratulating him on his plan to begin a new crusade against the Turks. He attended state banquets and indulged himself and his troops in revelry in Naples.

Meanwhile, the Pope quietly organized a league of Italian states against the French. The Pope even convinced the Duke of Milan, who had encouraged Charles to invade Italy, to occupy the pass barring the path of French reinforcements and the retreat of his army. Charles was trapped. All the Italian states except Florence were enlisted in the "Holy League." When news of the Holy League reached Naples, the people of Naples rose up against Charles and his army—for the French behaved worse in Naples than they had in Florence, robbing, carousing, and killing like common thieves and murderers. The Pope also persuaded the Monarchs of Spain, the Emperor of the Germans and the ruling house of Portugal to join with him in checking the French and driving them out of Italy.

Charles abandoned his plans for a crusade to drive the Turks out of the Holy Land and began a long and hasty retreat. He intended to stay in Florence, but he had Piero de Medici and his 2,000 mercenaries with him. The Florentine leaders were convinced that if they opened their gates to Charles he would force the hated Medici dictatorship on them again. The Florentines armed themselves against Charles, who was on the brink of wrecking his alliance with the only city in Italy that was still on friendly terms with France.

The Florentines were adamant in their rejection of the Medicis. Charles threatened to bombard Florence if the Signoria refused to let him in. As the king approached the city, the officials sent

Savonarola to speak to the king—with firmness, but not so as to provoke hostilities. Savonarola told the king that he, Charles, had broken his vow and neglected to fulfill his calling to reform the Church and punish the tyranny of the Italian states. He charged the king to take up his duty as he, Savonarola, had announced it in the name of Christ. It was God's will for Florence to remain his ally, but because the king had failed to do his duty toward God and had broken his promises to the Florentines, Charles was beset by many dangers. He would have to fight his way back to his homeland, but he would live to see his wife again.

Charles trembled at the Friar's words. He promised to come back with a larger army and do in a year or less what he had failed to do in this disastrous campaign. He marched past Florence and had to fight his way through the territory of the Duke of Milan. He lost most of his army in the battle. He returned to French soil with only a thousand troops. There he was greeted with the news that his only son and heir to the throne had died. The king wept. "Oh, Savonarola, Oh! Had I only listened to you!"[2]

Because Charles didn't listen to Savonarola, the Friar had troubles of his own. Inside Florence, the Arrabbiati were at work to undermine Savonarola and the Republic he had helped bring into being. They sent a message to the Pope urging him to transfer Savonarola to the Dominican community in Lucca. The Pope sent a brief ordering Savonarola to Lucca. The Florentine ambassador asked the Pope to reconsider his decision, citing the transformation the Friar had brought to Florence, and sending a bundle of Savonarola's printed sermons for the Pope to read. The Pope rescinded his Brief.[3]

Next, the Pope issued a polite invitation to the Friar to come to Rome and speak personally with the Pope. Savonarola was ill at the time and asked to be excused on the advice of his physician and his weakened physical condition. The Pope sent a messenger who informed the Friar that the Pope had accepted his excuses. Fra Domenico Buonvicini conferred with Savonarola and preached in his place while Fra Girolamo recovered.[4]

The Pope sent another Brief, this one not to Savonarola directly, but to the Franciscans of Holy Cross, whose Prior was known to be jealous of Savonarola. In it was a charge against Savonarola of disseminating false doctrine, an order demoting him from being Prior of St. Mark's, forbidding him to preach, placing him under the authority of the Vicar-General of the Lombard congregation, and demanding that he go wherever the Vicar-General should send him. Underlying it all was a threat of excommunication.[5]

Savonarola replied in a letter, in which he refuted the charges of false doctrine made to the Pope by Savonarola's enemies and submitted himself to the Pope and the Catholic Church for correction. The Pope responded by withdrawing all the orders against the Friar on condition that he abstain from all preaching, both in public and in private.[6]

The Pope's next move was a shocking one that provoked the Friar to a terrible resolve. Fra Girolamo was in the chapter hall with his fellow friars. On the walls the saintly artist, Fra Angelico, had painted saints and angels, representations of the cloud of witnesses to the scene unfolding in the auditorium. Two men dressed in rich black cloaks with the purple and scarlet insignia marking them as papal representatives, spoke in confidential tones with the Prior. Savonarola, dressed in his worn Dominican robe, his shoulders bent from sickness and fasting, listened in silence; his face registered shock and surprise. After a few minutes, Savonarola shook his head and the papal representatives departed. The heavy wooden door closed and the latch clicked behind them.

The Prior stood before his monks for a long moment. "I was not prepared for that," he said. "I have just been offered a cardinal's hat. The condition is that I stop opposing the Italian League and abstain from criticizing the Vatican's foreign policies."

There were gasps from many of the friars; they knew their Prior's uncompromising integrity, and that he has just been offered a bribe by the highest authority in the Church.

"The Pope has no understanding or care for the spiritual issues here," Savonarola continued. "He cares nothing for the work of God in this city. It doesn't matter to him whether Florence is saved or damned. It's all about his 'Holy League.' This I tell you, my brothers. I shall have no cardinal's hat. The only hat I shall have is that of a martyr, red in my own blood."[7]

The pressure mounted in Florence. First, the papal army attacked Florence to force the city to join the Holy League. The attack was repulsed. But the German Emperor, an ally of the Pope, invaded Italy, took Pisa, and cut off Florence from its port city of Livorno. The Italian principalities, members of the alliance, then threatened to destroy Florence unless it joined them in the Holy League. Florence was alone and in grave danger. There were stores of food inside Florence but Farmers outside the city in the war zones were starving. They came to Florence and the city, under Savonarola's compassionate policy, let them in, putting a strain on Florence's supplies. The grain ships from France had not arrived, and everyone supposed that they had been lost or wrecked in the bad weather. Heavy rains added to the misery. And on top of everything else, a plague broke out in the city. Wagons were drawn through the streets at night, and the call came, "Throw out your dead!" The corpses were collected and dumped into the Arno.

The people desperately needed a word from the Friar. But he was under the Pope's orders to remain silent. As conditions worsened, pressure mounted, and the Arrabbiati denounced Savonarola as a deceiver, and demanded that the city join the holy league and return the Medicis to power. Savonarola was convinced that if Piero de Medici returned to power in Florence, heads would roll as Piero avenged his banishment on the Florentine leaders. The very existence of the city would be imperiled. The Signoria insisted that Savonarola speak to the people, and at last he agreed. He encouraged the Florentines to hold to their policies, give of their means to support the republic, and he told them of his confidence that God would intervene on their behalf. He urged them to put away their sins and return to the Lord.

The response to the Friar's words of hope was overwhelming. The people's faith revived, and the authorities called for a solemn procession. The image of the Madonna dell Impruneta would be carried into Florence.[8]

The day of the event dawned dark and rainy but the procession went ahead as scheduled. Suddenly the rain stopped, the sun broke through the clouds, and as the procession of monks, clergy and the faithful reached the center of the city, a man on horseback arrived with good news, miraculous news. The enemy's fleet was driven off by the winds. The French galleys loaded with grain, men and weapons, arrived safely in Livorno, and the Florentine troops had opened the road from Livorno to Florence. The German Emperor's army was in flight and the first wagonloads of food were on their way to the city. The people wept and laughed and danced in the streets for joy.[9] But not everybody rejoiced at the miraculous deliverance. As Savonarola and the friars of St. Mark's walked back to the convent after the celebration, they were pelted by dirt thrown by Doffo Spini's gang of homosexual operatives.[10]

With the cooperation of the Signoria, the Friar planned a demonstration. He had a huge wooden pyramid constructed. It was fifteen stories high, with many compartments. He asked the Florentines to bring their vanities—their pornographic pictures and statues, their indecent objects of amusement and indulgence, whatever was used to excite their lust or indulge their impurities— to the city square and place them in the compartments of the pyramid. Savonarola's youth companies went door to door asking the Florentines to contribute objects for the holocaust.

On the day before Lent began—what is known as Mardi-Gras today—there was a great celebration. Instead of a wild fling, the Florentines found joy in praising God and disposing of objects used for shameful purposes. Instead of indulging the appetites of the flesh, they contributed their money to the relief of the poor. The great bell rang, the pyramid was torched and the forbidden objects exploded in gunpowder and burned in a great medieval display of fireworks as the people gave a great shout. A work of righteousness became the occasion of good fun.

The pyramid of vanities was controversial in its day. It still is. I remember hearing the television comic and talk show host, Steve Allen, fault Savonarola for the loss of some great works of art by Sandro Boticelli in the pyramid fireworks. Steve Allen made it sound as if the paintings had been taken from the great artist by force and destroyed. The truth is, Boticelli himself placed these paintings on the pyramid. He considered them pornography, paintings he made before his conversion to Christian faith to incite lust. Boticelli had sold some paintings of this kind, and on these Boticelli went to a great deal of trouble—in one case entering into a private house by stealth—to paint drapes and veils over his nude figures. It was not some kind of GESTAPO demanding the lewd objects at the point of a gun; the children of Florence asked their relatives and neighbors to give the objects voluntarily, and they did.[11]

It is true, of course, that not everybody in Florence enjoyed the fireworks. There were many who resented the destruction of their sensual toys, beauty products, and pornography. Many were angry, because their pleasures were publicly identified as sin and vanity. Although sin was not restrained by law, the conversion of so many in Florence and their adoption of an upright, moral lifestyle created social and cultural restraints on their self-indulgence. Savonarola's campaign of public righteousness made him many enemies. And the more the Friar pushed his reforms, the more adamant his enemies became.[12]

23

Martyrdom And Aftermath

Although the papal prohibition was still in effect, Savonarola announced his intention to preach on Ascension Day, May 3, 1497. The night before Savonarola's scheduled appearance, Doffo Spini and his thugs broke into the cathedral, beat the watchman unconscious, and spent the night carrying human waste from the city's latrines to the pulpit of the Duomo. As dawn was breaking, the watchman regained consciousness, dragged himself to St. Mark's and told the friars what had happened. The Dominicans worked hard cleaning up the mess and when the time came for the meeting at noon everything was back in order and clean.

Savonarola mounted the pulpit. Spini's activists were standing in the rear dressed in their finery, arms folded and sneers on their faces. The cathedral was packed. The atmosphere crackled with tension due to the presence of so many of the preacher's enemies.

"I must tell you, my people," the Friar began, "that tribulations are at hand. We will be warred against by excommunications, by the sword, by martyrdom...The wicked cry that I am no prophet; yet they do all things to fulfill my prophecies." The Compagnacci laughed out loud. Savonarola responded, "Lord, do not be angry with them for they know not what they do." He then addressed the agitators directly, "My friends, why do you not return to virtue? For then peace will be with you and God will show you his grace..."

Suddenly there was a loud crash. One of the Compagnacci had hurled a large collection box to the floor. The other gay activists then overturned benches and shouted as loudly as they could. The people panicked and ran for the doors. The Compagnacci, daggers in their hands, moved toward the pulpit. Some of the Friar's men surrounded the preacher, others ran for their weapons. Savonarola was surrounded by hundreds of his people and the Compagnacci could not reach him. When the other monks arrived with their weapons, Spini's mob fled. Savonarola's followers accompanied him to St. Mark's garden shouting, "Viva Cristo!" There Savonarola finished his sermon.

A report of the riot was printed and distributed throughout Italy. The Pope had a copy within a week. With this sign that Savonarola's support within Florence was eroding, Alexander made his Move.[1]

On May 13, 1497 the Pope sent a Brief excommunicating Savonarola. The cause of the excommunication was the Friar's disobedience to the Pope's order to suspend all preaching.[2] It was a valid case from the standpoint of Cannon law.

The rule was that the Pope's holiness resided in the office, not in his person, so even an unworthy Pope had to be obeyed. Savonarola knew the law. But he was driven by the course of events, directed by the Scriptures which he knew, perhaps better than any other man alive at the time, and compelled by the inner urging of the Holy Spirit. In spite of his professed beliefs, the Friar took a New Testament position even though, as a loyal Catholic, he was forbidden, hesitant, and extremely reluctant to resist the Pope. In the end he chose to speak and act very much as Peter and John did in the early days following Pentecost, and "obey God rather than men." The Lord's apostles kept preaching Jesus although the Jewish authorities of those days, with an official and exclusive claim to represent God, had forbidden them to preach in the name of Jesus.[3]

In following the example of the first century apostles, the Friar stepped over the line. He was excommunicated, and he and his followers became more and more isolated—we might use the term *marginalized* today—or in biblical terms, they went forth "outside the camp," bearing the reproach of Christ.[4] The difficulty for Savonarola was that the "camp" from which he departed was "Christian." It was the "official" camp, and the Friar believed and taught that there was no salvation outside of it. And yet the Scriptures and the Holy Spirit led him to take a stand on truth that put him outside of the establishment he believed in. The Pope demanded that the Friar be turned over to Rome for questioning in regard to his orthodoxy. When the Signoria refused, Alexander VI threatened to seize the assets of Florentine businesses in Rome.

In a few churches in Florence sermons were preached warning the faithful against having any contact with Savonarola or the brethren from Saint Mark's. Some of these sermons accused the Friar of evil ambition to replace the Pope. This encouraged the Compagnacci who gathered outside St. Mark's and continued to harass Savonarola and his friars night after night with verbal insults and disgusting graffiti, which they painted on the walls of the convent. They broke windows and some of them entered the building and damaged furniture. They wrote letters to the Pope asserting that the city of Florence was in open rebellion against the Vatican.

Meanwhile, with Savonarola's voice silenced, the city reverted to its former state. The taverns were back in operation, the red lights appeared again advertising the services of prostitutes, women reverted to immodest dress. Savonarola and the brothers of St. Mark's were slandered.[5] The Signoria requested Savonarola to return to the pulpit. There was opposition to this from some of the Florentine churches because Savonarola had been excommunicated.

The conflict was heating up. A research team from the University of Paris had been studying the election and reign of Pope Alexander VI. They published their findings: that Alexander's election was invalid, that the Pope was guilty of simony, bribery, immorality, and was an unworthy Pope. Savonarola was encouraged by this report. He accepted the invitation of the Signoria, and launched a series of sermons on the book of Ezekiel. The Friar became increasingly bold in opposing the Pope and calling for a church council to depose him and reform the church.

> The temporal power of the Popes is at the bottom of all the evils and abuses which have slipped into the Church. When the Church was poor, she was holy, but when she gained temporal power, her spiritual power collapsed.[6]

> I lay down this axiom, there is no man that may not deceive himself. The Pope himself may err. You are mad if you say that the Pope cannot err! How many wicked Popes have there been who have erred: if they have not erred, should we do as they have done, should we be saved? You say that the Pope may err as a man, but not as Pope. But I say that the Pope may err in his processes and his

217

sentences. How many constitutions have Popes issued, annulled by other Popes; how many opinions of Popes are contrary to those of other Popes? He may err by false persuasions; he may err by malice, and against his conscience. We ought, indeed, in this case to leave the judgment to God, and charitably suppose that he has been deceived.

The Friar defended himself against his excommunication with the logic of an Anabaptist:

Our doctrine has enforced good living, much fervor, and perpetual prayer, yet we are the excommunicated, they the blessed. Yet their doctrine leads to evil doings—to waste in eating and drinking, to avarice, to concubinage, to the sale of benefices, to many lies, and to all wickedness. Christ! on which side wilt thou be? -- on that of truth or lies, of the excommunicated or the blessed? The Lord will be with the excommunicated, the devil with the blessed.[7]

Savonarola wrote letters to the princes of Christendom: to Ferdinand and Isabella of Spain, to Henry VIII of England, to Charles VIII of France, to the King of Hungary. In them he wrote, "This Alexander is no Pope, is no Christian, and believes in no God." None of them reached these sovereigns. One was intercepted and taken to the Pope. Alexander was furious. "Such a challenge will not be passed over," he vowed. "After this Savonarola will be made to feel the full measure of our wrath!"[8]

The turning point came when one of the Franciscan friars at Holy Cross challenged Savonarola to a trial by fire.[9] They would both step into the fire and God would decide which one was in the right by burning the other to a crisp. The Campagnacci seized on that challenge as an opportunity to do Savonarola in. They persuaded the Franciscan to press the challenge but promised they would not let it come to the point of actually entering the fire. They would be armed with daggers, rush Savonarola and kill him during the public spectacle.

Savonarola ignored the challenge, but Fra Domenico, without consulting with his Prior, accepted the challenge in Savonarola's place. The Signoria at this time was composed of a majority of the

Arribbiatti, Savonarola's bitter enemies. They approved of the ordeal as an opportunity to discredit the Friar. Plans were made for the 7th of April 1498. The Florentines jammed the Piazza. Some came out of curiosity, some out of animosity to the prophet, most came to see a miracle.

The Franciscans stalled the proceedings on one technicality after another. The crowd, numbering about 50,000, was kept standing for hours without food or drink while an angry debate went on between the Franciscans and the Dominicans. Few of the spectators could hear what the friars were saying. The crowd became impatient. The Campagnacci meanwhile, five hundred strong and armed with knives, were shouting obscenities and blaming Savonarola for the delays.

At last, around five in the afternoon there was a cloudburst. Everybody ran for cover. The rainfall was heavy but short. When the rain stopped the people returned to the Piazza, but the contest was postponed. The Compagnacci were unable to get to Savonarola with their knives, but their tongues were effective enough. They shouted accusations at him, called him a false prophet, and the people, disappointed because the miracle they expected didn't happen, turned on the Friar. It was one of those strange shifts in public opinion that sometimes happens, and someone who is a hero one day is a villain the next. So it was with Savonarola.

There was a mob scene at St. Mark's. The Compagnacci broke in and were repulsed by the monks. The Signoria decided to exile Savonarola. But the brothers at St. Mark's refused to let him go. They were convinced that as soon as the Friar stepped outside the convent he would be murdered. Time passed in a standoff, and with it the deadline set for Savonarola's departure. Now the Friar was guilty of disobeying the order to leave the city and he was arrested. The arresting officers were barely able to take him through the angry crowd alive. He had a gash on his forehead and his fingers were cut by a Compagnacci knife.

The committee appointed to "interrogate" Savonarola included Doffo Spini and others who hated the Friar. The interrogation procedure was this: The Friar's arms were tied behind his back. A cable was attached to his wrists, and with it he was pulled to a height of twenty feet. He was then dropped to a foot or so above the floor where the cable caught him. His weight, the momentum and the sudden stop wrenched his arms out of their sockets. He was in excruciating pain. His interrogators then asked the Friar to confess to "crimes." There was nothing to confess, so the procedure was repeated. After several such sessions Savonarola, feverish and broken in body, made a confession which he subsequently retracted. The charges against him were patently false.[10] But Pope Alexander VI insisted, "Even if Savonarola is a saint like John the Baptist, he must die."[11]

On May 23, 1498, Savonarola was brought to the Piazza. With him were Domenico Buonvicini, who spoke for the Friar during his enforced silence, and Silvestro Maruffi, a simple brother in the order who somehow got caught in the coils of the judicial system. A scaffolding had been erected in about the same place where the structure for the ordeal by fire had stood. High above it was a gallows from whose crosspiece hung three iron collars. The three friars were dressed in their priestly garments which one by one were removed from them in the ceremony of degradation. A piece of glass was used to scratch their finger nails to symbolize the removal of the holy oil of consecration. Then a barber destroyed the tonsure, symbolic of their monastic vows, by shaving their heads.

A Bishop who had served under Savonarola was chosen to read the service of desecration. He stuttered, swallowed, and did not look the Friar in the eyes as he said, "I separate you from the Church Militant and Triumphant." Savonarola interrupted, "Not from the Church Triumphant, my dear son, for the Church Triumphant is in heaven...you have neither the right nor the power..." The Bishop corrected himself, but could not finish his office. He broke into sobbing.

The Papal legate, Bishop Romolino, read the charges against the three men. Then he added, "I have received word from His Holiness Alexander VI this very day that he grants you a plenary indulgence-in-the-article-of-death with release from all canonical censures and excommunications. His Holiness sets you back into your original state of sinlessness...You will not undergo the punishment of purgatory...Do you accept?" The three bowed in assent.

One by one the Friars climbed the ladder where the executioner placed the noose and iron collar around their necks. Fra Silvestro went first. "Father Girolamo, see how a knight of Jesus Christ dies with joy in his heart!" The executioner pushed him off the ladder and the body swung free. Fra Domenico was next. Halfway up the ladder he called out, "I assure you that all of Fra Girolamo's prophecies will go into fulfillment... The Church will be purified.

The Holy Spirit will send his heavenly fire!" The executioner ordered him to be silent. He dropped from the ladder and died instantly.

Savonarola was next. Somebody from the crowd shouted, "If you can do miracles, now is the time to show us!" The executioner tied Savonarola's hands behind his back and pushed him toward the Compagnacci; they spit on him, struck him and scratched his face. When he climbed the ladder his face was covered with blood. He looked over the crowd of Florentines as he had done so often from his pulpit. The executioner struck him and he fell. The pile of faggots below the bodies was ignited and the smoke billowed and obscured the bodies. Then the wind blew and dispersed the flames and the bodies were visible again.

The flames had burned off the ropes that held Savonarola's wrists, and by some nerve reaction, his right hand was raised to shoulder height with his two fingers extended as he had done so often in blessing his congregation. "A miracle! A Miracle!" shouted voices from the crowd. Women screamed and sobbed. A wail issued from the people, as if it suddenly dawned on them the terrible evil they had been a party to. The Compagnacci cursed. The people stampeded out of the Piazza. Many children were trampled in the rush. The officials scurried down from the tribunals and ran into the palace.[12]

Less than twenty years after the death of Savonarola, the reform of the church began, but not in the way the Friar had imagined. The judgments that he predicted would strike the Italian states—particularly Rome—came true in successive waves of devastation. During these fateful years, the aftermath of Savonarola's work and witness in Florence, the Medici family contributed two Popes to the Roman Catholic Church.

The first was Giovanni de Medici, the younger son of Lorenzo the Magnificent. He reigned as Leo X from 1513 to 1521. He was the Pope who inherited the heavy debt incurred by his predecessor, Julius II, for the construction of the new basilica of St. Peter. To pay the debt Leo X developed the fund-raising scheme of selling indulgences: money contributed to the papacy in return for a reduction of the sentence in purgatory for deceased relatives. It was this scheme that provoked Martin Luther to post his ninety five theses on the church door in Wittenburg in 1517, the act that launched the Protestant Reformation. The easy-going Leo X drew the line at a church reform and excommunicated Martin Luther.[13]

221

The other Medici Pope was Giulio de Medici, the illegitimate son of Giuliano de Medici, the murdered brother of Lorenzo the Magnificent. He reigned as Clement VII from 1523 to 1534. Prior to becoming Pope, Giulio was the guiding genius and detail man for the Pontificate of his cousin, Leo X.[14] Although Giulio was a promising candidate—able, shrewd and knew the ins and outs of the papacy—he lost his first bid for the tiara.

In between the Medici Popes Leo X and Clement VII there was a Pope named Adrien VI. He was what in American politics we call a "dark horse" candidate, elected because of a deadlock in the balloting for the real contenders. And so it was that an honest man was chosen who made serious plans for a real reform of the Catholic Church from the top down. One feature of his proposed reform was to deal with the abuse of power by the papacy and to restrict the overgrown influence of the office. Adrien VI never lived to implement his reforms. He died after twenty months in office. The probable cause of death: poison.[15]

At the next conclave, Giulio de Medici was elected and took the title of Clement VII. His was the most disastrous pontificate in the history of the Catholic Church. Charles V of Spain contributed heavily to get him elected, and Giulio purchased enough votes to win easily.[16]

King Charles V expressed his desire to convene a General Council of the church for the purpose of reforming it. Pope Clement VII professed agreement, but laid down a number of plausible obstacles to be overcome first, and then took steps to stir up trouble between the three dominant kingdoms of Christendom, France, Spain and England, hoping that these sovereigns of Christian states would soon be so preoccupied with making war with one another that they wouldn't have time to deal with church reform.[17] In this Clement was successful. He made secret deals with the king of France against the king of Spain, and with the king of Spain against the king of France. He kept king Henry VIII of England on the string for years with the hint that he might dissolve Henry's marriage to Katherine of Aragon so Henry could marry Ann Boleyn. Clement VII succeeded in turning most of Europe into a battlefield. He reaped what he sowed.

He betrayed Charles V and backed the king of France. But Charles defeated the French and took the French king, Francis I, to Spain as a prisoner, releasing him only when Francis promised to stay out of Italy. With the French neutralized, Charles invaded Italy and in 1527 loosed his troops on Rome in one of the most devastating sacks any city has ever had to endure. This time the Pope inspired no awe to restrain the violence and lust of the troops. Charles deliberately let his troops go without pay, and marched them through desolate, war-torn territory that could not support the army. He gave them the promise that they could do what they wanted when they reached Rome, and when they took the city there was no restraining them. When they finally withdrew after occupying the city for months, Rome was destitute and in ruins.[18]

Somehow, Clement survived. He made a humiliating deal with Charles V, but retained the papacy. In 1529, he crowned Charles V Emperor, but it was no triumph for the Pope as the crowning of Charlemagne had been centuries earlier. Dominated by Charles V, the Pope could not give Henry VIII of England a divorce from Katherine, the sister of Charles V's mother. Pope Clement VII kept postponing the decision, and Henry finally took matters into his own hands and created his own national church. Henry and the English church broke with Rome and Clement finally excommunicated Henry. England was lost.[19]

While Christendom was consuming itself in the West, The Muslim Turks were closing in from the East. The Turks invaded Hungary. Charles needed help from the Germans to resist the Turks. But the Germans were Lutherans, and Clement was forced to legitimize the Protestants in order to secure their help. Charles V repulsed the Turkish troops, but at a high cost to the Papacy. He had to make it legal to be Protestant.[20]

Clement succeeded in restoring the Medicis to power in Florence by force of arms. Charles V made part of his army available for the purpose. The Florentines held out bravely, but this time there was no Savonarola on hand to stir up their faith. The city surrendered and the Medicis were back in power. Clement installed his nephew, Allesandro, as Duke of Florence. Allesandro dissolved the Signoria, and gradually took away from the Florentines their cherished liberties. The final humiliation for the Florentines came when Allesandro had the bell removed from the tower of the palace where the Signoria used to meet. It was the bell that used to summon the men of Florence to decide on crucial civic issues, a liberty bell. The Florentines would not be needing it any longer.[21]

And so the prophecies of Savonarola were fulfilled. Italy was devastated by wars, and Rome was judged with terrible severity. Savonarola suffered martyrdom, but the reform of the church began. Florence was judged severely. She rejected her prophet and the proud, freedom-loving Florentines lost their Constitutional republic and were brought under the heel of a tyrant. Savonarola predicted the city's eventual restoration to holiness. That prophecy is yet to be fulfilled, perhaps at the Second Coming of Christ.

The reign of Clement VII was motivated by one supreme goal: the avoidance of a General Council of the church.[22] As a member of the Medici family, Clement knew too much to allow a reforming council. The new learning the Medici family had promoted with such zeal and expense during four generations uncovered, along with the classic Greek and Roman literature, "the knowledge of the fraudulent basis on which the Papal claim to supremacy in the church rested, the knowledge of a Christian age in which there had been no Papacy and all bishops had been of equal rank and authority, and the knowledge of a pre-existing scheme of Christian doctrine not overlaid by the errors and corruptions which had subsequently grown up in the Church at Rome. And as this knowledge spread, wider and stronger grew the determination to end the existing state of things in the Church, to cast off the usurped supremacy of Rome, and to return to a purer form of Christianity."[23]

The Medicis gathered all this explosive material. Martin Luther provided the spark that detonated it. And when it blew, there were members of the Medici family sitting on the papal throne. The papacy began to shake during Leo X's reign, but it was during the reign of Clement VII that the papal empire broke up. Clement stonewalled the convening of a reforming council of the church because he knew what a council was likely to do. He succeeded in his aim, but in the process turned Christendom into a desolate burned-out battlefield. Rome was in ruins. The Papacy lost most of its temporal power. Christendom fed on itself like a cancer. Jesus said Christians would be recognized by their love for one another. At this sad moment in history, however, professing Christians killed, robbed, brutalized, and raped one another on an international scale. The Pope himself led them on in these mad pursuits.

Roman Catholic scholar and author, Malachi Martin, a former Jesuit, commented on the history of the Church of Rome.

> From the days of Luther and Clement VII
> [there] has been a 400-year decline and fall.
> Through vicissitudes of exile, war, persecution,

and bankruptcy, the popes continued into our day, until at the beginning of the eighties in this century, the most definitive signs of inner and irreversible decay appeared in the church which Emperor Constantine made possible. In that 400 years, on three occasions, it looked as if external forces would level that church. They never did.

Yet the ecclesiastics in charge of the Roman structure never for an instant reflected on the long past of their churchly structure in such a way as to appreciate the fateful lesson of history: when churchmen tried to foment and propagate the Catholic faith by means of politics and money and worldly prestige, the condition of their church always deteriorated. No one ever reversed that single but complex decision of Pope Silvester I to accept the temporal power and influence Emperor Constantine offered him.[24]

That decision to accept the temporal power and influence offered to Silvester I, Bishop of Rome, by Emperor Constantine in the fourth century, was the real problem underlying the struggle between Savonarola and Pope Alexander VI in the fifteenth century. The Constantinian issue was never at the forefront of the conflict, but it was alluded to again and again by the Friar every time he attacked the wealth, influence, political power and corruption of the official church and compared it to the poverty, political weakness, purity, love and spiritual power of the New Testament church. The problem, as Malachi Martin said, is unresolved to this day. It surfaced in an unforgettable way with Savonarola.

The problem represented by Savonarola—a five hundred year old dilemma—is this: the Catholic Church has inherited the legacy of revival and reform as represented by Savonarola. The Friar sought to restore the integrity of the New Testament church. And because the Catholic Church has cleared the Friar of the false charges of heresy, Savonarola remains a valid part of the Catholic legacy. However, the Catholic Church has also inherited the legacy of Pope Alexander VI, who resisted the Savonarolan revival and reform, and of Pope Clement VII, who was willing to see the Church ravaged rather than reformed.

Ultimately, these two legacies are incompatible. The Church cannot continue to hold on with integrity to both legacies. In the years to come Catholics will have to decide between them. Someone once pointed out that not to decide is to decide. In this case, if you are a Catholic, not to decide is to agree with Alexander VI. That is, it will take no decision for Catholics and the Catholic Church to stand with Alexander VI and against Savonarola. The Church has already decided on that issue. Not to decide is to accept the decision made in the fifteenth century.

The power—the decision-making authority of the Catholic Church—is in the hands of the Popes. The Catholic Church, in the person of Pope Alexander VI, decided against Savonarola, his revival and his vision for reform. The Catholic Church, in the person of Pope Alexander VI, denounced the Friar and put him to a cruel death. And Alexander VI remains a valid part of the Catholic legacy, too. Alexander VI has never been declared an anti-Pope, nor have his policies been denounced by the Catholic Church as anti-Christian. And of course, the decisions of Pope Alexander VI carried the day. They were the decisions that determined the way the Church would go.

The position of the Popes is the default position of the Catholic Church. It is they who, in Catholic tradition, are said to be infallible and to carry final authority, not prophets and reformers like Savonarola. And therefore, while the revival and reform position represented by Savonarola is a possibility for the Catholic Church, it is the decisions of the Popes, including Alexander VI, that will prevail in the Catholic Church if there is not a decision to make a fundamental change. For the changes that have taken place in the Catholic Church, including the remarkable changes of the Vatican II Council, have not resolved the issues raised by Savonarola. The Friar remains a controversial figure more than half a millennium after his death.

24

A Catholic Dilemma

The person of Savonarola presents the Catholic Church with a dilemma. He was no doubt one of the holiest men ever to serve Jesus Christ, and he was an orthodox Catholic. On the other hand, he defied a legitimate Pope. The record is clear on that point. Alexander VI, with all his faults, flaws, weaknesses, and sins, was the official head of the Catholic Church from 1492-1503. There is no reason, on Catholic principles, to exclude him from the system. The rules of the Church and its theology make room for such men, even in the highest office of the Church.

The dilemma exists because the Church also makes room for men like Savonarola. Many true servants of God have arisen, particularly in the religious orders such as the Dominicans in which Savonarola served. But, whereas there was no way found by which Alexander VI could be dislodged from the papacy in spite of his flagrant sins and corruption, Savonarola, although a man of unquestioned holiness, broke a rule of the Catholic Church, and paid for it with his life. He probably would have been martyred anyway. The Compagnacci (by their unprincipled violence and relentless hate) and the Arrabbiati (by their deceit and political manipulation) were determined to rid Florence of the Friar. They might well have succeeded without the Pope. But the Pope's excommunication of Savonarola set the stage for his enemies to work their treachery and made their evil task easier.

Savonarola and Pope Alexander VI represent different and contradictory spirits: one of them, the spirit of holiness and of the coming kingdom of God; the other, the spirit of this age and of the present evil world. Ultimately, those two spirits are incompatible. The time appears to be at hand when a choice must be made between the two.

Savonarola still has a loyal following both inside and outside of the Catholic Church. There have been repeated efforts over the last five centuries from within the Church to have Savonarola declared a saint. His beatification is now under consideration again. It is being considered because Pope John Paul II, in the face of the third millennium, has called for an examination of conscience by the Church. The Pope has led the way in confessing some of the past sins of the Catholic Church in an attempt to make amends and promote Christian unity. The canonization of Savonarola would certainly help to achieve those ends. The Cardinal Archbishop of Florence expressed the hope that Savonarola's martyrdom and sainthood would be acknowledged by the 500th anniversary of his death, May 23, 1998,[1] but the date passed and it hasn't happened. It is hard to imagine how it could.

Had Savonarola defied a political leader in the pre-Constantinian era, there would have been no obstacle to his canonization. But the Friar defied a Pope in a Constantinian context. And so there are serious problems about declaring the Friar a saint.

The problems are not necessarily connected with the doctrine of papal infallibility, for infallibility can be and has been defined very narrowly. The Pope is considered infallible only when he speaks from his office on moral and spiritual issues for the purpose of defining an issue and establishing a doctrine. And the Catholic Church has not denied that some of its popes, including Alexander VI, were sinful men and unworthy to represent Jesus Christ. But the Roman Catholic Church has never been able to admit that the institution itself went wrong, as Protestants have charged.

Therein lies the dilemma. Protestants have claimed Savonarola as a sort of forerunner of the Reformation, like John the Baptist, who prepared the way for Jesus. And the Friar had this in common with all true Christian reformers and revivalists, that he looked to the New Testament and to the early church for his standard. But Savonarola was not a Protestant; he did not reach the same conclusions or stress the same doctrines as Martin Luther or John Calvin or the other Protestant reformers. He sought a remedy for the corruption of the Catholic Church within the framework of the Catholic system itself. He didn't find it. His martyrdom, however, initiated the era of church reform in spite of the built-in resistance of the Catholic system.

It has been argued cogently that Savonarola was a forerunner for both the Protestant Reformation and the Catholic Counter-Reformation. Although this may be true, I maintain that the Friar would not have been satisfied with either, for his goal in seeking to reform the church was the restoration of the church to the likeness of the original New Testament church. He held a New Testament standard before the people to whom he ministered. But the clincher is that Savonarola followed the New Testament not only in doctrine, but also in practice and procedure. He actually took up his cross and followed Jesus to a martyr's death. He did not fully understand his own leading or the logic of the Spirit of God, but he followed that leading and logic to its bitter end in martyrdom. And he will know its overwhelming joy in the resurrection. He suffered with Christ and he will reign with Christ in that day.

Savonarola anticipated the Protestant Reformation in that he defied the Pope on the grounds of conscience, as instructed by the Bible and the Holy Spirit. Nevertheless, Catholics have as valid a claim to the Friar as the Protestants. But Catholics have a problem with Savonarola that Protestants do not have. The problem with declaring Savonarola a saint in the Catholic Church is that it would set a precedent dangerous to the Catholic institution. Even when the issue is framed in an historical setting—in which holiness clearly lies with the individual reformer and villainy with the Pope and the institution he headed—it is the kind of precedent that could result in the dismantling of the whole Constantinian structure. That structure created and defined the Catholic Church and the Catholic Church has officially regarded it as the norm since its inception in the fourth century.

Sainthood is an invitation to Roman Catholics to follow the example of the person canonized. It could be argued that the precedent Savonarola set, in following the Scriptures and his conscience, resulted in a great part of Christendom being swept away from the Pope and the Catholic Church by the Protestant Reformation.

Traditionalist Catholics have argued that to raise questions about the history of the Catholic Church and its institutional development would be an invitation to apostasy. They point out that today there are "Catholics" who believe in abortion, birth control, and universal salvation. There are "Catholics" who believe in Marxism and practice armed violence in order to produce social and political change. There are "Catholic" feminists who think women should be priests, and "Catholic" ecumenists who think that the Catholic Church should open its arms to non-Christian religions.

Traditionalist Catholics have more in common with conservative Protestants than they do with many who are members in good standing with the Roman Catholic institution. They would find themselves in agreement with Savonarola on almost all points of doctrine. But they would hesitate to canonize the Friar for fear that his example of obedience to God rather than the Catholic Church and the Papacy would validate private judgment in matters of faith and morals and lead to the disintegration of the Catholic institution. They hope and pray for a strong, conservative Pope. They worry that a split today would lead to something even worse than Protestantism—to apostasy and unbelief.

The real issue facing the Catholic Church is truth. Telling the truth is an invitation to Catholics to put their faith in Jesus Christ, rather than in the power of money and political influence that an institution of this world can wield. The issue raised by Savonarola is a call to take up the cross, renounce the sword, and follow Jesus Christ. Yes, it is an invitation that may and probably will be rejected by most Catholics. Yes, telling the truth may be the occasion of unbelief and apostasy as well as faith and salvation. But that is what Peter said about Jesus Christ. He is the chief cornerstone for the believer and a stone of stumbling to the unbeliever.[2] And the Catholic Church has structured itself from the time of Constantine to accommodate both believers and unbelievers.

The issue is truth. If Savonarola was an exemplary believer worthy of emulation, if he was a true prophet of God, if God sent him to bear witness to the truth and to be His instrument for the reform of the church, then that truth must be acknowledged whatever the supposed consequences for the institution. For the truth, however painful, will ultimately issue in the salvation, not the destruction, of God's people. In any case, the problem will not go away by ignoring it. The issue keeps coming up. It remains unresolved after more than 500 years.

Consider the following facts: Pope Alexander VI undermined a great work of God that occurred within the Catholic Church during Alexander's pontificate. In the decisions made by the highest official in the Catholic Church, the temporal, political concerns of this age and this evil world took precedence over salvation, holiness, sound faith, good works and practical goodness. The Pope used the power of the Papacy to silence a man of God by bribery, threats, false accusations, torture, a rigged trial and finally by hanging and burning him.

Those are heavy burdens for the Catholic Church to support. But the burdens are there, and the failure of the Catholic Church to deal with them does not make them go away. It merely postpones the day of reckoning.

A relevant precedent exists in the New Testament in the dialog Jesus had with the Chief Priests and Sadducees. Jesus had driven the money changers out of the temple. They asked him by what authority He did it. Jesus answered by asking them a question. By whose authority did John baptize people? Was it from heaven or from men?

The chief priests and Sadducees conferred among themselves and came up with a dilemma. "If we say, 'From heaven,' He will say to us, 'Why then did you not believe in him?' But if we say, 'From men,' we fear the multitude, for all count John as a prophet." So they didn't give any answer. They said they didn't know.[3] The decision they made in rejecting John was only consistent with the decision that John's authority was not from God, that he was a false prophet. But they didn't want to say so publicly, because of the holiness of John's character and the soundness of his doctrine. The people recognized these qualities in John; the chief priests and Sadducees could not dispute them without raising a furor among the people. So they postponed the answer. They hoped that the people would forget the question. They tried to avoid the issue because they wanted to hold on to their places of power and influence. For their legitimacy had been challenged and they had not given an adequate defense.

The Catholic Church is in the same position in regard to Savonarola as the chief priests and Sadducees were in regard to John the Baptist and Jesus. As the Jewish establishment in the New Testament era condemned John and Jesus, so also the Catholic Church excommunicated Savonarola, and put him to death.

If the Catholic Church now declares the Friar to be innocent, moreover, if it declares Savonarola to have been a saint and a prophet of God, then the Catholic Church, in effect, confesses itself guilty of murder—the murder of a saint and a prophet of God. That is a very serious crime indeed. And such a confession could create a multitude of problems for the Catholic Church. Would every other questionable decision of the Catholic Church have to be reviewed? Savonarola's canonization could lead to a kind of class-action suit. No one knows where it would end.

But if the Catholic Church fails to deal with the Savonarola case, then the alternative is that God Himself will deal with it, and the result will be worse than if the Catholic Church makes confession and repents. Consider what happened in Judea.

When the authorities of Judea engineered the deaths of John the Baptist and Jesus, when they refused to confess their sins and repent, God Himself intervened. Judgment struck. The temple was destroyed in 70 A.D. and the Priesthood ceased to function. The Judeans who believed in John and Jesus were called out of mainstream Judea and became the church of Jesus Christ. The temple was gone and the church became separated from the synagogue. Many of the unbelieving Jews were scattered into the nations or put to death by the Romans. After the Bar Kokhba rebellion in 135 A.D., Judea ceased to exist as an independent state.[4]

There is another historical precedent that is relevant. During the reign of king David in Israel there was a famine for three years. David inquired of the Lord, and He answered that the cause for judgment during David's reign was a sin committed by king Saul before David came to the throne.[5] There is historical continuity to an institution, whether national, religious, commercial, or any other kind. Nations and institutions typically outlive the generation in which they were founded. When that happens, the institution is treated by God as a kind of corporate person. The institution remains long after the individual members have died. Their sins and crimes may and often do escape judgment during their lifetimes. Nevertheless, the institution continues and its guilt accumulates. If sin is not confessed and repented of in one generation, the debt grows and eventually comes due in some future generation. That is why it was necessary for David to make things right. In his times, David had to correct an act of his predecessor, king Saul. Saul violated a covenant Israel had with the Gibeonites. It was a violation which had been committed in the previous generation, under a different administration, even a different dynasty.

God has not changed. The same principle applies to the Catholic Church today. There is historical continuity to the Roman Catholic Church. The institution has survived and remains accountable to God. Sins committed in one generation that were not confessed and repented of can and will be dealt with in a later generation. Iniquity, like a field of grain, eventually reaches maturity and provokes a harvest of judgment. The responsibility can sometimes be postponed, but it cannot be avoided. Guilt can only be cleared up by confession and by repentance that rectifies the situation. If that doesn't happen, the only other alternative is judgment sooner or later.

What then can we expect to happen to the Catholic Church? One possible scenario is that the Church will make confession and repent. The Vatican II document on religious liberty appears to be a step in that direction. The statement contains the same logic the Donatists and Anabaptists used against Rome. The one weakness in the document is its attempt to evade the awful responsibility for centuries during which the Catholic Church routinely and as a matter of policy tortured and killed "heretics." That policy violated the doctrine the Vatican II document claims has always been the teaching of the Church. The document admits that in the vicissitudes of history, the Church has not always practiced that truth.[6] But can the Roman Catholic Church truly be said to have always believed a truth it denied in practice during sixteen centuries? Does not the practical policy of the Church over those many centuries indicate what the real belief of the Church was?

The confession must be much more detailed and candid than that. It is not acceptable as it stands. For one thing, it must deal with Savonarola. And then, assuming a full confession is made, what would be an appropriate repentance?

I will return for a moment to the question Jesus raised with the chief priests and Sadducees. If they had admitted that John and Jesus spoke for God, the logical result would have been to submit to their authority and repent. But that would have cost the authorities of Judea dearly. In all probability, they would have lost their jobs and their places of influence, authority, security and prestige in Jewish society.

It was the same with Alexander VI. Had he recognized Savonarola as a saint and a prophet of God, his repentance would necessarily have included repenting of his sins and submitting to the reform of the Church. That would have meant that he, Alexander, would almost certainly have been removed from office in disgrace and might have had to face other punishment as well.

But of course, Alexander is no longer on the scene. He cannot repent now. But what of the Church which has inherited the legacy of Alexander VI and has on its hands the blood of Savonarola? How would it clear itself? To canonize the Friar would be tantamount to a confession of having slandered and murdered a man of exemplary holiness and a prophet of God. What would constitute repentance for such sins? Would it not involve at the very least submitting to the thoroughgoing reform Savonarola was demanding? And what would such a reformation look like?

The repentance of the Catholic Church would have to include the renunciation of its complicity with Constantine and his successors. The Church would have to renounce the wealth and power it gained because of its illicit alliance with the state. Savonarola continually pointed out that its wealth and worldly power were the root causes of the Church's corruption. He called on Catholics to return to the New Testament pattern of Church life. Repentance in a Savonarolan context would mean returning to apostolic doctrine, and to a fellowship of believers who love one another as the early Christians did, and to following in the footsteps of Jesus Christ. That was clearly where Savonarola was heading, and where he would have led the Church if he had been given the chance.

When Pope John XXIII convened the Vatican II Council he said something very much like that, and showed Catholics what, in his view, the renewal of the Church would mean. He symbolically opened the windows of the Catholic Church and invited the Holy Spirit to come in and renew it. The renewal he had in mind was indicated by two memorable statements: "We must blow off the dust from the throne of Constantine which has been lying too long on the chair of Peter;"[7] and, [The ecumenical council must] "...restore the simple and pure lines which the face of Jesus's church wore at its birth."[8] He was calling for a renewal of the Catholic Church that would separate it from the legacy of Constantine, and restore to it the humility, simplicity and love that characterized the church of Jesus Christ at its inception.

In his novel, *The Final Conclave*, written when the reign of Paul VI was ending, the Catholic scholar and author, Malachi Martin, suggested such a scenario. In his novel, the princes of the Catholic Church recognized that they stood at a crossroads in history. In a scene that was frankly miraculous, the Holy Spirit overruled the plots, plans and ambitions of the Cardinals. The novel ended with the Cardinals about to do the unthinkable.

A young African prelate, inspired by the Spirit of Jesus Christ, set before his colleagues the policy he believed the Church should pursue. He proposed to the astonished assembly that the Catholic Church divest itself of all its wealth and political power—disband the diplomatic corps, renounce all territorial possessions granted the Holy See by the state of Italy in 1929 -- and rely instead on the power of the Holy Spirit.

The policy was affirmed unanimously by the Cardinals. The only remaining decision was to choose the man who would implement the policy.[9] There was a sense of finality to this act as the princes of the Church prepared to mark their ballots. It was the final conclave, the conclave to end all conclaves.

Malachi Martin's scenario did not take place in 1978, but something of the kind could happen at the next Conclave. Dr. Martin believed in a Marian prophecy that may have inspired his book. In the primitive town of Garabandal, Spain in the early 1960s four young girls claimed that the Virgin Mary appeared to them and spoke to them. One of the prophetic messages allegedly given to the young girls said that there would be three more Popes. When the reign of the third Pope ends, it will mark the end of "our Catholic times."[10] The end of Catholic times is not the time of the end of the world predicted in Scripture. Ordinary history and the present age will continue after the last Pope and the end of "Catholic times."

John XXIII was Pope at the time of the Garabandal prediction. Paul VI followed him, and then came Pope John Paul I whose reign was very short. He was followed by John Paul II, the third Pope, who is still reigning. If the prediction is correct, when the reign of John Paul II comes to an end "our Catholic times" will end.

Dr. Malachi Martin (d. 1999) believed the term "these Catholic Times," referred to the time period between the Council of Nicea (325 A.D.) until the present, during which the Catholic Church enjoyed a preeminence among the religions of the earth. Dr. Martin believed that period will end when the reign of John Paul II ends.[11]

"Our Catholic times,"then, is the Constantinian age. They are called "Catholic Times" because the Catholic Church was the chief beneficiary of the "favors" of the Emperor Constantine and of the policy he established linking the Church with the world and the state. The Garabandal prediction indicated that John Paul II would be the last Pope of the age of Constantine.

The prophecy, if accurate, would seem to mean that when the present Pope's reign ends, the worldly advantages conveyed to the Catholic Church by Constantine will be withdrawn. Presumably, the end of the Constantinian era would expose the Church to persecution by the state, for that is how it was before the time of Constantine. I find the Garabandal prediction intriguing. It deals with the Catholic Church, and suggests that a monumental change is about to take place in that institution. There have been many signs in the last few generations that some such change is coming. The Garabandal message doesn't tell us how it will happen. But if this amazing prediction comes true, it could happen as it has happened before, because the state will confiscate the wealth and property of the Church and will withdraw its protection from the Church.

When the state has turned on the Catholic Church in various countries at various times in modern history, the Church was always able to reclaim at least some of its former worldly wealth and power. If the Garabandal prediction is correct, this time the wealth and power will be lost and not recovered.

It is conceivable, however, that these worldly powers will be lost, not because they will be taken away by force and violence, but because the Catholic Church voluntarily renounces the wealth and power of this evil world, and seeks to recover the spiritual power of the New Testament church. It could happen as Malachi Martin suggested in his novel, *The Final Conclave*, by repentance, by a deliberate decision of the College of Cardinals in a conclave, to do, in effect, what the rich young ruler in the Bible failed to do,[12] and what Constantine never did. The Church could give away its riches and wealth to the poor, voluntarily renounce its worldly power and influence, disestablish itself, and follow in the footsteps of Jesus, as Peter said.[13] That would be a radical act, to be sure, and would run counter to the whole history of the Catholic Church and the Papacy. However, such an act would be perfectly consistent with the New Testament. And it would be the best way to deal with the great unresolved problems in the Church's history—by humbling itself, confessing its sins, repenting, and becoming a willing sacrifice. It is not impossible, but it would surely take a miracle of the kind Martin imagined in his novel.

The apostle Paul wrote, "If we would judge ourselves, we would not be judged."[14] The Catholic Church could do that. Or a part of the Church could do that. If it does not judge itself, however, God will judge it. I am confident that all of those within the Catholic Church who have a living faith in Jesus Christ will judge themselves, or will be chastened by the Lord so that they will not be condemned with the world. Those Catholics who in their hearts belong to the world and not to Christ will be judged and destroyed with the world.

There have been instances of national and institutional repentance. They are impressive but problematical. In the New Testament, John the Baptist, Jesus and the apostles, did not expect or receive that kind of a response from Israel. They did not address the institutional leaders of Judah and call the priesthood, the Sanhedrin and the synagogues to repentance. They addressed the common people and invited them to repent of their sins.

When the individuals and in some cases, whole families, repented they were immediately forgiven. They were not only forgiven for their personal and individual sins by repentance and faith in Jesus Christ, they were also separated from the national and institutional guilt that had accumulated through Israel's history. For they were called out of the world system and were hated by the world.[15] The act of separating themselves from the world alienated them from the social, cultural, national, and religious benefits and protection of Judean society. By virtue of their conversion, they became dependent upon God in a radical way.

It is not impossible that the Roman Catholic and other Constantinian churches could repent in a radical and institutional reversal of Constantinian policy. Maybe Malachi Martin's scenario will happen somewhat as he imagined it. It doesn't seem likely. But whether or not the institutions are converted, individuals and families certainly can and will be. And when they are converted, they will immediately be released from the guilt and saved from the punishment that is due to them not only as individuals, but as members of the institutions and societies they once belonged to.

As Peter said, "Be saved from this perverse generation." They will no longer be part of the world and its institutions, but citizens of the kingdom of God. Freed from the sins of the world, they will be morally and spiritually separated from the world. Therefore they will also escape the punishment that will come upon the world and its institutions and works.

The teaching of the cross means that the believer is separated from the world in such a way as to be alienated from it, no longer a part of it, and therefore a target of the world's hatred and opposition.[16] This was how it was in New Testament times. This is how it will be when the last revival restores the church's New Testament integrity.

25

The Importance Of The Church

There is a folk tale about a peasant who captured an elf and made the unfortunate creature tell the peasant where his treasure was hidden. The elf told the peasant that the treasure was buried under a certain tree in the forest. "Which one?" asked the peasant. The elf pointed to a tree, and the peasant tied a yellow handkerchief around the tree so he could identify it, for he was intending to go home and get his shovel and return for the treasure. The elf pleaded with the peasant to let him go, but the peasant refused, saying that the elf would remove the yellow handkerchief if he did. The elf promised to leave the handkerchief around the tree exactly where the peasant had put it. And since the word of an elf could be relied on, the peasant let him go while he went home to get his shovel. When he returned, however, he found yellow handkerchiefs on all the trees in the forest.

I think somebody made up that story to explain what happened to the church. When every tree in the forest has a yellow handkerchief tied to it, it's impossible to tell where the treasure is. And when everybody in the kingdom is a "Christian" it is hard to tell a believer from an unbeliever. It was this confusion that gave rise to the notion of the invisible church. The visible institution was composed of believers and unbelievers; obviously, as it stood, it could not be the true church. For the true church is composed only of believers; hence, the true church is invisible in this present age. So it was argued.

The early Christians didn't speak of the church in those terms. In New Testament times it was obvious who the Christians were. They confessed their faith in Jesus Christ in a public way and suffered the consequences. They loved one another like members of the same family. But they were excluded from the synagogues.

239

They were spoken of as evil by the societies in which they lived. They were hated and mistrusted. They were deprived of their rights and persecuted. Some were martyred. It was hard to be a Christian, but it was not hard to tell who the Christians were.

Jesus told his disciples that they were the light of the world. By their witness to Jesus Christ and their upright behavior, they stood out in sharp contrast to the rest of the world like lights in the darkness. If that analogy means anything, it means that the church, as revealed in the New Testament, is visible. It has to be to fulfill its task.

According to the New Testament, the basic unit by which God works in the world in this age is the church. I do not mean that God does not use individuals or that He does not deal with nations and states. God deals with nations and states as He always has. And He deals with each of us as individuals. We are saved and called into the service of Jesus Christ individually and personally. We are personally responsible to the Lord. He knows each of us by our name.

But our baptism is into the body of Christ. We are born again as individuals, but we are born into a family, the church. Apostles were sent out by the Lord and they sometimes had to stand alone, but they went out as members of the church, were sent by the Holy Spirit and by the church,[1] and they reported back to the church.[2] Normally they went out two by two. They represented a kingdom, and their plan was to establish churches, colonies of the kingdom of God. A church—a collective entity—was necessary, because the church was designed to demonstrate what life in the future kingdom of God will be like. Believers lived by hope, that is, they conformed to the lifestyle, not of the present world but of the world to come. They related to one another as brothers and sisters with a supernatural love. They walked in the truth of the gospel, and lived together in the unity and harmony of the Holy Spirit.

The truth Jesus came to reveal was not primarily conceptual, intellectual and academic; it was personal and relational. For instance, in the New Testament love is revealed in the relationship that exists among disciples. Love is the relationship between God and His believing people and finds practical, visible expression in the relationship of disciples to one another.[3] Indeed, that relationship of love is what identified them as disciples.[4] I remember as a young Christian reading the New Testament and seeing how the believers were knit together in a fellowship of love. I experienced something of that brotherhood in the Spirit among sincere believers, so I knew that what the Scriptures were talking about was real. But it was so rare in the church. And when I was a student preparing for the ministry, I was frustrated for the lack of it in so much of what was called church, even in churches that took the Bible seriously. The point seemed to be to make sure that our opinions about the teachings of the Bible were correct. I came out of a Sunday morning service one winter day and told my wife, "We're supposed to love one another, but we hardly know one another! Somehow the church has turned the narrow way into a ten-lane highway! There are lots of members but membership doesn't mean anything any more." I began to find out as I studied church history that my analysis was not far from the truth. The relational element, so crucial to the New Testament, was lost by the fourth century, and has not been restored to this day.

We live in a society that stresses the importance of the individual and the intellect. The church is typically conceived of as an institution providing religious indoctrination for individuals; it may be for a large number of individuals, but individuals are the usual focus. We urge people to establish and cultivate a personal, individual relationship with God. And we try to make sure that their understanding of biblical doctrine is sound. And that being done, we are satisfied. They come and go from a church meeting as they come and go from a super market, pretty much as strangers to the other people who shop there. They get what they need for themselves and their families and then they go away again—consumers of a religious service.

The New Testament church, on the other hand, was like a family. The lives of the believers were connected to God as their Father and to one another as brothers and sisters. Jesus made these connections. He who was God and man connected men to God and to one another. These relationships were supremely important. One did not quit one church and join a competing church, any more than one quit one's family and joined another. Families were not in competition with one another, and neither was the church in competition with itself. And the church was an even more important connection than that of one's earthly family. If, as the saying goes, "blood is thicker than water," then spirit is thicker than blood.

I was filled with the Spirit and zeal to serve God and I knew I was called into ministry. It seemed absurd to me that the minister did everything in the church while the congregation sat passively and listened. But apparently that was the only way to do it. I learned from what I saw in operation. So I went away to Bible school where I ingested a lot of information, and in time became a professional minister. Now I was providing the services. But the church was not changing, I was. I could preach as much as I wanted about a New Testament church, and nothing happened. We were structured for something quite different from a New Testament church. The people were paying me to be their minister. That was the foundational reality. By functioning within a system that was not the system of the New Testament church, I was contradicting by my actions everything I was saying from the pulpit. I was a religious professional. My job depended on keeping the institution going, because the institution was paying my salary. But the institution was taking the place of the church.

When in the revival of the 1970s, the Spirit called a multitude of young people into the kingdom of God, we tried to change things. We preached about the New Testament church and the priesthood of all believers. And for a while it worked. The Lord sent us a lot of young men, capable men who were potential leaders. And we began to train them. We didn't send them away to Bible school or seminary. We wanted to raise them up in the church. That was the New Testament way.

They responded well. They heard what we said. But they also saw what we were doing. We were professionals. We made our living by preaching the gospel. And they, of course, were following our lead. It didn't matter what we said, they were following us in what we did. They too wanted to be paid professionals. They wanted our jobs. We became competitors like executives in a business competing for the top jobs. Of course, we didn't explain it in those terms. Overtly our disagreements were about doctrines and procedures. But the doctrinal and procedural issues masked a power struggle. Our efforts to build a New Testament church broke down. In the end we gave up the New Testament vision in exchange for the security of the traditional institution. And broke a lot of implicit promises in the process. It was one of those inherited problems of the church. It has a long history.

When the Gospel penetrated the Greek world it influenced that world powerfully. But the Greek world also had a profound influence on the church and the gospel. The apostle Paul identified this problem in the first century in the opening chapters of his first letter to the Corinthians.[5] Paul was distressed because of the divisions that arose among the Corinthian believers. They were dividing up into competitive parties and making artificial distinctions based on a preference for one teacher over another. Paul told them to get their eyes on Jesus Christ rather than any one of his apostles, prophets or teachers. The problem was an incipient denominationalism, and Paul dealt with it definitively. But Paul's solution was not implemented. He attributed the divisiveness among the Corinthians to the Greek love of human wisdom and knowledge. Already the believers were treating the gospel as if it were a philosophy in competition with other philosophies after the manner of the Greeks. Paul put the cross in the center of his proclamation as something in a whole different category from Greek wisdom and philosophy. But in spite of Paul's admonition, the influence of Greek thinking and its methodology continued to grow. By the fourth century it was dominant in the church.

The influence of Greek ways of thinking on the church was more subtle, but it constituted as important, pervasive and serious a compromise with the world as the one the church made with Roman politics.

In a book written near the close of the nineteenth century, Edwin Hatch documented the remarkable changes that occurred in the church as a result of the impact of Greek philosophy and rhetoric.[6] Hatch admitted that his work was a pioneering trek in comparatively unexplored territory, and that he was vulnerable to the mistakes of a pioneer.[7] Nevertheless, he was convinced that what he found during a lifetime of study was a fair and accurate description of the landscape. I do not claim to have checked all the sources and verified all of Hatch's assertions. But what he revealed in his investigative report on church history jibes with the New Testament, with what I know of the influence of Greek thought on the institutional church, and with what I have learned and experienced during my lifetime in the contemporary church. His book has the ring of truth to it.

Hatch's book is old and out of print. So I will quote him at length and try to give you something of the flavor of his writing and his discoveries; you can judge for yourself. I will begin with his conclusion which he believed he had proved.

> [A] large part of what are sometimes called
> Christian doctrines, and many usages which have
> prevailed and continue to prevail in the Christian

Church, are in reality Greek theories and Greek usages changed in form and colour by the influence of primitive Christianity, but in their essence Greek still...Its ethics of right and duty, rather than of love and self-sacrifice; its theology, whose God is more metaphysical than spiritual—whose essence it is important to define; its creation of a class of men whose main duty in life is that of moral exhortation, and whose utterances are not the spontaneous outflow of a prophet's soul, but the artistic periods of a rhetorician; its religious ceremonial with the darkness and the light, the initiation and the solemn enactment of a symbolic drama; its conception of intellectual assent rather than of moral earnestness as the basis of religious society—in all these, and the ideas that underlie them, Greece lives.[8]

Hatch believed that the church's impact was greater before it took on the Greek characteristics and that the progress of the faith was retarded by absorbing them. So the Greek influence cannot be considered essential to the Christian church or its faith. Hatch saw,

on the far horizon—the horizon beyond the fields which either we or our children will tread—a Christianity which is not new but old, which is not old but new, a Christianity in which the moral and spiritual elements will again hold their place, in which men will be bound together by the bond of mutual service, which is the bond of the sons of God, a Christianity which will actually realize the brotherhood of men, the ideal of its first communities.[9]

First, Hatch described the character of the church before and after the impact of Greek thought on Christian faith.

To be a Christian was to be a member of a community. The basis of the community was not only a common belief, but also a common practice. It was the task of the community as an organization to keep itself pure...In other words, the earliest communities endeavored, both in the theory which they embodied in their manuals of Christian life, and in the practice which they enforced by discipline, to realize what has since been known as the Puritan ideal. Each one of them was a community of saints. 'Passing their days upon earth, they were in reality citizens of heaven.'... to be excluded from the community was to pass again into the outer darkness, the realm of Satan and eternal death.[10]

Hatch noted that in the last half of the second century and the first half of the third, an enormous change took place in the churches. The emphasis shifted from a moral and spiritual to an intellectual base, from godly behavior to correct theology, from purity of life to consistency of theological speculation. This changed the church from a company of people who lived right, to one that held correct opinions.

In both the production of this change and its further developments Greece played an important part. The net result...was, that the attention of a majority of Christian men was turned to the intellectual as distinguished from the moral element in Christian life.[11]

Another change occurred in the church from the influence of Greek rhetoric, the art of speech-making. It gradually changed the nature of the Christian meeting from a kind of family gathering around a common table, to a performance by a professional orator before an audience. Hatch described the change.

Christianity...came into the educated world in the simple dress of a Prophet of righteousness. It won that world by the stern reality of its life, by the subtle bonds of its brotherhood, by its divine message of consolation and of hope. Around it thronged the race of eloquent talkers who persuaded it to change its dress and to assimilate its language to their own. It seemed thereby to win a speedier and completer victory. But it purchased conquest at the price of reality. With that its progress stopped. There has been an element of sophistry in it ever since...many of its preachers live in an unreal world. The truths they set forth are truths of utterance rather than truths of their lives...Such are some of the indications of the influence of Greek Rhetoric upon the early churches. It created the Christian sermon.[12]

We have already considered the Christian scholar Origen, who sought to harmonize Plato's philosophy with the Bible by interpreting the Bible as if it were an allegory, as if the Bible wasn't intended to mean what it said, but was talking about something else. But there was more than that. Not only did the Greek mind alter the contents of the Christian revelation, it also modified the truth of Scripture by its methodology.

The Greek philosophical method required its devotees to define terms and then to speculate, that is, to "draw inferences from the definitions the philosophers made, to weave the inferences into systems, and to test assertions by their logical consistency or inconsistency with those systems."

> The earliest Christians had but little conception of a system. The inconsistency of one apparently true statement with another did not vex their souls. Their beliefs reflected the variety of the world and of men's thoughts about the world. It was one of the secrets of the first great successes of Christianity. There were different and apparently irreconcilable elements in it. It appealed to men of various mould. It furnished a basis for the construction of strangely diverse edifices. But the result of the ascendancy of philosophy was, that in the fourth and fifth centuries the majority of churches insisted not only upon a unity of belief in the fundamental facts of Christianity, but also upon a uniformity of speculations in regard to those facts.

> The holding of approved opinions was elevated to a position at first co-ordinate with, and at last superior to, trust in God and the effort to live a holy life.[13]

Hatch pointed out that while revelation applies to the facts of Christian faith, the speculation on those facts "are *dogmas* in the original sense of the word. They are simply personal convictions... The belief that metaphysical theology is more than [someone's opinion] is the chief bequest of Greece to religious thought."[14] As to ethics, Hatch declared that the victory of Greek ethics was complete. While Christianity was being transformed into a system of doctrines, the Stoical jurists at the imperial court were slowly elaborating a system of personal rights. The ethics of the Sermon on the Mount, which the earliest Christian communities endeavoured to carry into practice, have been transmuted by the slow alchemy of history into the ethics of Roman law. The basis of Christian society is not Christian, but Roman and Stoical.[15]

Hatch appealed to the experience of the people of his time—it is equally applicable today—that the Sermon on the Mount is not only dismissed as impracticable but is generally considered undesirable.[16] He concluded that the clash of the gospel with the Greek mind ended in a compromise. It appeared that Christianity had won a great victory, but that was a deception with serious ramifications for the church.

It was in reality a victory in which the victors were the vanquished. There was so large an absorption by the original [Christian] communities of the principles of their opponents as to destroy the main reason for a separate existence.[17]

With the church in a compromised relationship with the Greco-Roman world, the ideal Christian came to be exemplified by the hermits who separated from the compromised church in protest.[18] The father of this movement, called monasticism or asceticism, was Antony of Egypt. Antony was a hermit. The word *monastic* means one, or solitary. Another term, *anchorite*, is applied to the same movement. It refers to one who separates himself from others, or goes on a permanent and solitary retreat, not only from the world but from the impure church that has absorbed so much of the world. The other term applied to the movement, *ascetic*, refers to the discipline adopted by the monks. These disciplines were also picked up from the Greek philosophers.

Just as ordinary philosophers had sometimes found life in society to be intolerable and had gone into "retreat," so the Christian philosophers began to withdraw altogether from the world, and to live their lives of self-discipline and contemplation in solitude.[19]

Even when the monks joined together in communities, as they eventually did, the disciplines they adopted were essentially the individualistic disciplines developed by Antony in his lonely service to God. They were patterned on the disciplines of the Greek Stoic philosophers. An extreme example of this individualism that has survived to the present is the order of Trappist monks who, although they live together communally, do not speak to one another, but only to God.

> [T]o Greece, more than to any other factor was due the place and earliest conception of that sublime individualism which centered all a man's efforts on the development of his spiritual life, and withdrew him from his fellow-men in order to bring him near to God.[20]

In the main body of the church the waning commitment to God and the fading of hope in the future kingdom undermined the bond of love and unity that had once existed very powerfully and recognizably in the churches. That love had been a key part of their witness, and had given credibility to the Gospel which was preached by the apostles, prophets, and evangelists. The church illustrated or "adorned" the doctrine.

But when Christianity became the official religion of the Roman Empire, people poured into the church and the distinction between the church and the world was to all practical purposes obliterated. The bond of Christian love that characterized the early Christians disappeared when the illusion arose that everybody was a Christian.

The relational element, so crucial to the New Testament, was lost to the main body of the church by the breakdown of the standards of membership. And in the monastic discipline, which was held up as exemplary of a serious commitment to Christ, the ideal was a solitary search for God by especially virtuous and gifted individuals. The monks acted for the most part in isolation and independence from other Christians, even from other monks. The relational element was lost there, too. Monasticism and asceticism were themselves Greek ideas developed by the stoic philosophers and added to the Christian revelation like feathers on a horse.

The Stoics thought that a philosopher should adopt an austere lifestyle consistent with his doctrines. To live consistently with one's beliefs was a good idea, but the radically individualistic discipline of the stoic was alien to Christian faith, and the austerity of the stoics was in a whole different category from the cross of the New Testament. Nevertheless, the stoic ideal became the ideal of the monastic movement, and the monastic movement became the ideal of devotion to God in Christendom. In the spiritual quest, therefore, it was every man for himself in a church hardly distinguishable from the world.

The church ceased to be a family where believers were reared in the nurture and admonition of the Lord as citizens of the kingdom of heaven. It ceased to witness to the loving God by the love believers showed to one another. The church became instead a kind of preaching station where individuals might pursue their private quest for God. And if they merely attended services without pursuing God, that was all right, too. The system produced an occasional "saint," but the church as a whole was at best lukewarm with the large majority of members religiously indifferent. It survives today in the passive pew-sitters of what has been called spectator Christianity.

In the absence of the love and unity that characterized early church life, the relational test of true faith gave way to the intellectual. And because the church was conceived as embracing the whole society, there was no way that the established church could maintain the old standards of godly living that the church had held when it was composed of committed and regenerated believers only. Discipline broke down. Religious ceremony took the place of the experience of the Holy Spirit. Correct opinion was foremost, and that opinion was expressed in Greek categories and modes of thought. The official church became Greek in its thought patterns. And Greek thought was individualistic, intellectual, and competitive.

This is our heritage as the heirs of Christian civilization. The Greek mind is in our culture and in our churches. It is natural to us, for the Greek mind, after all, is simply the human mind, the mind of the flesh, refined, cultivated, educated, efficient, and independent. The Greek mind is the mind of the self—mankind—raised to its highest potential. It finds its expression today in the slogan, "be all that you can be." The slogan fails to take into account the fallen and corrupted state of mankind. The gospel, on the other hand, faces man's fallen condition head-on. It is not the means of doing your best and fulfilling yourself, it is the crucifixion of self, and putting one's faith in Jesus Christ. It is the end of independence, the restoration of the wholeness and oneness that Satan broke by his ambition to exalt himself and fulfill himself in heaven. Lucifer infected the whole human race with his independence and self-exaltation. And he found a way to insinuate his own evil passion into the Christian community. This particular deception works so well because it comes to us in the guise of something good, something that feels natural.

Greek philosophy gained access to the church, and provided a cover for the flesh, a place where the intellectual aspects of fallen human nature could hide out undetected and escape the cross. The devil had a button of flesh he could push whenever he needed to disable the church. He made room in the church for disputes, for bitter conflicts and power struggles among leaders, for selfish ambition and hatred, by hiding these fleshly impulses under the cloak of a doctrinal, an intellectual, issue. Christians could excuse their selfish ambition, their bitter competitive struggles by assuring themselves that they were defending the true faith. The combatants thought they were doing God service as they fought among themselves.

There is something in us, native to our fallen nature that wants to be independent—even when it addresses faith in God. It wants to create a theology or a church structure or an evangelism so good and so efficient that it can operate effectively even without God, independently of God. And of course, if we want to be independent of God, how much more will we want to be independent of other people. The irony is, we can do this with sincerity and earnestness, conviction and zeal.

T. Austin-Sparks put it in these searching words spoken not to sinners but to earnest, spiritual Christians:

> If we were asked straight out whether we wanted to please ourselves, whether we were after our own personal gratification, whether it was our pleasure and satisfaction that was motivating our lives and directing us, we would at once most vehemently repudiate the suggestion, and probably be very offended with whoever made the suggestion; and yet, beloved, deeper than our deepest honesty, deeper than our truest sincerity, there is that subtle constituent of fallen nature which so often unperceived by the believer himself or herself does just love to be gratified, personally

satisfied, and which does not like to be emptied out and have nothing. Gratification and glory is the very essence of the flesh even when we are engaged in the Lord's work. To set up something *for the Lord*, yes, but men point at it and say: 'That is his work and her work,' and how we like that! Something that will be a good testimony to faith, a great monument—yes, but subtly the monument to *our* faith. Such is this horrible thing that is always reaching out from beneath, under cover, and, quietly and imperceptibly, taking the glory of the Lord to itself.

The remedy for that is the Body of Christ practically applied in principle. Yes, it is! That is why it is so difficult to live a corporate life with other believers, because you have to be so thoroughly crucified. There is nothing that demands crucifixion more than to live with other Christians all your days. You say: 'That is a terrible thing to say,' but you know what I am talking about. You have to defer, refer, consult, submit, let go. In a thousand and one ways you have to put your own likes and dislikes aside if the Lord is to get His end. Oh yes, it is the body of Christ that is the saving thing. It is corporate life that is the remedy, but O beloved, that is the way of triumph, the way of victory. It is! It is a mighty remedy for the flesh, a mighty remedy for the work of the Devil, but it does represent the mighty power of God working in us. You see, you can never come into the Body of Christ until you have been crucified. It is because uncrucified flesh has impinged upon the corporate life of believers that there is such contradiction and denial, because the Body represents the exclusion of man, in himself—flesh.[21]

Austin-Sparks explained the importance of the Church's witness to Christ by its unity. Lucifer's rebellion consisted in his declaration of independence from God, his self-exaltation over God. The devil lured the original man into the same independence and rebellion on earth that he (Satan) had staged in heaven.

[F]rom that time the principle of the fallen race is independence, self-direction, self-realization, self-possession; the flesh is just that, and that lies back of the whole terrible history of the revolt in heaven and the wreckage in earth. There is no unity until Christ comes, God in Christ.

In His obedience unto death, Christ overcame the devil. God raised Him from the dead, and raised up the Church by the same power that raised Christ from the dead.

The Church, the Body of Christ represents God's victory over the disintegrating, dividing, schismatic work of the Devil. The Body is His victory in the sense that it is the reversing of all independence.

I shall have very little hope against the enemy in a detached capacity; but if I can bring in the Body, even if it is only in two or three gathered into His Name, that represents the Body, and the principle of the Body in function and representation is there...He is in the midst. The Lord's irreducible minimum for His Body is two, not one. Bring in the Body even by its minimum representation and the Lord recognizes the full value of the Body...If it is Christ, only Christ, central and supreme, we have got the answer to the Devil; we have got the secret of victory, we have got the secret of fellowship, we have the power of His resurrection.

But beloved, the unity is not in us, it is in Christ; the unity is not our unity, it is the unity of Christ...Now you see the necessity for Christ to be central and supreme...[I]f we have got any other interest that we are trying to further...perhaps a system of teaching, or a fellowship, or a denomination...the history will be still more divisions, it is bound to be...[For] independence of spirit or action is a violation not only of the truth of the Body of Christ, but of the power of His resurrection...[22]

The warning is necessary. Satan has succeeded in short-circuiting the power of the resurrection, not as it is in itself, but as it is appropriated by believers, by undermining their faith in the truth and unity of the body of Christ. He was able to do it by distracting the church from Christ with ideas, systems and methods of thought derived from Greek philosophy.

The recovery of the Bible with the Reformation of the fifteenth and sixteenth centuries began the process of church reform. But as Jesus Himself said, the Bible points to Him. It is only as we grasp the central position of Christ that unity and purity will be attained. The church is like a solar system with Jesus Christ as the sun and every member a planet in orbit around Him. The only way to avoid collisions is to make sure that Christ is at the center of everything we do as a church. If we are orbiting around anything or anybody else, or if we are trying to make ourselves a central sun with others in orbit around us, we will find ourselves colliding with one another.

The centrality of Jesus Christ is a hard lesson to learn. Church reform has therefore been a long, slow process requiring many revivals and experiencing many setbacks. It is not yet complete. In the process of revival and reform, the disentangling of Christian faith from Greek philosophy and Roman politics is the issue least understood, the last to be addressed, and the slowest to be implemented. That is partly because this particular deception is bound up with our ideas—Greek ideas—of orthodoxy.

26

New Testament Orthodoxy

Does the New Testament indicate some way by which to identify true disciples? Does it contain, in other words, the equivalent of a test of orthodoxy? As I pondered the question, I recalled a couple of verses I memorized years ago. Jesus himself spoke the words to his disciples on the night of his betrayal. They were among the last things he said to his closest followers just before His greatest ordeal.

Jesus said: "By this shall all men know that you are my disciples." That, it seems to me, is a statement about orthodoxy. It points to a standard by which one may know who are the authentic disciples of Jesus. Jesus did not want it to be a mystery. Evidently, He did not think it a mark of humility that his disciples should not know how to identify one another or discern true faith. The fact is, Jesus said there is a way by which all people will know who His real disciples are.

This test is not something discernible only by mystics or theologians or initiates of some exclusive inner circle. All will recognize the disciples of Jesus, even their enemies. But you have to know what to look for, and we haven't been taught to look for orthodoxy where Jesus told us to look. The standard he set up is a relational rather than an intellectual one. Jesus said, "By this all shall know that you are my disciples, if you have love for one another."[1]

That raises the question, what is love? And here is the genius of the Lord's kind of orthodoxy. Love is defined for Christians by the example of Jesus. He had just told them, "a new commandment I give to you, that you love one another; as I have loved you, that you also love one another."[2]

What is new about it? We have already been commanded to love God with all our heart and soul and mind and strength, and our neighbors as ourselves. Jesus stressed those two commandments as the key to the whole law.[3] The command to love was already revealed in the law of Moses.[4] What was new was Jesus in the flesh. The disciples knew the commandment to love; they did not know its full intent until Jesus lived it out before them. In Him we see the love of God in action. And that was why the commandment was new. Nobody had seen pure love in action before Jesus came. He revealed it. The command is inseparable from Jesus and his example.

New Testament orthodoxy, if I can use the term, consists in loving our fellow believers in the same way Jesus loved us. The Lord did not teach one thing and do another; His teaching explained His life and His life illustrated His teaching. And His teaching and His example were about love. So we are not talking about warm, fuzzy feelings, or the recitation of creeds, or the observance of rules; we are talking about the life of Jesus. We are not talking about disembodied doctrines, we are talking about the teaching of Jesus as expressed in His lifestyle of love, suffering and sacrifice. Love is defined by Jesus and the way He loved His disciples. He laid down His life for them, and for us. And we are commanded to love one another in the same way.

> Beloved, let us love one another, for love is of God; and everyone who loves is born of God and knows God. He who does not love does not know God, for God is love. In this the love of God was manifested toward us, that God has sent His only begotten Son into the world, that we might live through Him. In this is love, not that we loved God, but that He loved us and sent His Son to be the propitiation for our sins. Beloved, if God so loved us, we also ought to love one another. No one has seen God at any time. If we love one another, God abides in us, and His love has been perfected in us.[5]

In other words, the invisible God who is love becomes visible in the relationship among believers when they love one another. The disciples of Jesus demonstrate God's existence and character when they love one another in the same self-sacrificing way that Jesus loved them. That is, they demonstrate what the kingdom of God is like.

Discipleship necessarily involves fellowship. You can't live it in isolation. Neither can you live it in an impersonal institution in which most of the people are strangers to one another. Furthermore, Christian love is not developed in an institutional setting in which the officials are concerned about establishing themselves and their institutions in a place of preeminence over other leaders and other institutions. But if you want to follow Jesus and be His disciple, you can do it with a few others who share the same desire. It begins by asking, not what my brother can or ought to do for me, but what I can or ought to do for my brother. Scripture says that God is love. The kind of love that God is was translated, as it were, into human terms by the example of Jesus. His kind of love is one that gives, not one that takes. Jesus said, "It is more blessed to give than to receive,"[6] and His life shows us in practice what His teaching meant.

In the thirteenth chapter of John, in which Jesus gave the disciples his new command to love one another, he began his teaching with a simple amenity. He washed the disciples' feet. In that ancient middle eastern culture washing someone's feet was as normal as it is for us to help our guests take off their coats when they enter our houses. The streets were dusty. Sandled feet got dirty. It was conventional courtesy to provide a basin and towel and to wash the feet of a visitor, particularly a visitor one respected. Jesus did that for his disciples. It was love in the commonplace affairs of life, in the little things. Its design was to show the disciples in a small but important matter that He loved them, that they were important to Him.

But Jesus made a kind of sacrament out of that little act of kindness and respect. As He did with so many commonplace things, this became an object lesson, a sermonette. His conversation with Peter was like that. Peter thought it was beneath the dignity of the Messiah to wash a disciple's feet. Peter would have been glad to wash Jesus' feet. He didn't think the Lord should wash his feet.

Jesus told Peter, "If I don't wash your feet you have no part with me."

Peter responded something like this, "Well, then, give me a bath."

I imagine Jesus smiling at Peter's remark, and then making it clear he wasn't talking about conversion and salvation, represented symbolically by baptism, the bath of regeneration. He was talking about the ordinary affairs of life. Simply walking through this world leaves a film of dust on the skin, particularly on the feet which are closest to the ground. Jesus washed off that film of dust and dirt. It was an act of humble service.

There wasn't a word of criticism about the dirt. The Lord was not annoyed by it. He didn't rebuke His disciples for tracking in dust and dirt, didn't order them curtly to wash their feet. It was more like the attention a father shows to his son or a wife to her husband to make sure the wrinkles are smoothed out, the collar is straight, that this beloved person is at his best. It is an act done with an accepting and affectionate smile, not a frown or a rebuke. It is the spiritual side of courtesy. It's the way the nobility of the kingdom of God act toward one another. It is simply good manners, a small thing, but so very important. It was an act of love and affection. It is the lubricant of the body of Christ that allows the many parts to interact without grinding and causing pain.[7]

But much more was at stake in that final evening together. The Lord Jesus was about to go to His death. He was about to pick up the tab, not just to pay for the evening meal for himself and the disciples, but the price of sin itself. He was the responsible one, the way a good father is responsible for his family. The father pays the bills, puts in the long hours in the field or in the shop. He is there to provide, to protect, to instruct, to correct, to console, to encourage, to help. His eye is on the best interest of all His children. It is a long range vision. So it is with Jesus. "He who has seen me has seen the Father."[8] He sees the end—what His children will be at maturity and in the kingdom of God. He wants for them everything they need to attain to God's best for them. He wants nothing to damage them or rob them of anything they need to arrive at God's intended purpose for them. And that purpose is nothing less than everlasting life, joy, peace and happiness in the kingdom of God.

So He will stand between them and the devilish attacks that threaten them. He will do it Himself. Nobody else is able. But Jesus wants to inculcate in His disciples the same attitude He has. He wants them to be responsible ones who, like Him, will be protectors and providers, correctors and consolers, encouragers and helpers, too.

The cycle has to be completed. We touch the Savior and we are saved. Then, with the salvation He has given us, we touch others in His name and they too are saved. They in turn touch others, and so on.

It's not a numbers game. The object is not competitive, to see how many more lives you can touch than somebody else, but how purely and unselfishly you can touch those you touch, whether many or few. For you cannot be a clean conduit for the love of Jesus if you are trying to promote your church over somebody else's church. You cannot be a clean conduit for the love of Jesus if you are trying to make a name for yourself in the process, or gain material benefits. You cannot be a clean conduit for the love of Jesus if you are trying to impress somebody with your gifts and graces, or demonstrate your superiority over somebody else. That's not how Jesus did it, nor why He did it. All He wanted to do was the will of God. That's all that was required of Him. And all we can do is the will of Jesus for us. That's all He requires of us. Love is enough. And that pure love is recognizable.

The pagans recognized the pure love of God in the early days of the faith when the church was still pure. They cried out in amazement tinged with envy and frustration, "These Christians! How they love one another!" On the one hand, they hated the Christians. On the other hand, they saw something real and wonderful that they couldn't help respecting and wanting. They gave the early Christians a grudging admiration. The reason was, the early Christians, in contrast to the typical pagans, cared for one another and helped one another. They laid down their lives for their brothers and sisters. They loved one another and the pagans noticed it and recognized them as disciples of Jesus.

The Pilgrims, who came to this continent when it was a "howling wilderness" to set up the first Christian settlement in New England, loved one another. They were called "separatists." They separated from the Anglican Church and were persecuted. They fled to Holland where there was greater freedom to practice their faith. But life was hard there and they were Englishmen. They wanted to preserve their English culture. So they came to the new world under an English charter.

There were a hundred and two passengers on the Mayflower, a ship about ninety feet long and twenty four feet wide with three masts. There was a crew of between fifteen and twenty men who were not serious Christians. The boatswain, a crude and arrogant young man, made it a practice to mock and curse the believers. It was a long voyage and they landed far north of Virginia, their intended destination. It was not a hard winter as New England winters go, but it was more than they were prepared for and they lacked adequate shelter.

During that first year there was a lot of debilitating sickness. All but two were sick at one time or another. Forty-six died that first year. Those who were able cared for those who were sick. The Christians looked after one another. They did those little, unpleasant tasks like cleaning up the vomit and the excrement of their ailing brothers and sisters who were too weak and sick to help themselves.

There was sickness among the crew, too. The boatswain who had cursed the passengers, confessed to William Bradford, "O, I now see that you show your love as Christians to one another, but we let one another lie and die like dogs." The crew recognized the Pilgrims as true disciples of Jesus by their love for one another as they risked their lives to establish a colony of the kingdom of God in the new world.[9]

Love of believers for one another is the identifying mark of true disciples. But that love also reaches out to neighbors and even enemies. Mother Teresa attracted a lot of attention by the sacrificial care she and her Sisters of Charity showed to the poorest of the poor. But she and her little band of Christian women cared for the poor that they found on the streets of Calcutta for a long time before anybody noticed. And they never did it to be noticed.

Somebody once asked her about her work. "There are millions of poor and homeless people living on the streets of Calcutta. The task must seem overwhelming. How do you do it?"

Her answer was simple and beautiful: "One at a time."

In her book she explained her conviction more fully. "Remember, it is the individual that is important to us. In order to love a person, one must come close to him or her. If we wait until there is a given number of people, we will get lost in numbers and will never be able to show respect and love for one concrete person. To me, every person in the world is unique."[10]

I am sure there are points of doctrine about which I would disagree with Mother Teresa. But I find myself in agreement with her central message: the love of Jesus Christ. And I have found some personal encouragement in her words which explain her life and work.

My wife takes care of elderly people. She doesn't have an RN degree. But the professionals who know her and have seen her work respect her. They say she has the gift. She makes sure the old folks are clean and fed and comfortable. She makes sure they look good and smell good. She cleans them up and does things for them that they are too feeble to do for themselves any more. And she does it in a way that doesn't rob them of their dignity. Her gift is that she loves them. And people recognize it and appreciate it. I can testify that she also loves me and our children and grandchildren. She gets it from Jesus. Charity begins at home, as the saying has it. She doesn't reach the number of people Mother Teresa reached. But the few people whose lives she touches she touches with the love that God is and that Jesus exemplified in a human body. And for now, that's all the Lord is asking of her.

Like a lot of other people, I have been hurt and disappointed by the church in its present condition. But I have known some Christian people who, in spite of their human weaknesses and limitations, really loved with the love of Jesus Christ. They were honest with one another, didn't take advantage of others, and they sacrificed and suffered in order to help their brothers and sisters. They took the time, opened their hearts, and shared the things, the personal things that were dearest to their hearts. They shared what they had learned of God and His Son, Jesus. And when the situation called for it, they shared their money and their muscle, their skills and their possessions.

There was something precious and real there—more precious than money or fame or power. It's the love that God puts into the hearts of His people. I have tasted the real thing. And in spite of the pain that comes my way, I can't deny or forget that I have also known and experienced the real thing: the love of Jesus Christ. And I haven't given up hope. I still believe in the church. One day soon I shall see the orthodox New Testament church, walking in truth, motivated by love, characterized by good works, purified and united.

Real love is hard to counterfeit. People know when they are being patronized or used rather than loved. Jesus did not exploit others to promote Himself. He exploited Himself in the interest of those who believed in Him. What He said and did led to His being opposed by the powerful and wealthy. He was a threat to them because He was genuine, and His love for the poor and needy exposed the hypocrisy of the leaders. Those who wielded power and influence plotted against Him, set a trap for Him, rigged a phony trial, and arranged for His death in the most painful and degrading manner possible.

He taught and lived the truth, not for the sake of money; he was and remained a poor man. He didn't do it to make a name for Himself in this world; the fact is, He didn't have a good reputation in the society into which He was born and in which He lived and died. The influential and powerful in that society made sure of that. He didn't do it for the sake of power. He never sought a place of influence and authority in the society of His time.

What could possibly have motivated someone to do what Jesus did? His own explanation is the only one that makes any sense. He did it out of love for God and for the people God the Father had given Him. People recognized the purity of His love. He laid down His life for His friends. There is no greater love than that.

It is interesting the way the Lord put his teaching about orthodoxy. He said, "by this all will know that you are my disciples, if you have love one for another." He didn't give a test for recognizing institutions, organizations, and structures as being composed of His disciples. He exposed the institutions of His day by their failure to measure up to this test. Perhaps the structures that we know today as churches are likewise incapable of being identified as Christ's. Perhaps one reason the theologians resorted to a doctrinal or philosophical and theological test was because it was obvious that their institutions were not living up to the standard Jesus actually set.

But it remains true that when the disciples of Jesus are living in the kind of love Jesus exhibited, it will be recognized by all people. It may not be appreciated and people will not necessarily want to join such a group. In fact, those who express this kind of love will be hated and persecuted. But their love will be recognized even by their enemies.

One day the secret and hidden things will be revealed.[11] But even before that awful revelation, there will be on this earth a church that is indeed the church. The disciples of Jesus Christ will be recognized by their love for one another. All will know that they are disciples of Jesus. They will live the kind of life He lived. They will not seek for power and money. They will not try to embrace the whole world with a diluted and impure love; rather they will love one another in truth and purity as Jesus has loved them.

We are God's beloved children, not His clients or subjects. Our leaders are brothers, friends and servants, not executive officers or bosses. Our goal is righteousness, truth and love, not wealth, knowledge and power. We seek to glorify God, not ourselves. Our goal is the glory of God and Christ and the well-being of the whole body. Together, we are the bride of Jesus Christ. All are beloved, valued and cared for. Those who are the strongest, wisest and most gifted among us are the most humble, make the greatest sacrifices, and are watchful that none are neglected or belittled. Our ambition is not to rule, but to serve. We are neither exploiters nor exploited, neither slaves nor masters. We are not divided by race or class or economic status or education or intellect or occupation. We are not competitors, but brothers and sisters. We are not an institution, but a family.

What does a healthy family do? Lots of things—as many different things as there are different gifts and callings among the members of the family. The important thing is not what they do but why. They do it because they love God and love one another. And that, in Jesus' view, is Christian orthodoxy.

27

The Church At The End Of The Age

Back in the seventies Juan Carlos Ortiz confessed, "Our church grew from two hundred people who didn't love one another to six hundred people who didn't love one another."[1] Ortiz was more candid than most pastors. They would be satisfied with the amazing church growth and not raise any question about the quality of the relationship among the members. But the question Ortiz raised is a crucial one. It has to be raised. Statistics show that millions of Americans claim to be born-again Christians. But those statistics stand side by side with others that point to an astonishing increase in immorality and violence. A Gallup poll concluded that there is little difference in moral behavior between those who go to church and those who don't.[2]

The church revealed in the New Testament is a church characterized by love of the members for one another, by their unity and their practical righteousness. Unity, love and righteousness among believers are crucial issues. They are crucial issues because Jesus made them so. Consider His prayer for the unity of His disciples. He asked the Father "that they may be one, as thou and I are one."

Jesus asked for the church to be united with the supernatural bond that holds the Father and the Son together. That is an astonishing request. That prayer will certainly be answered. How could the prayer of the Messiah, the Son of God, not be answered? And the answer will be obvious. Jesus framed the prayer in such a way as to make it clear what kind of answer He expected. It would be visible. He asked "that they may be one in Us, that the world may believe that You sent Me."[3]

It is clear from the context that the word *world* in this passage (John 17) is used to denote the evil system under the control of

265

Satan, a system opposed to God and Christ, and will oppose the kingdom of God with an unprecedented intensity at the end of the age. Even this evil world will be convinced that Jesus has been sent by God. And how will the people of the world come to believe that Jesus is the Messiah? By the unity of those who believe in Him, those who are His true followers.

The world has tried repeatedly to unite mankind, and has not been able to accomplish it. But Jesus will bring about a unity among His true disciples in the last days. The world has a different agenda and is bitterly opposed to the purposes of God, but it will be in awe of the unity produced by Jesus Christ in the Holy Spirit. The world will attempt to achieve such a unity and will not be able.

The prayer of Jesus will be answered, but it is clear that the prayer has not yet been answered. For the church is divided into thousands of pieces. The church is a joke in the world for its many divisions. Our human efforts have not achieved the unity for which Jesus prayed. But God will do it. The time is coming when God will unite the people of Jesus in a way that will convince, not just believers but the world—the skeptics, the unbelievers, even those who hate God and Christ—that Jesus is the Messiah sent by God the Father. They will see and believe because the unity men have tried in vain to create since they first began to build the tower of Babel, will have been accomplished in the church by Jesus Christ.

The belief of which Jesus speaks in this prayer is, of course, not the redemptive belief that converts the soul to God. The world will believe only because its representatives will be unable to deny a fact that is too obvious to dispute. It will be like the situation in the book of Acts in which it is recorded that the Jewish authorities who wished above all things to silence and discredit the apostles, could not deny that a notable miracle had been done through them. There were too many witnesses. It will be that obvious to the powers arrayed against the church in the last days, that the church is united and pure. This unity will be a sign. The sign will draw some people to Christ and the church. For the rest, it will be evidence against them in the day of judgment. They saw a miracle. They recognized the truth and believed it to be genuine, but rejected both the church and its witness to Jesus.

I say that it will happen in the time of the end, for it is part of the church's witness to Jesus as the Messiah. The unity of the body of Christ is the matrix in which our testimony is set, like the gold band in which a diamond is set in an engagement ring. We are engaged to Christ. The church is the band, the setting in which Christ is displayed like the shining, multi-faceted diamond. The ring signifies our unity. Our unity sets off the splendid truth about Jesus in a beautiful and compelling way. We ourselves, in our life together, are the evidence of the gospel we proclaim and of its power to change human nature. We demonstrate by our lives that Jesus gives human beings the capacity to love other human beings and to be united in a society of justice, peace and truth. Only Jesus can do that.

This is an important part of our testimony to Jesus. It is a testimony that must come in ordinary history, prior to the Second Coming of Jesus Christ. Some say it will come only when the Lord Jesus returns to the earth with His heavenly army in power and glory. I believe this witness of the church must take place before the Lord's return. For when Jesus comes in power and glory, He will bear witness to Himself and the whole world will see His glory. There will be no need for the church's testimony in that day. Now is the time when this testimony by the church is needed.

Now is the time for us to repent, for we have been depriving the Lord Jesus of the witness He deserves. We have hindered the unity of His people for which He has prayed. A friend of mine once said, "it is better to be divided over the truth than united in a lie." It is a clever saying, but it masks an evasion of responsibility. It is not the truth that has divided us, it is our selfishness and greed, our pride and self-exaltation. We have wanted to be lords instead of servants. We have insisted on building our own kingdoms rather than God's. We have been competitors rather than brothers. We have pursued the riches, the power and the wisdom of this corrupt world, rather than the truth, justice and love of the world to come. We have been more solicitous of Caesar than of Christ. We have wanted Caesar's protection and Caesar's favors, and we have not felt the need to depend on Christ. We have made the interests of this world our own, but we have not represented Christ's future kingdom. We have fought with one another over the issues of this corrupt world. And we have masked our power struggles with theological doctrines and rationalizations. We are like paper hangers trying to cover up gaping political and economic cracks with religious wall paper. Of course we are divided!

If we were willing to repent, take up the cross and follow in the footsteps of Jesus in practical obedience to the New Testament

Scriptures, and if we were in fact suffering for the sake of Jesus and the gospel, then we would not be fighting with one another over the details of theology.

During an historic naval battle between the English and the combined forces of the French and Spanish fleets, Lord Nelson, the British commander, came up on deck to find two of his officers arguing bitterly. They were so involved in their debate that they didn't see the commander approaching until he had grabbed both of them by a shoulder and spun them around until they were looking out to sea and the enemy ships. "Gentlemen," said Lord Nelson, "There is the enemy!"

Jesus is approaching His servants and they don't even notice. Soon they will feel His hand on their shoulders and hear His rebuke. He will spin them around until they see the battle and their real enemy. They will see the devil and his deceptions and the Lord will tell them as Nelson told his officers, "Gentlemen, there is the enemy!"

We, His church—and in particular the leaders of the church down through the ages up to and including the present—have given the enemies of Christ an occasion to blaspheme His name, challenge His Messiahship and mock the church. They can appeal to the New Testament itself, for the devil knows the Scriptures, and he will show his servants how to use it to advantage. Exhibit A for the accuser of the brethren is the New Testament prayer of Jesus. Exhibit B is a divided church. I imagine an enemy of God some time in the near future addressing the court of public opinion on television or the internet like a clever trial lawyer making his case:

> Jesus prayed that His people would be one—as the Father and the Son are one, no less. We have it on record. Those are His words. And then the "Messiah"—ah yes, the Messiah, the Christ—says that this marvelous, miraculous unity will convince the whole world that He—Jesus Christ—was sent by God. Wonderful! We are so indebted to the New Testament—the, ah, word of God—for those wonderful words—words which prove conclusively, do they not?, that Jesus cannot possibly be the Messiah, the Christ. For—on his own terms—if it takes the unity of the church to convince the world that Jesus is the Messiah, then

> there is no reason why anyone should believe in
> Jesus. For there is no company of people
> anywhere on the face of the whole earth more
> divided than the Christians.

The world and its prince have grounds to make this case and we have given it to him by our selfish ambition, our greed, our illicit compromise with the politics and philosophy of this corrupt world. Of course, it is the strategy of the Devil to sow division and hatred in the church. And then he mocks us for it. But the church fell into his trap and gave him the opportunity he wanted to mock our Lord. And therefore we must repent. We must take up our cross and follow Jesus. That much we can do by His grace. Other things must take place that only God and His holy angels can do. But we must do what Jesus tells us to do. God will take care of the rest.

For there will be—there must be—a united church on the earth before this age is over. There was a credible witness in the early days because the church, by its love and integrity gave its witness. There will be such a witness with integrity at the end. The Messiahship of Jesus requires it. His prayer requested it, and God the Father will surely grant it. This expectation is corroborated by other New Testament Scriptures which tell us that the Lord will present to Himself a bride (the church) who has made herself ready, who is pure and spotless when He comes to claim His kingdom and take His bride.[4]

But there is other scriptural evidence that in the last days there will be tremendous conflicts among those who are professing believers in Jesus Christ. Matthew 24 speaks of a time of crisis on the earth: wars, famines, epidemics, earthquakes, and persecution of believers.

> Then they will deliver you up to tribulation and
> kill you, and you will be hated by all nations for
> My names sake. And then many will be offended,
> will betray one another, and will hate one another.
> Then many false prophets will rise up and deceive
> many. And because lawlessness will abound, the
> love of many will grow cold. But he who endures
> to the end shall be saved. And this gospel of the
> kingdom will be preached in all the world as a
> witness to all the nations, and then the end will
> come.[5]

These prophecies seem contradictory. The Scripture says on the one hand that the church will be united, purified and will exhibit the love of God in the relationship of believers to one another. It says, on the other hand, that in reaction to the persecution and lawlessness of the last days, many will betray and hate one another. It is clearly referring to professing believers. Which of these prophecies are we to believe?

We must believe both, for both are true. The persecution of a lawless world will present a terrible crisis to the church. In response to the opposition and hatred of the world, professing Christians will have to decide whether to remain true to Jesus and the gospel or compromise with a lawless and anti-Christian world in order to avoid persecution. And of course, cooperation with an anti-Christian world will cause some professing believers to betray and hate those with whom they once worshipped as fellow Christians.

There is a revealing passage in the writings of Dietrich Bonhoeffer, the German theologian who lived during the church struggle in NAZI Germany in the 1930s and 40s. The passage gives us a close-up picture of what it was like when a powerful delusion was drawing many people to believe a lie, walk away from Jesus Christ and embrace a new and anti-Christian political faith. Here is how Bonhoeffer and his fellow believers experienced that apostasy during the Hitler years in Germany.

> There is hardly one of us who has not known what it is to be betrayed. We used to find the figure of Judas an enigma, but now we know him only too well. The air we breathe is so infested with mistrust that it almost chokes us. But where we have managed to pierce through this layer of mistrust we have discovered a confidence scarce dreamed of hitherto. Where we do trust we have learnt to entrust our very lives to the hands of others. In face of all the many constructions to which our actions and our lives have been inevitably exposed we have learnt to trust without reserve. We know that hardly anything can be more reprehensible than the sowing and encouragement of mistrust, and that our duty is rather to do everything in our power to strengthen and foster confidence among men. Trust will

always be one of the greatest, rarest and happiest blessings of social life, though it can only emerge on the dark background of a necessary mistrust. We have learnt never to trust a scoundrel an inch, but to give ourselves to the trustworthy without reserve.[6]

Bonhoeffer described the separation of the unconverted from those who truly believed in Jesus Christ during an era that anticipated so vividly the last days and the rise of the anti-Christ. The crisis Hitler precipitated divided the professing Christians from the confessing Christians, the false from the true. And the crisis itself, dangerous as it was for those who dared to believe in Jesus and follow in His steps, drew the believers together in a bond of love and trust they had never known before. The danger seems to have been necessary to produce that purification and unity.

Those who wear the white robes of purity are those who come out of great tribulation. They wash their robes and make them white in the blood of the Lamb.[7] Believers in the Lamb of God are purified by faith in the blood of the Lamb, but the purification occurs at a time of great suffering, persecution, and martyrdom.

Love, trust and unity are not easily learned. But they are the unmistakable characteristics of believers in Jesus Christ. Where these qualities exist and are exhibited, there is the church. It is a church which lives by hope, for its present experience is typically bitter, as it was for Jesus Himself in this world. No doubt Jesus experienced joy, but it was a joy based on what was to come, what His suffering would accomplish.[8] In this world He was "despised and rejected by men, a man of sorrows and acquainted with grief."[9]

Jesus in His Messianic ministry drew crowds of people who were said to believe in Him. But He did not accept their belief at face value. For example, we are told in John chapter eight that many believed in Jesus when they heard His teaching. At this point, modern evangelists have an altar call, end the meeting, and publish the results: so many (dozens, hundreds, or perhaps thousands) were saved. But Jesus didn't end the meeting with an altar call. He kept on preaching.

"If you abide in My word," He said, "you are My disciples indeed, and you shall know the truth, and the truth shall make you free." This raised objections. The people insisted that they were children of Abraham and were already free. Jesus went on to talk

271

about slavery to sin and their need to be set free from sin by the Son of God. He told them that if they were really children of Abraham they would do as Abraham did. They would believe in the Messiah who had now come as Abraham believed in the Messiah who would come in the future.

They challenged Him: "you are not yet fifty years old, and have you seen Abraham?"

Jesus answered, "Most assuredly, I say to you, before Abraham was, I AM." His words were profoundly offensive to that Jewish audience, for the name I AM is the name of God, a name so sacred that the Jews rarely spoke it. The people who initially believed in Him, now picked up stones to stone Him. Jesus hid himself from them, and miraculously passed through the crowd unhurt. His time had not yet come.

If it is Jesus who has gathered the crowds, the millions and millions of "believers" in our time, I do not deny it; He drew the multitudes in the first century. But we must expect that His appealing message will be followed by His "hard sayings." For it is a mixed multitude that is following Him, and they have come to Him with mixed motives. Many have come with earthly and selfish motives, looking for Jesus to make them rich in the material goods of this world. Others have come to Him for power and influence in this present evil world. Some want to harness the power of heaven to their own human and earthly agenda.

To them Jesus will say what He said in the first century to that large company of believers, "if you continue in my word, you shall know the truth, and the truth will make you free." And as in the early days, many will be offended. And many of those who started out believing will end up with stones in their hands ready to kill Him and His followers.[10]

But those who endure the hard sayings, and the persecution that will follow, will find a freedom and a love, a hope and a holiness that they have longed for but hardly believed was possible in this world. It will only come, however, as they renounce their earthly hopes and dreams and embrace the hope of the gospel and of the world to come. They will hear that word, "Arise, shine; for your light has come! And the glory of the LORD is risen upon you."[11]

When will this occur? At a time when "darkness shall cover the earth, and deep darkness the people; but the LORD will arise over you, and His glory will be seen upon you." The morning star appears at the darkest hour of the night. But it is the darkness just before the dawn. The morning star is a herald of that dawn which is not yet visible, but is about to break in splendor over the earth. The Lord's coming is near, and the morning star is arising in the darkness of this age.[12] It is arising in the hearts of those who not only believe but continue in the word of Jesus, who endure the offense of the cross and the hostility of sinners, and set their "hope fully upon the grace that is to be brought to you at the revelation of Jesus Christ."[13]

One of the most gut-wrenching pictures that came out of World War II was taken in Poland during the invasion in September 1939. Polish civilians were fleeing from the German troops. A wave of German Stuka dive bombers swooped down and strafed the crowded road. The picture shows a little girl kneeling beside her mother, tears running down her cheeks, her face registering anguish and terror, her hands on the lapels of the fallen woman's coat, shaking her mother in desperation, trying to wake her up.

The picture tells the tragic story of the cost of false hope and of a false Messiah. Under the spell of the false Messiah, Adolph Hitler, the German people built a war machine that in its day was a marvel of technical efficiency. Poland fell in a matter of days, like the mother who was machine-gunned to death and fell in the road, leaving a helpless child clinging to her coat.

We have seen a number of these false messiahs in our time. We shall see at least one more, far more evil and terrible than all the rest. And the technology he shall wield in that day will make him seem invincible. In fact, no earthly power will be able to resist him. God will allow it for a short time. He will allow it to show us what godless government is like, what it ends up doing, not only to its enemies, but also to the people it promises to save. We shall see evil stripped of its deceptive cloak and revealed as it is in all its horror, in all its ugliness and barrenness, in all its lies and bitter disappointments. It will be brief, but unforgettable.

In that day we shall hunger and thirst for righteousness, and for righteous government. We shall cry out for the true Messiah, Jesus Christ, to come again as He has promised to do.

The coming revival will bring about the return of the New Testament church. It was a church that lived by its hope, looked for the return of her Lord, and represented the future rather than the present. For the sake of that glorious hope the church kept itself pure and endured persecution and martyrdom in the present world.

The question is, how do we get from the kind of church we are now to that New Testament kind of church?

28

What Are We To Do?

The parable of the Wheat and the Tares shows us a panoramic view of Church History and calls our attention to two major turning points. One was caused by the devil; he corrupted and weakened the church by filling it with false believers. The other will be caused by the angels who will reverse the process at the end of the age, remove the false believers, and restore the church to its original vitality, purity and unity in time for the Lord's return.

The devil has messed everything up. The angels will fix it. The human servants of the Lord were instructed not to try to correct the situation by pulling weeds. Is there then anything for us to do? There is.

1. Be Careful About Assigning Blame

Christians have blamed one another for false doctrines, hypocrisy and various evils committed in the name of Christ which have disgraced His cause. There is truth to what they say about one another. For if there are weeds in the Lord's field, if there are false believers in the church, then it is inevitable that there will be false beliefs and evil behavior in the church as well. But we have to be careful here. Christians have a tendency to make generalized charges of corruption against other churches and other Christians. Those charges often contain an element of truth. But one can speak the truth and still be in error, if one's heart is impure, if one is, for example, holding on to bitterness and unforgiveness. And if so, one's truth, even if factually accurate, does not truly represent the heart of Christ.

Jesus laid the blame for the deplorable condition of the church on the devil. Both the plan and its execution were laid at the doorstep of Satan himself. And the entire church, while not altogether innocent, is a victim of the devil's cunning. Like Adam

275

and Eve, some of the church leaders succumbed to the devil's temptation. Adam was not exactly incorrect in his analysis of the problem when he blamed Eve, but a bitter quarrel between Adam and Eve was not going to solve the problem. Likewise, accusations hurled at Christians by other Christians is not going to solve the problem of the fall of the church that occurred during the reign of Constantine.

Furthermore, our Lord does not disown any part of this field simply because it is an ugly mix of wheat and weeds. It is "His field" and "His kingdom." Neither does He regard any part of the field as free of weeds. Jesus acknowledged it all, and He will deal with it in the time and way indicated in the parable of the Wheat and the Tares.

2. See The Church As Jesus Sees It

Jesus sees His church today as a field of wheat and weeds. He also sees it as it will be at the end: pure, holy, true and faithful. But He does not confuse the church as it is now with the church as it will be in that glorious day. Right now it is like a field of wheat and weeds. And that's how we have to see it.

The church today is not the church as it was on the Day of Pentecost when it was new and young, in love with Jesus, and when the believers loved one another dearly and sacrificially. It is a church which the devil has invaded, penetrated, defiled, and wounded deeply. But Satan has not destroyed it.

The church's sickness is not permanent, and it is not unto death. But it is real and undeniable. The church as we have inherited it is a church whose purity has not yet been restored. It is a divided church, whose original unity was broken because there can be no unity of wheat and weeds, of believers and unbelievers. And that's what the church is today, and what it will be until the angels gather the weeds out of the Lord's field. For that's not something we men can do and we shouldn't try to do it. But we do try. Like the farm hands in the parable, it is the first thing that occurs to us when we seriously contemplate a defiled church. We must make up our minds to leave that work to God and to the angels.

3. Don't Pull Weeds

The most grandiose church split in history occurred when the Pope of Rome and the Patriarch of Constantinople excommunicated each other and divided the institutional church in two. The church split occurred ostensibly over a point of doctrine.

After almost a thousand years there seems to be no way to remedy the regrettable situation. Because for either the Pope or the Patriarch to admit to error—not as men, but as heads of churches—would call into question the infallibility of one or the other church or maybe both. And that could undermine the whole structure and perhaps bring it (or them) crashing down to ruin.

It was a world-class split, but it is just a big example of the way Christian leaders often treat other Christian leaders and their churches. Protestant churches have been credited (by Roman Catholics) with more than 20,000 splits from the sixteenth century to the present. Division is one of the bitter fruits of Constantinian Christianity, and it is nothing more than weed-pulling. It is Christians defining one another, and often whole churches and denominations, out of the kingdom. We act and speak as if we men had somehow accomplished what the Lord has not assigned to us men, but to the angels. We act as if the job had already been done and our church had already emerged as pure wheat while the rest have been exposed as tares.

In the sixteenth century, Protestants and Catholics did this to one another. They declared one another heretics and apostates and anti-Christians in the same way that Communist dictators in the twentieth century declared their countrymen non-persons and then proceeded to imprison, torture and kill them. Christians also did this to one another, as if to prove the correctness of their doctrines by a body-count. In their zeal for a pure church or pure doctrine they went after other Christians they regarded as weeds with a fury. In the process, they uprooted much that was wheat. Fortunately, God has set limits on the damage a man can inflict on another man. Men may kill the body, not the soul.

Jesus will surely support whatever is right and true and He will oppose whatever is evil and false. But He will not take sides in our power struggles, our acrimonious disputes over doctrine and practice, or our mutual accusations and recriminations that have characterized so much of church history. Sometimes these disputes have broken out in bloody battles and carnage.

The teaching and the example of Jesus show us that we may suffer for the truth and we may die for the truth, but we may not kill for the truth. The only blood Jesus shed was His own.

It is instructive to consider the attitude our Lord took toward the competing sects of Judaism at His first coming. Presumably they all thought the Messiah would stand with them and against their competitors when He came. As a matter of fact, Jesus confirmed some of the central doctrines of the Pharisees. It turned out they were right in their beliefs about angels, spirits, and the resurrection of the dead. But the Messiah was devastating in His criticism of the Pharisees.

Jesus did not confirm the claims of the High Priests and the Sadducees in their disputes with the Pharisees. He had nothing to do with the Herodians. There is no mention in the New Testament of the Essenes, a separatist community. And although there were Zealots or rather, ex-zealots, among His disciples, the Lord's non-violent methodology was radically different from the Zealots' theology of armed revolt against Rome.

We may hope that the Lord will keep His church from the selfish insensitivity of so many of the leaders of Judea in the first century. But the Lord asked a searching question in regard to the state of His church as it will be at the time of His return. "When the Son of man comes, will He find faith on the earth?"[1]

His viewpoint is higher than ours. We are still in a field of wheat and tares. There have been many revivals that have anticipated the crisis of the last days as the power of the world-to-come broke into human history at various points and challenged the present evil world. At such times the church has been purified, and many of the offensive elements have already been removed. But all of those revivals were precursors of the last revival in which the final purification will occur.

Many of the sins and errors of the competing churches are due to the tares among them. As the angels remove the tares many offensive doctrines and practices will also disappear. Let us walk softly before Him and be careful how we deal with our fellow believers. In the words of the Apostle Paul, "Therefore judge nothing before the time, until the Lord comes, who will both bring to light the hidden things of darkness and reveal the counsels of the hearts. Then each one's praise will come from God."[2]

4. Confess Your Church's Sins

The work of restoring the Church's unity and purity is beyond our human capacity. We cannot do it, even instrumentally. It is a work expressly assigned to angels. But there is something we can do. We can pray.

Daniel's prayer at the end of the Babylonian captivity was a powerful and appropriate example for us. It moved the powers of heaven. The angels arose and the course of history was changed. The content of his prayer is especially instructive.

It was essentially a prayer of confession. Representing Judah and Israel before God, Daniel took responsibility for the sins of generations of Jews—the people, their kings and princes—sins of which Daniel was for the most part personally innocent. But instead of accusing and condemning others, he confessed those sins as if they were his own. And God moved heaven and earth to restore the Jews to their land.[3]

Does the New Testament show us an example of this kind of confession? The New Testament covers a relatively brief period of history, but we can infer that something like that happened even before the close of the New Testament period.

For example, consider the letter to the church at Ephesus, one of the seven churches addressed in the book of Revelation. The Lord held the church at the end of the first century responsible to maintain a corporate commitment made by the church at an earlier period in the church's history. It is possible that twenty five or thirty years (a generation) had elapsed between the time of the founding of the church at Ephesus and the time the letter was delivered. We can assume that the membership had changed substantially during that time due to the death of some members and the addition of new converts. But the letter is addressed simply to the church in Ephesus.

The church is assumed to have a continuing existence, a corporate existence that can outlive the individuals who comprise it at any given time. The church had a certain corporate personality, a corporate history, and a corporate responsibility. It was a divinely established corporation, if you will. Different individuals may be its representatives, may speak and act in the name of that church, at different points in its history.

It doesn't matter whether the individuals alive at the time were personally and individually responsible for the loss of the church's first love. As representatives of the corporate body, they were held responsible to repent as a church when the call for repentance was issued by the Lord. And repentance implies confession of sin.

This is not a case of one individual confessing the sins of another individual, but of representatives of a corporate body confessing sins committed in the name of that same body at an earlier period in the history of that body.

For instance, I do not claim to be able to make a confession or to repent on behalf of another person, say, Martin Luther. But I think I can and should, as an heir to the Protestant tradition and a member of a Protestant church, make confession and repent for the remarks Luther made against the Jews. I believe Luther was wrong and I believe it would be sin to do as he advised, that is, to persecute Jewish people. If that confession has never been made explicit, it needs to be now. The Jewish people need to know that Protestantism as it stands today has repudiated the sixteenth century error that the leader of the Protestant Reformation made in his time. As an individual, Luther will give account of himself before the Lord on the day of judgment, as I will have to give account of myself. But if I am given an understanding of Scripture in my times that Luther did not have in his times, I can and should act and speak according to the increased light the Lord has given in my times. In that sense, as a representative of a corporate body and a certain tradition within the Christian church, I can and should make confession for the corporate sins of the past within that church or tradition. If I know of an error in my church and tradition, and fail to renounce it, by my silence I give my tacit approval to wrongs my church or tradition has committed in the past. And I may thereby give encouragement to others in my church or tradition to repeat the same errors.

I read in a Youth With A Mission publication some time ago a touching story written by Ed Silvoso of Harvest Evangelism, about that kind of prayer. It took place in Aloha Stadium in Honolulu, Hawaii, following a March for Jesus. There was a dramatic sketch with music and dance of the history of the Church in that land, recalling that about 130 years ago Hawaii had the world's largest Church and a huge population of Christians.

But descendants of the missionaries who had brought the Gospel to the islands conspired with American businessmen to take away the land from the Hawaiian people. There was a political upheaval. The U. S. military got involved in a coup that deposed Queen Liliuokalani. In the wake of that betrayal, multitudes of Hawaiians left the Church. Silvoso wrote:

> Native Hawaiians sang and danced a song
> written by Queen Liliuokalani, forgiving those
> who had betrayed her and her people and pleading

with God for her nation...At that moment a direct descendant of the early missionaries...began to weep uncontrollably. He moved toward the native pastors and knelt before them, asking forgiveness on behalf of himself and his ancestors... Representatives of the U.S. Armed Forces did the same.[4]

It would have been easy to disclaim responsibility for that deed, and blame it on hypocrites and false believers who were not really part of the church. It would have been easy, but it would not have been altogether true, and it would not have changed anything. The confession did. Something stirred in the hearts of the people gathered in the stadium, and something broke in the heavens. A healing began.

It led to another spontaneous confession. "Dr. Paul Ariga from Japan said, 'I am here to repent on my behalf and on behalf of my nation, Japan, for Pearl Harbor and World War II. We have sinned. We have wronged you. We have committed indescribable atrocities....' His sobbing carried all over the stadium. A group of Christians representing many nations that had been victimized by Japan during World War II quickly surrounded Dr. Ariga and extended forgiveness."

If we confess our own sins, and forgive those who confess their sins against us, wonderful things will happen. It works for individuals, but also for nations and institutions. It will work for churches and religious traditions that have long histories. For God's forgiveness can span the centuries and heal ancient enmities that continue to this day from old grievances. Assigning blame and guilt to others, even if we are correct in our judgments, is usually a dead end. In any case, it will not work until we have first confessed our own sins. In the affairs of the church, if we will confess the sins of our own tradition first, rather than insisting on our own purity and laying the blame on Christians from other traditions, we will be closer to the truth and closer to the heart of God. The Spirit of God will move in the heavens, and on the earth in the hearts of believers. And the church will be purified and united. That is revival.

29

What Are We To Do?
(Continued)

5. Don't Try To Produce A Pure Church

God the Father, His Son the Messiah, and the angels will produce a pure, united church in the only way it can be done. The entire professing church, the whole field of wheat and tares, is the raw material for this coming church. And the time designated for this work is the time of the end. In the last days, the Lord will send His angels to do the job of separating them. First they will gather the weeds out of His kingdom, the false believers out of the church.

The method will be apostasy, a world-wide revolt against God and Christ, activated by a powerful delusion. Those whose hearts are not truly committed to God through Jesus Christ will find this delusion irresistible. They will renounce their faith in Jesus and follow the anti-Christ in an open revolt against God and His Son.

But the very pressures of that apocalyptic struggle will draw God's people close to Him, intensify their love for God and for one another, purify them and unify them. All this is crucial to prepare the church for its work for the kingdom and the battles of faith in the last days. For the final conflict is coming, and there will be no neutral parties and no way to avoid the struggle.

When Julius Caesar invaded Britain he left a few soldiers behind with instructions to burn the boats while the rest of the army marched to battle. From a hillside, Caesar's legions looked back at the smoke and saw that their boats had been destroyed. There was no escape. Retreat was not an option. They had no alternative but to fight. They did, and they won. The struggles ahead will be like that for the church. It will be clear in that day that there are only two choices: Christ or anti-Christ, God or the devil, eternal life or eternal punishment. Daniel foresaw these days and wrote:

> Those who do wickedly against the covenant he [the anti-Christ] shall corrupt with flattery; but the people who know their God shall be strong, and carry out great exploits. And those of the people who understand shall instruct many; yet for many days they shall fall by sword and flame, by captivity and plundering. Now when they fall, they shall be aided with a little help; but many shall join with them by intrigue. And some of those of understanding shall fall, to refine them, purify them, and make them white, until the time of the end...[1]

The purified, united church is what is left after the apostasy has run its course. As Scripture says, "But he who endures to the end shall be saved."[2]

6. Hear The Voice Of The Good Shepherd And Follow Him

Jesus has assured us that there will be one flock and one shepherd. But the way to make sure that we are part of His flock, is not by taking sides and slugging it out with other Christians in the doctrinal squabbles among competing churches. We are part of His flock by keeping close to the Good Shepherd, hearing His voice, and following Him.

> [Jesus said], I am the good shepherd; and I know My sheep, and am known by My own. As the Father knows Me, even so I know the Father; and I lay down My life for the sheep. And other sheep I have which are not of this fold; them also I must bring, and they will hear My voice; and there will be one flock and one shepherd.[3]

Whatever fold we belong to, we can be sure that the Good Shepherd has other sheep in other folds. Our concern is to stay close to the shepherd who gave His life for us. As we listen to His voice and follow Him, we will find ourselves in the same "one flock" with everybody else who is also listening to His voice and following Him.

7. Discern The True Servants Of Christ And Help Them

The voice of the Lord Jesus will often come through His servants in whom He dwells. Jesus told His apostles:

> He who receives you receives Me, and he who receives Me receives Him who sent Me. He who receives a prophet in the name of a prophet shall receive a prophet's reward. And he who receives a righteous man in the name of a righteous man shall receive a righteous man's reward. And whoever gives one of these little ones only a cup of cold water in the name of a disciple, assuredly, I say to you, he shall by no means lose his reward.[4]

It is the same message as in the parable of the sheep and the goats.[5] The sheep are those who enter into eternal life. The goats go into eternal punishment. The difference between them was that the sheep were those who ministered to Jesus in his need; the goats did not. But the sheep did not in fact help Jesus, Himself; they helped believers who were representing Jesus and doing His work.

Because they were doing His work and representing Him, they were in prison, or in want: hungry, thirsty, sick, a stranger needing lodging, naked and in need of clothing. The sheep did what they could to meet the needs of the servants of the Lord. Jesus said, "Inasmuch as you did it to one of the least of these My brethren, you did it to Me." The goats represent those who did not help the Lord's servants in their need, and therefore did not serve Jesus.

The Lord will judge us on our discernment, that is, our ability to recognize Christ in His people, even the least of His servants, and our willingness to help them. The issue is not simply ministering to the needy, although that is a good work. The parable tells us that we will be judged on the basis of service to Jesus, by serving those who are suffering and in need *because of their commitment to God and Jesus Christ and their service to Him.*

It is not simply doctrine or truth that we must discern, but the presence of Christ. The issue is not simplified for us by membership in a particular institution or denomination. There is no reward for those who support a minister who does not truly represent Jesus Christ, however faithful he may be to his church institution or tradition. We must recognize Jesus in the living human servants who represent Him, and help those people *because they are servants of our Lord.* There may be nothing wrong with belonging to a particular church or denomination, but that is not the basis for the Lord's judgment for or against us. He will judge us on our ability to recognize the servants of the Messiah when we encounter them and on our practical help in meeting their needs.

We must be prepared to encounter some of them outside our own denomination or church or tradition. Otherwise, we may not be ready when the defining moment comes to us and we meet one of Christ's brothers or sisters and are in reality encountering Jesus. We will find some of them in unexpected places.

8. Hold On!

In a football game a ball carrier has to expect to get hit. The tacklers will do everything they can, not only to knock him off his feet, but to jar the ball loose and make him fumble. In the same way, Christians must be prepared to be hit. The enemy will do what he can to strip Christians of their faith.

The apostle Paul exhorted the Thessalonian believers to hold on. That is essentially all it takes to survive the apostasy. Hold on to Jesus Christ. Hold on to your hope. Hold on to your faith in spite of trouble and persecution.

Paul had just taught them again about the revolt against God and Christ that is coming. He told them about the powerful deception, the delusion that will grip people who have no love for the truth. The deception will persuade them to believe the lie, and draw them away from Christ, out of the church and into the ranks of the rebels. But Paul fully expected these believers to whom he wrote to survive with their faith intact. Why?

Because they were people with a growing faith. Their love for one another was abundant. They clung to their faith in the midst of persecutions and tribulations. To Paul this was evidence that God counted them worthy of the kingdom of God, for which they were suffering.[6]

Paul thanked God for these believers. His wording is important. He did not congratulate them, he thanked God for them.

> But we are bound to give thanks to God always for you, brethren beloved by the Lord, because God from the beginning chose you for salvation through sanctification by the Spirit and belief in the truth, to which He called you by our gospel, for the obtaining of the glory of our Lord Jesus Christ.[7]

Paul saw their faith, and he wanted them to see their faith, as rooted firmly in God, and not in men. Their salvation began with the choice of God in the hidden counsels of eternity. It entered into their consciousness when they heard the gospel and believed. They were coming to salvation through the sanctification of the Holy Spirit and belief in the truth. There was credible evidence of their salvation in the purification the Holy Spirit was accomplishing in their lives through faith in the truth. And it will be consummated when the Lord Jesus returns. In that day they will share His glory, His eternal life, His victory over all evil, His righteous reign, when at last peace and justice, truth and love are established on the earth. That was their hope.

That's what they had and the apostle told them to hang on to it steadfastly. "Stand fast and hold the traditions which you were taught, whether by word or our epistle."[8] Paul had delivered these traditions himself, in word when he spoke to them in person, and in his letters. It wasn't enough just to listen to a teaching or read a letter. The teaching had to become a habit, a tradition, something put into practice on a regular basis.

This is not a general endorsement of any and all traditions that may take hold in the church in its trek through history. These were traditions which had already been established, and the Thessalonian letters were among the earliest documents in the New Testament. Jude made the same point. He wrote to the early believers exhorting them "to contend earnestly for the faith which was once for all delivered to the saints."[9] It had already been delivered before the end of the first century—once and for all!

In his letter to the Galatians Paul wrote, "Brethren, I speak in the manner of men: Though it is only a man's covenant, yet if it is confirmed, no one annuls or adds to it."[10] But the covenant of which he spoke was not a man's covenant, but God's. That covenant was confirmed by His oath to Abraham and His seed, the Messiah, Jesus, who sealed the covenant with His own blood.

It is this tradition to which believers must cling. It is the original covenant. It must be maintained in its integrity. Nothing must be added to it or taken from it. In the same vein the Apostle urged the believers in Colosse not to be moved away from the hope of the gospel, but to be firmly grounded in the faith and steadfast.[11]

287

9. Prepare For A Church-State War

The church-state alliance was at the heart of the devil's deception, the means by which he scattered weeds in the Lord's field. The Lord will break that alliance before He returns. The partnership between church and state is so pervasive and long-standing that it is hard for us to imagine what life would be like without it. We have some hints in recent history in the struggles of faithful Christians in Nazi Germany, in Marxist states and in Muslim countries. And of course we read about it in the New Testament and early church History and in missionary advances in various times and places.

We will experience what life is like without the friendship of the world and the favor and protection of the state. Whatever was dependent on that church-state partnership will fall, including tax exemptions for churches and Christian ministries, freedom of religion, even police protection.

To some it will seem incredible that a nation founded for the purpose of establishing freedom of religion, in whose Constitution that freedom is explicitly spelled out and guaranteed, could ever be a party to religious persecution.

The Constitution, however, is celebrated today chiefly for its flexibility. The truth is, the Constitution is like wet clay in the hands of the Supreme Court. It means whatever the Supreme Court says it means. And the Court has demonstrated repeatedly that it can make the Constitution mean the opposite today of what it meant yesterday. It is commonly recognized that there has been a judicial revolution in this nation over the last half century. The American judiciary is like a runaway train, out of control.

Religious liberty hangs by a slender thread. All it will take is some provocation, some incident that can be puffed in the media to justify an anti-Christian reaction, and the thread will snap. The state will be pressed into a war against the church that remains faithful to Jesus Christ and the Gospel. And the Constitution will be interpreted in such a way as to support and even applaud it as a noble, all-American act in defense of liberty itself. We shall find, however, that when the state abandons the church, the Lord Himself will come to the church's aid. Whatever is truly essential to our salvation and to the work of the church will survive intact.[12]

10. Get Rready For A Change Of Direction

We're going to go through the process that restores the church's vitality, purity and unity. We must be prepared. We are like vehicles on a super highway travelling at a high rate of speed. Up ahead a huge green sign appears. On it are depicted two arrows pointing in two opposite directions. The fat arrow veers to the left. It is made up of three of the four lanes indicated by dotted white lines. The single remaining lane veers right. The three left lanes are marked "Mainstream", and in smaller letters, barely visible until you are almost into the turn, it reads "Destruction." The right lane is marked "Marginal Drive", and in smaller letters visible only at close range, it reads, "Life."

There is no other alternative. We do not have the option, even if we wanted it, of remaining on the same course and in the same direction we have been travelling. Separation is coming, a parting of the ways, and there is no way we can avoid it.

The liberal and conservative designations, which have been helpful guides in the past, will not help us here. The issue is the temptation to establishment. That is, if people aspire to power and influence in the mainstream, if in heart they belong to the present world, they are part of the left arrow and in the final analysis their differences won't matter. Whether they call themselves liberals or conservatives or something else, the truth is, all three lanes turning left are making a radical swing away from God and Christ.

The right lane is making a radical turn to God and Christ. It is neither conservative nor liberal. Those who take this course are making a radical choice of the future kingdom of God over the present world and all its works. The issue is the refusal to be established and in power in this present evil world. That world is coming to an end.

The only option for those who will remain faithful to Jesus Christ is to recover what has been lost since the fourth century, that is the integrity of faith and the love of God, rather than the love of this present world. The New Testament bears witness to it. The various reform movements through history, including many of the monastic orders and certain facets of the Anabaptist, Protestant and Pentecostal movements, tried valiantly to define it and model the integrity of the New Testament church. But the time had not yet come.

We are beginning to see the sign ahead on the horizon, in our own time, in our own history. For those who will be faithful to Jesus Christ and the kingdom of God in these rapidly and violently changing times, it is the only way open to us. It is God's will for us, for His church today. It indicates a recovery of the church's lost purity, unity, and holiness born of the Spirit of God.

These are dangerous times. Terrible things are beginning to happen. But it was of just such times that Jesus told His disciples— He's telling us now—"Now when these things begin to happen, look up and lift up your heads, because your redemption draws near."[13]

I have prepared a petition which is a model of what I believe the church must now ask from God. Like Daniel's prayer for Israel as the Babylonian captivity came to an end, it begins with a confession of the sins and failures of the past and ends with a plea based on the promises of Scripture, a plea which I believe God is now ready to hear and grant.

> Merciful and mighty God, and our Lord Jesus Christ, we your church do not feel ready for the final crisis that is now impending. The devil has invaded and weakened your church. Lord Jesus, You refused the kingdoms of this world and their glory when the devil offered them to You, but we and our fathers have accepted them. We have rejoiced in the wealth and the wisdom, the power and the pleasures of this sinful world. We have forgotten the hope of the kingdom of God to which you called us. We have avoided the cross in favor of the sword. We have sought the honors of men rather than the honor that comes from God alone. And we have presented a disgraceful image to the world of a church deeply divided, of believers acting like competitors and enemies rather than brothers and sisters, quarreling over money and power, sometimes even killing one another.

> We confess the sins of the church; they are our sins. Forgive us, and dispose us to forgive one another. Restore to us the integrity and truth, the unity and the love, the faithfulness unto death that characterized your church at the beginning.

Intercede for us, Lord Jesus, as you did for Peter,
that our faith may not fail in its final ordeal.[14]
Amen.

The final ordeal for faithful Christians will include persecution, and for some it will mean martyrdom. Persecution will be the key feature of the next revival, the missing piece to be supplied in the final reform of the church to prepare her for the coming of the Lord. Maranatha!

30

THE MISSING PIECE

The missing piece to be supplied in the coming revival is the cross—not the ornamental cross of Constantinian Christianity, but the real cross of persecution and martyrdom that was characteristic of the New Testament church.

In first century Israel, the appearance of Jesus caused a division in Jewish society. Those Jews who followed the Lord Jesus drew the fire of opposition from their fellow Jews who rejected Him, and there was a separation.

The difference between the two was important enough that it mattered, and substantial enough that there was no way to resolve the differences; in time the two groups separated. The believers were different in a way that made them offensive to their unbelieving families, friends and neighbors. They were like aliens, as if they had adopted a new identity and a new loyalty. All their previous connections and commitments, goals and ambitions, were cast into the shade by the power of a new and dominant commitment. They rearranged all their priorities under this new master-passion that demanded and received top-priority status.

To those who were the custodians of traditional values, this new commitment by so many of their fellow Jews seemed threatening. The converts had received a revitalization of the historic faith. More than that, they had received a partial fulfillment of what the faith had promised. What the institutional authorities had worked for for years by long study and discipline, the converts were claiming to have discovered by a kind of direct, immediate revelation. And there was an appeal, an infectious quality to the faith of the converts that was missing in the institutions and their curators. There were miracles of healing and transformations of character that could not be ignored by their enemies. Let's try to think how those curators must have felt by an analogy from our own world.

Imagine that you are a doctor. You have studied long and hard and are making a good living treating people who have sicknesses and diseases. One day you become aware that there are several healers out there who haven't studied medicine, never went through the ordeal of medical school, internship, and all the rest of it, but they are healing people and doing a better job of it than you are. They are not only making people well, but happy, too. Some of your patients (or former patients) are going to these upstarts. How would you feel?

All at once your job, your financial security, your place in society, are at risk. You would be troubled and angry, would you not? You would want to see things return to normal, that is, to what they were before these unauthorized healers came on the scene. For they have invaded your world and turned it upside down. If you don't do something, they are likely to destroy your practice. Your first move might be to charge these people with practicing medicine without a license. You would want to warn your clients against these healers. And in order to justify the warning you would want to find something wrong with the new healers—their methods, their ethics, anything to discredit them and get rid of them.

For those very understandable reasons the early believers were a threat, not to the historic faith—they were excited about the faith—but to the people who made their livings and their reputations or found their security in the traditional institutions that had grown up around the faith. The lawyers, the scribes, the chief priests, the officials of the synagogues, the members of the Sanhedrin had all fenced off a part of the religion as their own domain. They had franchised the faith, packaged and marketed it, and made it a profitable service industry which they controlled. The believers who identified Jesus as the long-awaited Messiah were a threat to the professionals who operated these institutional franchises. And so the believers were persecuted.

It was easy for the authorities to convince themselves that they were protecting the people from theological and moral error, and only incidentally protecting their incomes and their positions in society. The charge they made against the believers was something like practicing and especially propagating their unconventional teachings without a license, that is, without the authorization or the credentials of the establishment.

The gospel came from outside the regular institutional channels by unauthorized teachers. The believers accepted the gospel as the word of God, repented and began a new life of practical godliness and truth. There were a lot of them, but they were a relatively small minority in Judea, and they were almost entirely outsiders to the corridors of power, influence and wealth. They were therefore vulnerable. The teachings of Jesus were designed to keep them vulnerable.

The Lord anticipated persecution and told His disciples not to retaliate when it happened, but to turn the other cheek, to go the second mile, in other words, to return good for evil. On the one hand, they were directed to act in such a way as to make enemies. On the other hand, they were told to love their enemies, not to punish them. The disciples of Jesus drew the wrath of the officials and their followers much as a lightning rod attracts the bolts of lightning. They were out in the open and exposed, and presented the perfect ground. The very blessing of God made them targets. The believers, following the Lord Jesus and His words, took the angry stroke and refused to retaliate. They would not return evil for evil. Their goal was not to destroy their enemies but to convert them.

The gospel can only be preached with New Testament integrity when it is proclaimed from a position of vulnerability. As a minister once told me, you must always lead from weakness, not strength, when presenting the gospel. The New Testament preachers were given the blessing of God, but they lacked the recognition of men and the credentials of the institutions of society. So they presented the gospel from a disadvantaged position. They were always the underdog, always working against the odds. Like Jesus, His followers were "despised and rejected by men,"[1] a sign to be spoken against.[2] This was by design of God, who intended that the only strength of the gospel would lie in its spiritual qualities and nowhere else. The gospel is the power of God in contradistinction to every kind of human and earthly power. The triumph of the gospel points to God because it is not the triumph of anything or anybody else. It cannot be attributed to human wisdom or human power or human riches or earthly institutional power of any kind.

This is why the faith was so distorted when it allied itself with Roman politics and Greek wisdom. It allied itself with human and institutional power. It didn't matter whether the message remained the same or almost the same. It came across as a very different thing when it was backed with the power of this world. The kingdom of heaven had been the consolation and the hope of those who were deprived of the blessings and advantages and pleasures of this world. When the faith of the poor, the disenfranchised, the weak, the despised and the persecuted became the property of the wealthy, the powerful, the respected, the influential and the persecutors, it wasn't the same faith any more. Even when the words were the same, the message was different. In the first case, it came from outside and was a threat to the establishment. In the second case, it came from inside the establishment and was a support to the status quo.

The possession of the power of this world resulted in the loss of the power of the world to come. Miracles waned. Love decayed. Hope faded. Persuasion gave way to coercion, sometimes subtle, sometimes blunt and harsh, but it was always there. Faith became a duty instead of a joy, something forced on the people by the establishment rather than a free choice offered by God. The word of God was interpreted in the interests of the powers of this world. It became, in other words, the religion of the realm, a matter of law rather than grace, like every other religion on the earth. It became an instrument to enhance the power of the powerful and to exploit the poor and the needy. What God had ordained to set people free, men used to put them back in bondage. In the hands of the power brokers of this corrupt world, the gospel became bad news.

Did that mean there was no salvation? No, it didn't mean that. The words of Jesus, "seek and you shall find," remained true. Those who earnestly sought for God found Him, even in a compromised church. And from time to time God sent revivals in answer to the prayers of His people.

Dr. A. B. Simpson, founder of the Christian and Missionary Alliance, told a fascinating story that illustrates the power of accumulative prayer.

> In the city of Rangoon...the largest and finest temple bell in the East had been sunk in the river during one of the battles in the Anglo-Burman wars. Efforts by various engineers failed to raise it. At last a clever priest asked to make the attempt on condition that the bell be given to his temple. He had his assistants gather an immense number of bamboo rods. These hollow, light bouyant rods can scarcely be kept from floating on the water.

The bamboo rods were taken down one-by-one by divers and fastened to the bell at the bottom of the river. After many thousands of them had been securely fastened, it was noticed that the bell began to move; and when the last bamboo rod had been added, the buoyancy of the accumulated rods was so great that they actually lifted the enormous mass of bronze from the silt and mire of the bottom and bore it to the surface of the river. So faith-filled prayer can lift the heaviest burdens. That heavy burden you have faced may begin to rise with the very next prayer that you pray in faith![3]

God seems to collect the prayers of His people for revival—sometimes over centuries—and answer them all at the same time in great revivals. So I believe it will be in a preeminent sense in these last times. For the Scriptures focus on the last times as the period when God's righteousness will at last be vindicated, His people resurrected and saved, and the earth finally redeemed from the oppressive hand of Satan. That is why the hope of God's people has been drawn to this period from the very beginning and during the whole course of redemptive history. The prayers of God's saints down through the ages have been especially focused on this time. It is not unreasonable to believe that the greatest of all revivals has been reserved for the time of the end.

It is the time when the reformation of the church will be completed and the church restored to the integrity of its first love. It is the time when a renewed and restored church will proclaim with integrity the gospel of the kingdom of God to all the nations. It will be a time when the people of God will be visited with great power from on high. But it will also be a time of great persecution of God's people in all nations. Persecution and martyrdom will be important signs of the end and of the last revival.

In the final analysis, persecution is the work of the state. It only happens when the powers of this world either determine to pursue persecution as a policy of the government, or allow it to happen by refusing to protect the persecuted group from its enemies. And so persecution is an indicator of the withdrawal of the protection of the state from the people of God. It has happened at various times in the history of the church, but in a special way it is a sign of the last times. It is happening in our times.

Missiologist David Barrett reported that in 1989 there were an average of 25,000 Christian martyrs every month worldwide. That number is expected to reach 41,000 every month by the year 2000. Although it is not considered news by the secular media, more Christians have been martyred for their faith in the twentieth century than in all the other centuries of church history put together.[4]

God has cancelled the illicit partnership of the church with the state. This is already a fact of modern history in many nations of the world. It is a key feature of the revival that is now beginning in our own country. And the church here in America should not resist this trend but welcome it, for it indicates the recovery of the church's integrity and of her blessed hope. The church at the end of the age will resemble the church at the beginning—faithful to her Lord and Savior Jesus the Messiah of Israel unto death.

Another sign of the impending revival at the time of the end is the recovery by the church of its prophetic voice. When the church realizes that she is no longer dependent on the state, she will be free to speak the truth to the powers that dominate this corrupt world. In the United States, the state has taken the initiative in breaking the bonds of God's law and breaking the partnership with the church. The state did this by such acts of the Supreme Court as declaring prayer and Bible reading in public schools unconstitutional, and by legalizing abortion. The church has resisted these secularizing moves by the state, but without success. I believe it was the Lord's doing; His purpose was to return the church to its New Testament independence of the state. For it is only as the church is independent of the powers of the present evil world that she can truly represent the future kingdom of God, and speak prophetically to the powers of this world.

The time has now come for the church in America and the West to take the initiative in canceling the partnership with the state that has compromised her integrity and undermined her calling. It will be a painful, but wonderfully liberating, decision. Believers must now nullify the unscriptural agreement by which the church traded its prophetic voice for the protection of the state, and preached a kind of civic righteousness in support of the ruling powers of the present sinful world.

There has never been a national religious establishment in the United States, but there has been and continues to be an informal partnership between church and state. The church has had an influential voice in determining state policy, and has enjoyed a place of influence and protection in this nation. We take for granted a paid chaplaincy program in the military and tax exemptions for churches and church-related organizations. These favors by the state have not been without compromising favors granted to the state by the churches, notably a religious sanction to the present society, its government and culture with all of their attending evils. Most American Christians still think that the United States is or at least ought to be a Christian nation, and that America's policies, including her wars are righteous and deserving of the support of American Christians.

In World War I Sergeant York was perhaps America's most celebrated hero. As a young man, Alvin York had experienced a dramatic conversion to faith in Jesus Christ. With the nation in the war, York agonized over the question of whether or not, as a Christian, he could in conscience fight for his country in the armed services. After a long struggle, he decided to accept military service. York was an expert shot with a rifle and was instrumental in a remarkable American victory.

The American news media were delighted to make Sergeant York's heroics front page news and after the war a movie was made celebrating the military exploits of this committed Christian. It confirmed for many Americans the God-and-country alliance of Protestant revivalism and American nationalism. It was a reaffirmation of Constantinian Christianity, but with this difference, that for York the decision to participate in armed combat was a question that was not automatically settled by the traditional stance of the religious institutions. He struggled with the decision.

Most American Christians remained confident of the justice of their country's cause during both World Wars in the twentieth century. Conscientious objectors to military service were allowed to accept alternatives to combat, but they were relatively few and there was not much sympathy for their non-violent convictions by most American Christians. Most American church-goers continued to perceive America and Christianity as working hand-in-hand for righteousness and truth, even when it involved killing enemies instead of loving them, as the New Testament taught.

With the increasing secularization of American society and its culture, Christians today are much less confident of the justice of the American government, including its military adventures. The Vietnam war was unpopular in some quarters of the Christian community, and no military expedition has been without its critics, sometimes on religious grounds. But the idea of Christian America dies hard, even though with every passing day it is increasingly difficult to see any connection between the policies of the American government and the teachings of the Bible, and particularly of the new Testament.

The New Testament calls the Christian community to represent the future kingdom of God, not any earthly nation or its government during this present age. The next and last revival will restore the people of God to their New Testament responsibility to represent the future kingdom of God. It will also return the church to its non-violent stance as given in the New Testament. The church's non-violent commitment will include the renunciation of all recourse to any kind of coercion in the proclamation of the gospel, and the refusal of Christians to participate in the wars of mankind. The church will have to learn again the lesson taught by Jesus and the believers of the first century, to trust in God alone for their protection, provision and salvation, even at the risk of their lives in this world.

I am a Christian and an American. I think of the history of my country in the light of the New Testament. I see this country as the chosen stage on which a great deal of the reform of the church has been worked out. Here the experiment in religious liberty has found its fullest expression. And here we have learned, as Savonarola learned in Florence as America was being discovered, that the freedom to believe implies the freedom to disbelieve. The faith of the New Testament, applied honestly and consistently, has to insist on both freedoms during the whole of this present age. And since "the way is narrow" and a relatively few in any generation find it, Christians must be content to be a minority faith. Moreover, since ours is a prophetic faith that stands for and proclaims the truth which is unwelcome and alien in a fallen world, Christians will always find themselves at risk in this world during this age. According to the New Testament, this is going to be true at the end of the age in a particularly severe way for those who are faithful to the Lord Jesus and the gospel.[5]

New Testament Christians will find themselves not only a minority, but a persecuted minority. This is true because Christianity is unique in history for its insistence on the freedom of choice in matters of faith. Where Christian belief as revealed in the New Testament is not found, or where it is supplanted by some other doctrine that is held to be sacred (it need not be "religious" in the traditional sense), that political religion will not tolerate the freedom of faith the New Testament demands. Especially, it will not tolerate a reformed and restored New Testament church.

A new anti-Christian faith is arising in the United States of America today. At the moment it is known as humanism and liberalism (humanism its content, liberalism its methodology). It gained the upper hand by its propaganda in the past several generations. In the last generation, it has become dominant in law and government. And while in its ideological stage this humanistic philosophy cried out for tolerance in order to open the way for its own message, now that it has tasted power, the new anti-Christian religion is becoming increasingly intolerant. It will persecute dissenters, as has every other society except for those profoundly influenced by the truths of the New Testament.

The "brave new world" that now exists in the United States has pressed its liberty to the point of absurdity. It tolerates the intolerable. But ironically, it will soon curtail the religious liberty that our country has stood for from its earliest colonial beginnings. For the very liberty that made possible a free church has also made possible the triumph of an anti-Christian humanism. And now that it is established in power, humanism and liberalism will exhibit their illiberal and inhuman character. Our brave new world will not tolerate the truth. It will persecute New Testament Christians.

This persecution is now at hand here in the United States. It will serve God's purpose in that it will be the acid test of the church in the final stage of its reformation and restoration. The lawlessness of the end of the age will provoke the church to speak the gospel in prophetic power. And the gospel spoken in uncompromising terms will provoke opposition. It will be an opportunity for disciples of Jesus to love their enemies, to bless those who curse them, and to pray for those who despitefully use them and persecute them.[6] The opposition is there. Soon it will be coercive and violent. It will happen here in the United States. And that persecution will help, though unintentionally, to finish the church's reformation and to restore the New Testament church. For it will mark the return of the cross, persecution and martyrdom. At the same time, the persecution will restore the church's integrity, and quicken her hope.

There will be many martyrs here. And there will be many who will flee. This is as it should be. Jesus said, "When they persecute you in one city, flee to the next." When the church was persecuted in Jerusalem, the believers fled to the surrounding nations. And they preached the gospel wherever they went.

There is a sense in which the church of the last times will resemble a company of migrant farm workers. They reap one crop and then move on to the next as it becomes ripe, and so on. I believe the last field to be reaped is the field which was the first to yield the fruit of the gospel: Israel.[7] But when the fullness of the other nations has come in, Israel will turn to her Messiah.[8] Many signs of Israel's restoration are already present: a Jewish state in the Promised Land able to maintain itself in the face of its enemies, the land itself becoming fruitful, a significant Messianic movement in its midst.

The challenge we face is unprecedented in its intensity. But God will be with us in the difficult times ahead. His word to us is a familiar one: fear not. He is sending a revival, a spiritual awakening like that of New Testament times that will return the church to the character of the New Testament original. For the New Testament church was born into a hostile environment, into the very kind of world in which we find ourselves today. And the New Testament church overcame its enemies.

> Now salvation, and strength, and the kingdom
> of our God, and the power of His Christ have
> come, for the accuser of our brethren, who accused
> them before our God day and night, has been cast
> down. And they overcame him by the blood of the
> Lamb and by the word of their testimony, and they
> did not love their lives to the death.[9]

The word of God assures us that victory over the devil is possible. Jesus showed us the way. His strategy is martyrdom.

31

Martyrdom: The Strategy Of Jesus

Jesus was crucified. But few Christians have faced the implications of that fact. Jesus was rejected by His own society and in particular by the leaders, the people of influence, wealth and power in His society.

Jesus was a non-conformist. He pressed His non-conformity to the point where the leaders had to do something about Him. He became a threat to the established order. He spoke a truth the authorities could not dismiss or disprove. He exhibited a power they could neither ignore nor overcome. Yet He did not resort to the obvious, the ever-present option that is always available to anyone who wishes to change the existing order and replace it with another: He did not resort to arms and coercion. That is to say, He did not try to implement a political solution, either revolution or the gradual, piecemeal changes that can be made within the existing order, by changing policy or personnel without disturbing the system and organization already in place. Jesus did not teach nor did He exemplify political action, which is defined by its use of coercion in one form or another.

Jesus' strategy was martyrdom (He provoked persecution and He practiced non-retaliation); and hope (He believed, and He taught His disciples to believe, in a better world to come). He did not try to bring about that better world, except by obedience to God the Father. And that led to disgrace, disaster, apparent failure and death in this world. He took the way of the cross, the way of suffering unjustly for the sake of the truth and the hope.

He trusted in God. And He clearly believed in a supernatural and apocalyptic intervention by God at the end of the age. He said He would come again leading an invasion of the earth, accompanied by the holy angels of heaven at the end of the present

n the future known only to God the Father. That's what
that's what He believed.

resent evil world, Jesus taught and modeled a way of
nged to the coming kingdom of justice, truth and love.
He and His followers exposed the lies and hypocrisy of the world
and its leaders. Jesus and His disciples lived obediently within the
existing order as far as that was consistent with doing the will of
God, but there were limits to their obedience to the reigning
authorities of the time. There were laws they refused to obey and
conventions they would not observe. They challenged the
authorities when the established order failed to do justice. They did
it in hope. For the primary loyalty of Jesus and His disciples was to
the coming age and the future kingdom of God.

The rejection of Jesus by His own people, His own nation and
His own generation was not an accident of history. It did not occur
because He was dealing with a uniquely evil society or a uniquely
difficult historical situation. It was typical of the present age for as
long as the present age lasts. It was the result of a collision of the
just and holy kingdom of the future with the present world of evil. It
happens whenever the kingdom of God confronts the kingdom of
the devil.

We shall all know when the kingdom of God is established on
the earth in power and glory. Every eye will see Jesus in that day.[1]
The power of God will be revealed in all its terrible and
overwhelming reality.[2] The dead will be raised.[3] True justice will
prevail,[4] and the reign of sin will be over. Until that glorious day
comes, evil prevails on the earth. It is in control everywhere,
including our own country.[5]

The assumption that the world has already been changed by
Jesus, and that our loyalty to the kingdom of God can be expressed
by an unqualified loyalty to our nation and its government, is a
denial of the hope Jesus taught. Such an assumption confuses
hypocrisy with reality, and encourages belief in a false notion that
the kingdom of God has already come in power and glory to the
earth. That false triumphalism does not and cannot satisfy the
human heart and conscience. The final triumph of the kingdom of
God on the earth, according to Scripture, will occur when Jesus
Christ comes a second time, and not before.

The "triumph" of Christianity in the Roman Empire and other
places, was a clever deception of the devil. Despite appearances, the

result was the conversion of the church, not the state. For the Empire remained what it was, an unregenerate political and social order. The church made peace with that social and political order in exchange for worldly power and wealth for some of its leaders and the cessation of persecution for cooperating clergy and church members. But in doing so, church leaders modified the church's faith and hope and compromised the church's integrity from that day to this.

To regain her integrity will require an act of God. But it will require the faith and cooperation of disciples, too. We will have to consent in our hearts to a restoration of the faith and hope to what they were at the beginning. We must be willing to relinquish worldly power and wealth, and be willing to endure the inevitable return of persecution and martyrdom. We must be willing to do the will of God at the risk of provoking persecution and even martyrdom. For the truth has not changed.

The crucifixion of Jesus has to do with a living faith and hope in a truly righteous King and a truly just society. It was the result of a particular method of representing that King and kingdom of the future in a world that is essentially evil and under the control of the devil. In all essential matters, everything remains as it was in the first century when Jesus first appeared. The same method will sooner or later produce the same results in this evil world so long as the present age lasts.

The Uniqueness Of Jesus

The uniqueness of Jesus is a great truth. He is the only begotten Son of God.[6] But we must not let His uniqueness become an excuse and a cop-out. It is all too easy to draw the wrong conclusions. I recall a talk I had once with a member of a church of which I was the pastor. The man had done something unethical in business. In the course of our conversation, I appealed to the example of Jesus. He smiled broadly and said, "Sure, Bob, but He was God. You can't compare me to Him. That's not fair."

Because of the incarnation, we can and must compare ourselves with Jesus. That's one reason why the Son of God became the Son of Man.

It is true, of course, that Jesus is unique. His uniqueness means that Jesus is the only Messiah and king of Israel, the only begotten Son of God, and the only Head of the church. He is the only One who could or did make satisfaction for sin. And so it is in His name and His alone that there is forgiveness and justification for the sinner. Because only in Jesus is the penalty of sin fully paid and discharged.[7] An old hymn bears witness to the truth:

"There was none other good enough to pay the price of sin; He only could unlock the gate of heaven and let us in."[8]

Jesus died so we could live. He became poor so that we could become rich. Yes, but the riches are mostly spiritual and mostly future. And the life is realized on the other side of the cross. It also is mostly future.

The key to those riches and that life is forged in the shape of a cross. The way to life is the way of death. And Jesus calls His disciples to take up their crosses and follow Him, not just admire Him. Follow Him where? Along the same path that He Himself took: the path of love and truth and justice. And in a fallen world, that involves suffering and death, persecution and martyrdom, and hope.[9]

Jesus did not take the way of the cross so that we could avoid the way of the cross. He took the way of the cross to show us the way, so we could take up our crosses and follow Him. That's what He said. That's what He meant.

Jesus is the first born of a whole new divine-human race. We who have believed have become partakers of the divine nature by faith in Jesus Christ. We are made like Him in our redemption as we previously bore the image of Adam. Jesus now calls us to live as He lived in this present world,[10] in hope of the glory that will be ours in the world to come.[11]

Jesus is the only begotten Son of God; we are adopted sons and daughters of God. He is the original and we are the copies. We bear His image. As we have resembled Adam with his sin, misery and death, so we bear the image of Jesus who overcame sin by suffering, death and finally, resurrection.[12]

Our salvation begins in this world and in this age, and teaches us to swim against the current of this age. Most of our salvation is still future. We are called to live in hope. And in this world and this age we are called to take up our cross.

Apart from hope, we couldn't endure the cross. But with hope we can endure the cross. And our hope will never disappoint us.[13]

As the next revival approaches (the last revival), I have a word to share with Christian leaders, in particular, with those who were part of the revival of the 1970s and who were wounded in the struggles and splits of the 1980s. I have a word, too, for the young leaders who do not remember those times.

32

A Word To Leaders:
The Wounded And The Young

Those of us who were leaders are responsible for the way in which the revival of the 1970s was mismanaged in the 1980s. There is no way we can avoid that judgment. What we can avoid is repeating it. That whole era was a kind of dress rehearsal designed to work out the bugs before the big event opens. God let us make mistakes and yes, commit sins, in order to make the issues clear to us. Leadership itself was the key issue during those times. Leadership is a high but dangerous calling in which our human nature faces especially difficult temptations. There is no easy way to learn how to do it.

Leadership was the issue that brought on Lucifer's rebellion. It was the issue Adam and Eve faced in the Garden. It was the reason for Abraham's long and difficult testing while he waited for God's promises. It was the reason for David's struggles before and after becoming king. It was the reason for the Lord's temptation in the wilderness. And leadership was the reason we went through our struggles in the seventies and eighties. The purpose of our Father was to show us the truth we need to know about ourselves, our temptability, and the exacting requirements of our calling.

I have often been drawn to the twenty-third chapter of 2 Samuel and some lessons God taught David. These are King David's last words, the distillation of a long and hard discipline in leadership. "Thus says David the son of Jesse; Thus says the man raised up on high, the anointed of the God of Jacob, and the sweet psalmist of Israel:"

> The Spirit of the LORD spoke by me, and His
> word was on my tongue. The God of Israel said,
> The Rock of Israel spoke to me: 'He who rules

over men must be just, ruling in the fear of God. And he shall be like the light of the morning when the sun rises, a morning without clouds, like the tender grass springing out of the earth, by clear shining after rain.'[1]

David is a man we can relate to. He had a heart for God, and he made a lot of mistakes, including one huge one that nearly destroyed him. His final word is that right leadership is a good thing. But it must be done in the fear of God.

I won't dwell on David's sin with Bathsheba and the attempted cover-up. They are probably the best known facts about him. Instead, I want to recall a couple of instances that show the kind of man David was and why, in the final analysis, he was a great leader.

The first is a scene in David's camp outside of Bethlehem, his home town. On this occasion, the town was occupied by a garrison of the enemy, the Philistines who had overrun Bethlehem and possessed it.

David remembered his boyhood, and was reminiscing about it out loud. He yearned for a taste of the cool water from the well in the center of the town. Some of David's soldiers determined to satisfy that craving of their beloved leader. They broke through the Philistine ranks at the risk of their lives, filled a canteen with water, and brought it back to David.

David was profoundly grateful for the devotion of his men. But he would not drink the water. It would be like drinking the blood of his men. Why? Because they risked their lives to get the water for him. And David knew—the Spirit of God revealed it to him, I believe—that not he, not any man, was worthy of that kind of sacrifice. Only God is worthy.

And so, in the fear of God, David poured out the water on the ground. He gave it to God, in effect. And in that act David showed his refusal to use his position of leadership for his own gratification. He would not take for himself the honor due only to God. David knew his place in the grand scheme of things, and refused to make personal use of what belonged to God alone.[2]

The second incident in David's life I want to refer to was the return of the ark to Israel. David truly loved God, and longed to see Him pleased and satisfied. So he wanted to bring the ark of the Covenant of God, the centerpiece of Jewish worship, to Jerusalem, the city God had chosen for his name. He brought it on an oxcart, the same way the Philistines had returned the ark to Judea after they had captured it. David's heart was right in the matter. His motives were mostly pure. He was just a little too sure of himself and a little careless. The oxen pulled the cart over an uneven place in the road and the ark slid and it looked as if it would fall out of the cart. So Uzzah, one of David's men, grabbed the ark to steady it. It was an instinctive act on Uzzah's part. I don't believe he had any sense at all that he was doing something wrong or offensive to God. He was doing something he considered a good work on behalf of God and His glory. He was struck dead on the spot.

David was surprised and upset, angry at the Lord. The joyous celebration ended suddenly in tragedy. David had the ark moved into the nearby home of Obed-Edom, and David and his group of worshippers trudged home in silence, broken-hearted and confused. But two things happened after that.

The first thing to happen was that David noticed the Lord's blessing on the home of Obed-Edom. The second thing was that David did a little research into the Scriptures. As he read, he learned that there was a proper way for the ark of God to be transported. It was to be covered by the priests, the sons of Aaron. The Levites of the family of Kohath were the only ones authorized to carry it. They were to use long poles that the priests slid through the two rings on each side of the ark. Two Levites, one at the front, the other in the rear, grasped the ends of the poles and carried the ark that way. Carried that way the ark would not fall.[3]

So David researched the problem and found a biblical solution. Then after a long time, he once again had the ark moved and continued the celebration. And this time the ark arrived safe and sound and nobody was hurt. There was great joy in Israel.[4]

The example of David teaches us that we can be sincere, rightly motivated as far as we are able to discern, and guided by the Spirit as to the thing to be done, and we can still be wrong as to the method, the way we do the job, the proper people assigned to do it, and perhaps the timing. There are so many factors to be considered, and they all must be according to God's will, not ours.

In the 1970s and 1980s we were a lot like David. I think we had the right goal in mind. But we used some traditional methods bequeathed to the church like the Philistines' cart to Israel. And we unthinkingly employed them without really asking God, researching His word diligently, or examining our own hearts for impatience or hidden impurity of motive. Some innocent people got hurt, like Uzzah, because we weren't careful enough about how we went about doing God's work.

Isaiah wrote, "'My thoughts are not your thoughts, nor are your ways my ways,' says the Lord. 'For as the heavens are higher than the earth, so are my ways higher than your ways, and My thoughts than your thoughts.'"[5] This is simply the truth about our relationship with God, as T. Austin-Sparks said.

> This ordinary mind of man, at its best, is another mind. This will of man, at its best, is another will. You never do know what lies behind your motives until the Holy Ghost cleaves right down to the depths of your being and shows you...our best intentions are defiled, our purest motives are unclean before those eyes. Things that we intended to be for God, somewhere at their spring is self. We cannot produce from this nature anything acceptable to God. All that can ever come to God is in Christ alone, not in us. It never will, in this life, be in us as ours. He is other than we are... That is one of the hard lessons.[6]

Christ is in us, but He is utterly other than us. It remains that way. And so we must have constant recourse to prayer, the leading of the Spirit, and the insight the Spirit of God gives us into the word of Scripture, or else we will blow it one way or another.

Our trust in God must grow out of a profound mistrust of ourselves. As Isaiah said in speaking for the Lord, "Heaven is My throne, and earth is My footstool. Where is the house that you will build Me? And where is the place of My rest? For all those things My hand has made, and all those things exist," says the Lord. "But on this one will I look, on him who is poor and of a contrite spirit, and who trembles at My word."[7]

God will not be impressed with our building projects. He doesn't need us or our great efforts. But He will look to the one who is poor and of a contrite spirit, and who trembles at His word. Yes, He will. "The sacrifices of God are a broken spirit, a broken and a contrite heart, O God, you will not despise."[8]

I am sometimes tempted to think that God is waiting for me to mess up so He can flatten me. But that is not the character of our

Father. He seeks to bring us to the end of ourselves, yes, so that He can remake us in the image of His Son. And whatever it takes to accomplish that great end is mercy, sheer mercy, and grace, the kindness and love we do not deserve and could never earn.

That kind of mercy and grace is expressed in the covenant God made with David. David wanted to build a house for God. Nathan the prophet had encouraged him. But that night the Lord spoke to Nathan and gave him a message for David. He would not build a house for God, rather, God would build a house for David, a dynasty. And it would be David's Son who would build the house. That was Solomon initially, and the Messiah ultimately. God would take this son of David as His own Son. God promised to rear up this Son. And in that promise is a provision that didn't really fit the Son of God, the Lord Jesus, for it had to do with God's discipline for iniquity. Jesus endured that discipline and punishment on man's behalf. And in a mysterious sense the Son of Man had to learn by suffering the obedience the Son of God already knew. The application of that clause is a mystery in regard to Jesus. But it certainly has to do with us who are adopted sons.

> If he commits iniquity, I will chasten him with the rod of men and with the blows of the sons of men. But My mercy shall not depart from him, as I took it from Saul, whom I removed from before you. And your house and your kingdom shall be established forever before you. Your throne shall be established forever.[9]

David himself experienced that blessed provision of the covenant of God. When he committed iniquity, God did not reject him. Instead, He corrected him with the rod of men, and the blows of the sons of men. In David's case, it was his own son, Absolom, who rose up against him. David's reign was troubled. For a while it looked as if he would lose his throne. But David was chastened, humbled, brought to confession and repentance, and restored to his post.[10] It happened to David and to Solomon. It happened to all those who are descendants of David and believers in David's greater Son, Jesus.

As I pondered the Scriptures, it occurred to me that it also happened to me: the rod and the stripes of men. The men were some of my fellow ministers, and in particular one with whom I worked closely. He was a rod to me and I to him, because there was iniquity in both of us, and the same kind of iniquity. We hurt each other, but it was for our correction, not our destruction.

I was hurt and angry at some of my fellow leaders, but they were God's instruments. What they gave me—and what I gave them—was what we needed at the time, given the condition of the church and of our own sanctification. Whatever the intentions of men, God's purpose in it all was our correction, to make us faithful to and dependent upon God alone. The painful work of the rod produces the peaceable fruit of righteousness.[11] The church is being purified. That accomplished, we will recognize that our enemies are in the world, rather than in the church.

The time has come to forgive, as there came a time when Joseph forgave his brothers who had despised his gifts and his calling and treated him despicably when he was a young man and vulnerable. Joseph needed the discipline he received in Egypt to understand that his gifts and calling were not given to him to exalt himself and put his brothers down or humiliate them, but to serve them, to save them. God's intention was also different from the intention of his brothers. It wasn't clear initially, but ultimately God's purpose was to save and bless them all.[12] Together they were humbled before the amazing providence and grace of God. And so the word of the Father to us who are estranged from one another and cannot help feeling ill used on the one hand, but cannot really deny complicity and responsibility on the other, is simply to forgive. It is time to speak a word of reconciliation and hope to the church.

The prophet Jeremiah confessed, "O LORD, I know the way of man is not in himself; it is not in man who walks to direct his own steps. O LORD, correct me, but with justice; Not in your anger, lest You bring me to nothing."[13]

Jeremiah, who was a man, who was even a man of God, knew that it was not in a man to direct his own steps. God must do this. There are too many factors outside a man's control. But God knows all and is in control of all things. Jeremiah knew, moreover, that he needed more than direction, he needed correction. And he pleaded with God to do it. But Jeremiah appealed to God to correct him with justice and not in anger, "lest you bring me to nothing." He stood in awe of the power of God. And yet, he trusted God not to destroy him, though the Almighty could easily have done so. And He could easily have found grounds to justify doing so. But Jeremiah knew that the justice of God contains an essential element of mercy and grace, not as an alloy added to the mix, but as an essential part of His justice.

It was a good prayer that Jeremiah made. It was the kind of appeal we have to make to God in these times. We cannot settle the issue with our theology or with our plans or our accomplishments. We must put our case in God's hands and trust Him to make it all work out well in the end. And we must do so, knowing that we cannot represent ourselves to Him as if we were deserving of what we ask and need. We ourselves are in need of correction, and we have to ask for that, too. Such a prayer leaves us in a kind of tension. For we learn to trust God at the same time that we learn to distrust ourselves. It has to be that way.

We look back today as we approach a new millennium on a scene that is not pretty. God sent us a revival and we didn't handle it very well. But God's justice is full of mercy and grace. He reminds us that God is a consuming fire, but He also encourages us to come boldly to His throne of grace. He will correct us and direct us, and the lessons we have learned in the last quarter century will be important as the new millennium opens up to us and we face the tremendous conflict of the last days. We will meet it as sadder, perhaps, but wiser men and women who have learned to walk humbly with their God, and to love one another.

The task before us is a formidable one. But we have a salvation that was designed for formidable challenges. Part of the church's mistake was like that of using a high-powered racing car to run errands around town. An engine tuned for high speeds will sputter and cough if it is used for shopping trips to the mall in start-and-stop traffic. So it has been with the church. Designed by God for great and noble deeds as a representative of Jesus Christ and a kingdom of truth, justice and love, she has been content to serve as one of the pillars of a corrupt and doomed world. She has coughed and sputtered doing tasks that were far beneath her true calling.

And so I say to my brothers and sisters who were part of the revival of the 1970s and were wounded in the debacle of the 1980s, take heart as we approach the new millennium. As the saying goes, "All's well that ends well." God has not cast us off; He has simply corrected us according to the covenant promise given to David and His great Son, our Lord Jesus Christ.

To my younger brothers and sisters who were not part of that scene, I say this: you haven't got the time or the liberty or the energy to waste on exalting yourselves and your ministries and indulging your flesh. Learn from our mistakes and avoid them. Keep your hearts pure and humble before God. And Jesus will build a house whose beauty will astonish you. In that house you will find joy, hope and blessing beyond reckoning and that will never end, in a new and glorious world in which righteousness dwells.

And to all of us together, in the words of the Lord, let each of us take up our cross, and follow Jesus. Samuel Rutherford once said, "I find in the cross only such a burden as wings are to a bird." As we embrace the cross, we will wonder how we ever got along without it.

33

Summary and Conclusion

Revival is the method by which God restores the church to the integrity of the New Testament original. That is my conviction, and the message of this book. But it raises questions, like this one, for instance: how can a church with 2,000 years of history and a worldwide expansion become again what it was when it was a small, new sect in Judea?

Size, growth, and history do not raise serious issues with God. Sin and distortion do. Size, growth, and expansion led to changes in style, language, location, and culture that were only incidental to the church's character and mission. These changes in the course of history, however, presented the church with temptations that affected essentials. For instance, when the church became so numerous that it began to be influential in the affairs of the surrounding society and its government, when it began to attract people it did not convert, when it drew to its banners many who wished to use the church for their own worldly ends simply because the church became politically important in the world due to its size and influence, that was a temptation. To say the least, the church didn't handle that temptation very well in the fourth century.

But temptation need not have led to sin. Had her leaders kept their hearts pure and walked in humility, truth and love, had they repented when they made mistakes and committed sins, the church could have adapted to its new situations without compromise and corruption.

Once you get into corruption and compromises, however, you get stuck in them. They are like addictions, easy to start, hard to stop. A vehicle can easily drive into muck that it cannot drive out of under its own power. In the same way, the church needs more than its own resources to get out of the mess it got itself into. God must intervene before we can even repent. He has intervened repeatedly, by stirring up His people to pray and by sending revivals. Over the last five hundred years in particular, God has sent many revivals with the purpose of restoring the church to her New Testament integrity.

The revivals I have highlighted in this book occurred at the beginning of the period of reformation and indicated, like a weather vane, the direction God was taking in the process of reform. Again and again, the reform movements pointed to the New Testament scriptures and to the early church. Essentially, the direction was toward a renewal of the faith once delivered to the saints. The Catholic revival in Florence highlighted the return of prophecy and of martyrdom which is usually the price attached to prophetic ministry.

The Protestant revival in Germany was typical of all genuine revivals, for it sounded the call to return to the original sources—to the Scriptures—as the blueprints for revival. The Protestant Reformation brilliantly illuminated a path it was slow to take.

The Anabaptist revival was a radical attempt to walk along the narrow way of the cross. It represented the long, hard struggle to return to the New Testament. The Anabaptists sought to apply the New Testament scriptures as a way of life, and not only as a source of doctrines, confessions and proof-texts. They wanted to shake off the worldly influences that had perverted the faith and turned the church into a power of the present world. Anabaptists fervently desired to reestablish the New Testament church. Their many martyrdoms, like seeds that fell into the ground and died, brought forth much fruit. Their patience and persistence in spite of persecution, have won for them at last a respectful hearing for their beliefs and practices from other Christians.

When God moves in a revival, the church is enabled to repent and reform itself. But repentance involves more than the things we commonly think of as sins. Methods, systems, attitudes and teachings which the church has adopted but which are subversive of the church's true character and purposes, are discarded during times of revival, and the church recovers some of her lost powers and truths.

In our time, the church will recover her purity by recovering the cross, and that involves repenting of all that undermined her purity and made of the cross a kind of museum piece or ornament. The church must repent of her compromising relationship with the powers of the present evil world. The most glaring example of a practice that must be discarded, is the church's use of force and coercion of various kinds to supplement the gospel, and to pressure people to believe. Whatever organization the church employed to accomplish that end, whatever doctrines were created to support it or excuse it, must now be scrapped as part of the church's repentance.

The restoration of the church to what she was at the beginning involves the return of the church to her first love—love for God the Father and Jesus Christ her Lord, and for one another as fellow disciples. It requires the restoration of her unity and purity, her hope and faith as at the beginning. Those are the essentials that must be restored by repentance and faith in order for the church to be prepared for the Second Coming of Jesus. This restoration is beyond human power; it requires the intervention of God for which we must pray and prepare.

Peter made reference in his sermon soon after the day of Pentecost to the "times of restoration of all things which God has spoken by the mouth of all His holy prophets since the world began."[1] He spoke as a Jew to a gathering of Jews from all over the world to Jerusalem for the feast of Pentecost. He spoke in a Jewish historical context. His idea of restoration surely included as a key point the restoration of the kingdom to Israel, the return of the monarchy and the dynasty of David. Jesus, after all, is the son of David and heir to David's throne.[2] If today the church is composed largely of gentiles (non-Jews), she has nevertheless a Jewish future. The church is engaged to the Messiah of the Jews. She is soon to be married to the coming King of Israel and the ruler of all the nations.

The church has to be purified in preparation for that glorious supernatural event. For one thing, she has to get over her anti-Jewish prejudice. For another, she must break off her affair with the Roman Caesar and his successors. And she needs to get over her fascination with Greek wisdom and philosophy that has dimmed and distorted her apocalyptic faith and hope. All these items for repentance are different aspects of her love for this present evil world, the world which God commanded her not to love.[3] It is these worldly influences that have caused most of the sins, divisions and distortions in the church.

The time has come. The last revival is at hand and in fact is already here. In this last and greatest of revivals God will complete the church's reformation and restore the church to the purity, unity, love and integrity of the New Testament original. The church will live the gospel and preach it in its purity to every tribe and tongue and people and nation, and finally bring the revival back to Israel where it started so long ago.

That is a great hope, but it is not our ultimate hope. The church bears witness to the kingdom and to the King, our Savior and our Lord. It is the only kingdom that will survive the judgments of the apocalyptic future that is upon us. As the climax of that final conflict between God and Satan, Christ and the antichrist, the Lord Himself will return in power and glory to the earth. The dead will be raised, the last judgment will be pronounced and a redeemed mankind will at last live together in peace and justice, love and truth in a kingdom that will never pass away. Peter's closing admonition is relevant and important for us today.

> But the day of the Lord will come as a thief in the night, in which the heavens will pass away with a great noise, and the elements will melt with fervent heat; both the earth and the works that are in it will be burned up. Therefore, since all these things will be dissolved, what manner of persons ought you to be in holy conduct and godliness, looking for and hasting the coming of the day of God, because of which the heavens will be dissolved, being on fire, and the elements will melt with fervent heat? Nevertheless we, according to His promise, look for new heavens and a new earth in which righteousness dwells. Therefore, beloved, looking forward to these things, be diligent to be found by Him in peace, without spot and blameless.[4]

It is this glorious hope that will sustain us in the coming conflict when the church will once again face persecution and martyrdom.

Epilog

There is nothing quite so unsettling as an earthquake. In recent years earthquakes have interrupted the World Series and the Olympic games as a stunned world watched. These earthquakes were signs to this sports-minded world of a great shaking that is coming, that has in fact already begun.

The Bible gives this warning from Him who speaks from heaven: "Yet once more I shake not only the earth, but also heaven."[1] We know something of earthquakes. The Scripture predicts earthquakes at the time of the end, but it also predicts something more: a heavenquake. What could that mean?

The ancients believed that the conflicts on earth, not only wars, but natural disasters, were the repercussions of conflicts going on in heaven. As thunder follows lightning, so our earthly, cultural and physical explosions follow the massive electric charges in the heavenly realms, as effect follows cause.

What Scripture is saying is that in these last times God is not only dealing with earthly and physical matters, but with their heavenly and spiritual counterparts. He is going right to the source and dealing with root causes this time. There will be a final and thorough upheaval, a shaking like nothing that has ever been seen before. Evil will be allowed to develop and reach maturity.[2] It will dominate the earth for a short time.[3] And God Himself in Christ will reveal Himself in overwhelming power and glory and destroy the kingdom of evil, and will establish in its place the kingdom of God which will stand forever.[4]

Those who have experienced an earthquake never forget it. But all other quakes will seem like mere toys in comparison with the quake that is to come. The magnitude of what is coming will be off the Richter scale. That quake will never be forgotten.

But what will be involved in a phenomenon that will shake not only the earth but heaven, too? Scripture tells us that Satan will be cast out of heaven. There is something evil established in the very heavens that will be shaken loose and displaced in the last days. The heavens themselves will be cleansed. This shaking will affect the heavenly realms. The coming quake will shake spiritual things as well as physical things.[5]

What kind of things? God will shake—He is already shaking—not only the things we commonly think of as evil, but many things we consider good, things that are not simply earthly, but spiritual. Satan is called the prince of the power of the air.[6] If the time is coming when he will be cast out of heaven, until that time comes he has a certain presence in the heavenly realms. Scripture tells us that he masks himself as an angel of light.[7] We are accustomed to think of him only as the prince of darkness who rules in the caverns of Hades and the dark places of the earth. I think it is fair to say that the devil in the form of an angel of light has done far more damage and destroyed many more souls than he has as the prince of darkness. For the devil has not only built casinos, crack-houses, brothels, crime syndicates, terrorist regimes and concentration camps; he has also created churches and universities, businesses, political parties and governments of all kinds, democricies as well as dictatorships. Satan is the father of lies wherever they may be. And they exist not only among petty thieves and con-men, but among those who play for much higher stakes. Satan has invented theologies, religions, hierarchies, whole cultures, civilizations, traditions, philosophies and economies. He is the architect of many things built by men and angels. These are the things that will be shaken by the "heaven quake" of the last days. Whatever things can be shaken will be shaken when the heavens quake—and not only shaken, but removed. They will disintegrate. They will be no more.

"Every plant that my heavenly Father has not planted will be rooted up,"[8] Jesus said, every one of them. What then will survive? Only what the heavenly Father has planted. Only what cannot be shaken.

"Now this, 'Yet once more,' indicates the removal of those things that are being shaken, as of things that are made, that the things which cannot be shaken may remain."

There are things that cannot be shaken. They will survive, and they alone. What are those things? Only that which is born of God, only that which partakes of His nature, only what God has breathed, what has been spoken into existence by the Logos, the word of God, the Messiah, will be left standing after the shaking.

A lot of what has seemed secure and solid will be gone. Much of what has seemed good and even holy will not survive, including a lot of what has been built in the name of God and of Jesus Christ. What will survive is that which is pure and genuine and truly holy.

"Therefore, since we are receiving a kingdom which cannot be shaken, let us have grace, by which we may serve God acceptably with reverence and godly fear. For our God is a consuming fire."[9] The word was spoken to servants of God, not to unbelievers.

> For no other foundation can anyone lay than that which is laid, which is Jesus Christ. Now if anyone builds on this foundation with gold, silver, precious stones, wood, hay, straw, each one's work will become clear; for the Day will declare it, because it will be revealed by fire; and the fire will test each one's work, of what sort it is. If anyone's work which he has built on it endures, he will receive a reward. If anyone's work is burned, he will suffer loss; but he himself will be saved, yet so as through fire.[10]

It is not that which is impressive, but that which is pure and precious that will stand. Wood, hay and straw may make an impressive pile. They take up a lot of space. A wooden building may stand for years. But it is not in its very nature capable of withstanding the test of fire. It will burn.

For sheer volume, gold, silver and precious stones cannot hope to compete with wood, hay and straw. But the gold, silver and precious stones will survive the test of fire; the wood, hay and straw will not. Wood, hay and straw stand for what is natural. The gold, silver and precious stones represent the precious, the durable, the pure and the truly spiritual. We are instructed to build with purity, precision, and to build with materials that are precious in God's sight and enduring.

Over the last quarter century or so, God gave many of us an opportunity to try our hand at building. And He sent a fire to try it. Much of what we built was destroyed. It was a test run on a relatively small scale. But it gave us a key to understanding what it means to walk with God and to work with Him. And it is a key to evaluating, not only our own work, but whatever has been built in the name of God and of Jesus Christ. Much of it was a waste of time and effort, and worse; it was worldly, designed to impress men rather than to please God.

The story is told of Augustine on his death bed. He was surrounded by friends who came to watch with him during his last hours. As the end approached the great theologian sat up in bed and said, "I have seen the Lord. Everything I have written is straw!" And then he lay down again and was gone.[11]

This scene can be understood as a kind of revelation of the vast difference that exists between the reality of Christ in comparison with anything we can say or write about Him. That is no doubt true. But it can also be understood as an illustration of the text of Scripture we are considering, a text Augustine knew well. It can be understood as a confession that what he had built on the foundation of Christ will not stand the test of fire on that day when Christ shall be revealed in power and glory. The death scene was a hopeful one for Augustine, personally. "He himself shall be saved, yet so as by fire." But what he built will not survive.

Augustine was the main propagandist for the imperial church when it formed an alliance with the Roman Empire. His writings set the policy of the most numerous and most influential part of the Christian church, a policy which began with Constantine and has continued to this day. Augustine's prestige as a theologian is so firmly established that nobody wants to point out that in some very important respects the man was seriously in error. Augustine was instrumental in establishing a false alliance of church and state which has stood through centuries. The shaking has already begun that will destroy that false alliance.

Even to this day, the theology and structure of that ancient alliance still stands in many places. But the heavens have begun to quake and that theology and structure have begun to sway. One day soon, the great shock will hit, heaven will quake, and that theology and structure will be no more. But while it still stands, it remains possible to build our church structures either on Constantine or Christ. Much of what now stands in the churches of America is Constantinian. In this country today, we still have the option of building either on a first century plan or a fourth century plan. We can work for the world to come, or we can work for this present, evil world. But we cannot have it both ways, just as we cannot serve God and mammon.

The kingdom of this world is built on a shaky foundation. It may stand high, but it does not stand secure. It has already begun to shake because it can be shaken. It will be shaken. And it will certainly fall.

The kingdom of God and of His Christ comes with a cross. It is humble, lowly. It suffers in this world. But it stands on a foundation that will not collapse. It will still be standing after the shaking. Nothing else will remain.

In the revival that comes in connection with the end of the age, God will give us an opportunity to cooperate with Him as He rebuilds the church of Jesus Christ. Let us build on the one foundation that will stand the shakings that will certainly come. Let us build on the one foundation of Jesus Christ. And let us build this time with nothing but gold, silver and precious stones. Let us work with Jesus as He restores the New Testament church.

Notes

Introduction

1. Matthew 24:14
2. Matthew 28:20
3. Revelation 5:9
4. John 13:12-17
5. 1 Peter 2:21
6. 1 John 4:11
7. 1 Peter 2:4, 5
8. John 10:16
9. Ephesians 4:4
10. John 6:66
11. Luke 9:23, 24
12. Two books documenting the persecution of Christians in Marxist and Islamic countries were published in 1997. *Their Blood Cries Out, The Worldwide Tragedy of Modern Christians Who Are Dying for Their Faith,* by Paul Marshall with Lela Gilbert, Word Publishing, Dallas, Texas; and *In the Lion's Den, A Shocking Account of Persecution and Martyrdom of Christians Today and How We Should Respond,* by Nina Shea, Broadman & Holman Publishers, Nashville, Tennessee. They were the basis of an article in Reader's Digest, August, 1997, "The Global War on Christians," by Ralph Kinney Bennett, alerting American Christians, many of them for the first time, to this shocking contemporary reality.

Chapter One

1. James Burns, *Revivals, Their Laws And Leaders,* Baker Book House, Grand Rapids, Michigan, 1960, p. 21, a reprint. Originally published by Hodder and Stoughton, London, 1909.

2. See Luke 3:21, 22; Luke 4:1-14. The Holy Spirit descended on Jesus, the voice of the Father gave His approval and acknowledged Jesus as His Son. Then, the Lord being *filled* with the Spirit, was led by the Spirit into the wilderness where He was tempted by the devil. After the temptations, the Lord returned in the *power* of the Spirit, and began His public ministry. I believe that represents a general pattern that applies to Christian leaders. There is a filling with the Spirit, a period of testing, and then ministry in the power of the Spirit. The testing of Jesus took forty days. It is conceivable that for His disciples, the testing may take considerably longer.

3. "'I Have Sinned Against You' The Sex scandal—and the religious vendetta—behind the fall of Jimmy Swaggart." Cover story, People weekly, March 7, 1988.

4. Jeremy Rifkin with Ted Howard, *The Emerging Order, God in the Age of Scarcity*, G.P. Putnam's Sons, New York, N.Y., Copyright by Jeremy Rifkin with Ted Howard, 1979. Rifkin was a Jew who recognized the potential power of the evangelical Christian community in the 1970s in the wake of revival. In a chapter entitled, "America's New Spiritual Awakening," Rifkin wrote, "Of one thing there is little doubt, the evangelical community is amassing a base of potential power that dwarfs every other competing interest in American society today. A close look at the evangelical communications network and infrastructure should convince even the skeptic that it is now the single most important cultural force in American life" (p. 105).

5. Jimmy Carter confessed he was "born again" and was elected President in 1976.

6. Richard Wurmbrand, *Tortured For Christ*, p. 84, Living Sacrifice Book Co., P.O. Box 2273, Bartlesville, OK. 74005-2273, Copyright 1967 by the Voice of the Martyrs, inc.

7. Ibid., p. 90

8. John 12:42

9. Matthew 10:34-38

10. Acts 22:22

11. John 16:2

12. Acts 5:40-42

Chapter Two

1. Acts 3:1-8

2. Revelation 2:1-7

3. Philippians 2:5-11

4. Dietrich Bonhoeffer, *Letters and Papers From Prison*, p. 46, Macmillan Paperbacks, Edited by Eberhard Bethge, Translated by Reginald H. Fuller, 1953, paperback edition 1962.

5. Malachi 2:14-16; Hosea 1:2

6. Hebrews 6:13-20

7. Jude 24

8. 2 Peter 1:2-4

9. 1 Corinthians 12:12-14

10. John 8:54

11. John 5:17, 18; John 8:55-59

12. Acts 5:3, 4

13. Deuteronomy 6:4; James 2:19

14. Mark 10:6-9

15. 1 Peter 2:4,5,9,10

16. John Donne, *The Complete Poetry And Selected Prose Of John Donne*, Edited and with Introduction by Charles M. Coffin, p. 440, XVII Meditation, Modern Library, Copyright 1952 by Random House, New York, N.Y. The passage reads, "No man is an Iland, intire of it selfe; every man is a peece of the Continent, a part of the maine; if a Clod bee washed away by the Sea, Europe is the lesse...any mans death diminishes me, because I am involved in mankinde; And therefore never send to know for whom the bell tolls; it tolls for thee."

17. 1 Corinthians 12:13

18. Acts 2:44-47

19. Jeremiah 31:31-34

20. Matthew 26:27, 28

21. Jude 3

22. Galatians 3:15

Chapter Three

1. Isaiah 50:4-7
2. Acts 2:31
3. Acts 2:42-47
4. Acts 5:1-16
5. Acts 5:17-33
6. Zechariah 9:9
7. Luke 22:66-71
8. Luke 23:38
9. Acts 2:36
10. Matthew 28:18
11. Zechariah 12:10; Revelation 1:7; Romans 11:24-27
12. Matthew 7:13, 14
13. Matthew 24:9; John 15:20
14. Richard Wurmbrand, op. cit., p. 90.
15. Hebrews 12:2

Chapter Four

1. Edward Gibbon, *Decline And Fall Of The Roman Empire,* p. 276. An Abridged Version, Edited and with an introduction by Dero A. Saunders. Penguin Books, Middlesex, England and New York, N.Y. Copyright 1952 by Viking Press. Reprinted in 1985 by Viking Penguin.
2. Hebrews 11:10, 16; 13:14
3. William Ramsay, *The Church In The Roman Empire, Before 170 A.D.,* p. 274, Baker Book House, Grand Rapids, Michigan, 1954.
4. Matthew 10:40-42; 25:31-46
5. 1 Peter 3:15, 16
6. 1 Peter 2:18-21
7. Hebrews 11:1
8. Romans 10:9,10
9. John 2:23-25; Luke 14:25-27; John 8:31, 32
10. Dietrich Bonhoeffer, *The Cost Of Discipleship*, Macmillan Paperbacks, New York, N.Y. 1963, p. 99.

11. Romans 3:25, 26
12. Richard Wurmbrand, Op. Cit., pp. 53, 54

Chapter Five

1. Matthew 24:37-39
2. Matthew 24:4,5,11
3. Hebrews 11:7
4. 1 Corinthians 1:25-29
5. John 6:44
6. Judges 7
7. Matthew16:18
8. Ephesians 1:22, 23

Chapter Six

1. John 12:42
2. Romans 10:9, 10
3. Luke 14:26, 27
4. Matthew 10:39
5. Luke 14:28-33
6. Matthew 26:14-16, 17-25; 27:3-5
7. Acts 5:1-13
8. 1 Corinthians 5:1-13, 2 Corinthians 2:1-11
9. Philippians 2:5-9
10. Luke 2:34
11. Philippians 3:5-8
12. Galatians 6:14
13. Philippians 3:20, 21

Chapter Seven

1. John 11:6
2. Mark 9:31 32
3. Matthew 22:15-22
4. Luke 10:30-37
5. Daniel Chapter 7

6. Romans 13:6, 7

7. Revelation 2:10, 13. It is the political authority that puts people in prison; this act is attributed to the Devil. Pergamos, a seat of Roman governmental authority in Asia (modern Turkey), is referred to as the place of "Satan's throne."

8. 1 Timothy 2:1, 2

9. 1 Peter 2:13-17

10. 1 Corinthians 2:6-8

11. Matthew 10: 24-28

12. Matthew Chapter 23

13. Matthew 12:1-8. As Messiah, Jesus had the right and duty to interpret the law of the Sabbath and to overrule the existing authorities when they were wrong. That has always seemed obvious to Christians. But to most of his contemporaries, that behavior of Jesus looked like disrespect for established authority.

14. Matthew 21:12, 13

15. Acts 4:18-20

16. Matthew 5:38-48

17. Romans 12:17-21

18. Romans 13:1

19. Matthew 11:21-24

20. Philippians 3:20

21. Hebrews 1:8, 9

22. Acts 4:13

23. Hebrews 13:12, 13

24. Philippians 2:5-11

25. Matthew 15:14

26. Hebrews 13:8

27. Hebrews 2:5

28. Hebrews 6:5

29. Acts 1:6-8

30. 2 Timothy 2:11, 12

31. 2 Thessalonians 2:3, 2 Timothy 1:12, 18; 4:8.

32. Matthew 10:16-26

33. See United States Code Title 4, Sections 1, 2, and U.S. Army Regulations 840-10.

34. The Christian flag often displayed in Protestant churches is white with a red cross on a square blue field in the upper left hand corner. Perhaps it is time for someone to design a new flag to represent the kingdom of God. Images might include the lion of the tribe of Judah and the lamb with the scroll, which depict the suffering and the triumphant Messiah, and the apocalyptic end time era from Revelation 5; or the cross and the crown and the rod of iron. These images point, as they should, to the two advents of the King, His suffering in His incarnation in the past and present (in His body, the church) and His glory in the future when the kingdom is established in power on the earth. Other themes will come to mind; the scriptures are rich in imagery. It seems to me that there could be many flags representing the kingdom of God. I believe the unity of the people of God can be displayed and celebrated without imposing uniformity. The insistence on uniformity began with Constantine, not with Jesus and the twelve apostles.

Chapter Eight

1. 1 Corinthians 1:18
2. 1 Corinthians 1:25
3. Matthew 16:21
4. Matthew 16: 22, 23
5. Matthew 16: 24-28
6. 1 Corinnthians 2:6-8
7. Luke 18:22
8. John 6:15
9. Zechariah 9:9
10. John 2:13-17
11. Mark 12:37
12. Matthew 26:50-54
13. 1 Corinthians 15:19, 30-32

Chapter Nine

1. Ramsay, Op. Cit., p. 277

2. Edward Gibbon, Op. Cit., p. 215

3. Kenneth Scott Latourette, *A History Of Christianity, Vol. 1, p. 91 Beginnings to 1500 A.D.,* Revised Edition, Harper Collins, Harper San Francisco, copyright 1953.

4. Gordon F. Snyder, *Church Life Before Constantine, Ante Pacem,* Mercer University Press, copyright 1985, 2nd Printing, 1991, The Seedsowers, PO Box 285, Sargent, Georgia 30275, p. 27.

5. Ramsay MacMullen, *Christianizing The Roman Empire, A.D. 100-400.* Yale University Press, New Haven and London, pp. 46, 47.

6. *Encyclopedia Brittanica, 9th edition, 1890,* volume XX, p. 776, Rome; quoted in Terry Sullivan, *The Church Of The Empire Versus the Christian Church of North Africa, 312-430 A.D.,* copyright by Terry Sullivan, 1997, 1526 E. 35th Ave., Denver, Colorado 80205, p. 51. Terry Sullivan's book is a limited edition published by the author. I disagree with some of his assumptions and conclusions. Nevertheless, I am indebted to him for his extensive research into the struggle between the Donatist assemblies and the imperial church in the fourth and fifth centuries. Sullivan's analysis includes a perceptive and detailed look at the political and economic realities of the time, and their bearing on the doctrinal conflict. His unique insights derive from the significance he attributes to the overwhelming political and economic impact of a Roman Emperor when he joins the church without renouncing his office, pays the salaries of cooperating bishops from the public treasury, calls church councils and sets the agenda for those councils. Sullivan, rightly in my opinion, refuses to deal with the struggle as if it were a merely theological dispute.

7. Ibid., XX, p. 757, quoted in Sullivan, p. 51

8. Ibid., XX pp. 757, 766, in Sullivan, p. 51

9. Augustine of Hippo, Epistle CLXXXV, *Nicene And Post Nicene Fathers, Vol. 4,* pp. 634-651, Hendrickson Publishers, Peabody, Massacusetts, 2nd printing, June 1995.

10. John 15:20

11. Acts 14:22

12. Franklin H. Littell, *From State Church To Pluralism*, Macmillan, New York, N.Y., 1962, 1971, pp. 72, 73.

13. C. Wright Mills, *The Causes Of World War III*, p. 169, Balantine Books, New York, N.Y. 1958, 1960.

Chapter Ten

1. Ephesians 2:1

2. Matthew 16;13-19

3. Roland H. Bainton, *Christian Attitudes Toward War & Peace*, p. 53. Abingdon Press, Nashville, Tennessee, 1960, 16th Printing, 1988.

4. Mark Hatfield (U.S. Senator, Rep., Oregon), *Between A Rock And A Hard Place*, a Key-Word Book, Word Books, Waco, Texas, 1976, p. 83.

5. Latourette, Kenneth Scott, Op. Cit., Vol. 1, p. 132

6. Ibid., p. 132, 133

7. Ibid., p. 188

8. Ibid., p. 133, 134

9. 1 Corinthians 4:8-12

10. Verduin, Leonard, *The Reformers And Their Stepchildren*, Baker Book House, 1980, p. 41. copyright Eerdmans Publishing Co., Grand Rapids, Mich.

11. William L. Shirer, *The Rise And Fall Of The Third Reich, A History of Nazi Germany*, p. 236, Simon and Schuster, New York, N.Y.

12. Matthew 21:1-11; Zechariah 9:9

13. Romans 11:25, 26

14. Daniel Gruber, *The Church And The Jews: The Biblical Relationship*. Part I: The Historical Development of Anti-Judaic Theology, pp. 14-42. Serenity Books, Hagerstown, Maryland 21742-3595, Copyright, Dan Gruber, 1997.

15. Galatians 4:21-31

16. Justin Martyr, *Dialog With Trypho, Chapter LXXX. Ante-Nicene Fathers*, Op. Cit., Vol. 1, p. 239.

17. Eusebius, *Church History*, Translated by Arthur C. McGiffert, Chapter XXXIX, *Post-Nicene Fathers*, Vol. 1, p. 172, Hendrickson Publications, Peabody, Mass.

18. Gruber, Op. Cit., p. 15

19. Harvey Cox, *The Secular City, Secularization and Urbanization in Theological Perspective,* Revised Edition, p. 2, Macmillan Company, New York, N.Y. 1965, 1966.

20. Gruber, Op. Cit., p. 40

21. Ibid., p. 15

22. Mars Hill Audio Journal, Tape #34, P.O. Box 7826, Charlottsville, Va. 22906-7826

23. 2 Thessalonians 1:6-10

24. Revelation 1:7

Chapter Eleven

1. Mattthew 13:24-30, 36-43

2. Jacques Ellul, *The Subversion Of Christianity,* P. 40. William B. Eerdmans, Grand Rapids, Michigan, 1986.

3. Malachi Martin, *The Decline And Fall Of The Roman Church,* pp. 19-52, G.P. Putnam's Sons, New York, N.Y. 1981.

Chapter Twelve

1. Mimi Mann, "Simeon's Pillars Still Stand" N. H. Sunday News, November 11, 1990.

2. Kenneth Scott Latourette, Op. Cit., Vol. 1, pp. 226, 227.

3. Martin, Op. Cit., pp. 38-41

4. Matthew 5:11, 12

5. Martin, Op, Cit., p.41

6. Athanasius, Bishop of Alexandria, 4th century, *The Life Of Antony, And The Letter To Marcellinus,* Classics of Western Spirituality, Translation and Introduction by Robert C. Gregg. Copyright 1980 by the Missionary Society of St. Paul, Paulist Press, Mahwah, N.J. 07430.

Chapter Thirteen

1. Daniel 10

2. Revelation chapters 8 and 9 are typical.

3. Revelation 1:7

4. Matthew 4:29 -- 31

5. Matthew 24:24

6. 1 Kings 22:19-22

7. 2 Thessalonians 2:1-4

8. 2 Thessalonians 2:7-12

9. 1 Thessalonians 4:16-18

10. Matthew 24:9-14

11. Matthew 24:13

12. Matthew 24:14

13. P.A. Sorokin, *Man And Society In Calamity*, pp. 316, 317, E.P. Dutton and Company, Inc., New York, N.Y. 1942.

Chapter Fourteen

1. Robert H. Bork, *Slouching Towards Gomorrah, Modern Liberalism and American Decline*, Copyright by Robert H. Bork, p. 341, Regan Books, 1996, An Imprint of Harper-Collins, 10 East 53rd Street, New York, N.Y. 10022.

2. Francis A. Schaeffer, *A Christian Manifesto*. Copyright 1981 by Francis A. Schaeffer. Published by Crossway Books, a division of Good News Publishers, Westchester, Illinois 60153, Chapter 6, pp. 73-88

3. Benjamin Wills Newton, *Prospects Of The Ten Kingdoms Of The Roman Empire*, p. 44. Third Edition, Revised and Abridged; Wembley, G.L. Silverwood Browne, 32 Hillcroft Crescent, England, 1955.

4. Luke 13:34, 35

5. Luke 19:42-44

6. Wilbur M. Smith, D.D., *World Crises and the Prophetic Scriptures*, Copyright by Moody Bible Institute, 820 N. LaSalle St., Chicago, Illinois, 1950, pp. 169-172

7. Matthew 24:14

8. Revelation 11:15

9. Psalm 2: 1-3

Chapter Fifteen

1. Time Magazine, April 8, 1966, cover story.

2. John Neville Figgis, *The Will To Freedom, or The Gospel Of*

Nietzsche And The Gospel Of Christ, Bross Lectures Delivered in Lake Forest College, Illinois, pp. 63-66, Charles Scribner's Sons, 1917, New York, N.Y.

3. *The Portable Nietzsche*, Edited and Translated by Walter Kaufman, p. 656. Penguin Books, Viking Press, 40 West 23rd St., New York, N.Y. 10010, U.S.A.

4. 2 Thessalonians 2:8

5. 2 Thessalonians 2:9-12

6. Matthew 24:9

7. Matthew 24:13, 14

Chapter Sixteen

1. Philip Schaff, *History Of The Christian Church, The German Reformation, 1517-1530*, Vol. 7, p. 1, Hendrickson Publishers, P.O. Box 3473, Peabody, Massachusetts 01961-3473.

2. Earl E. Cairns, *Christianity Through The Centuries*, Third Edition, pp. 297-301, Zondervan Publishing House, Grand Rapids, Michigan, 1958.

3. Schaff, Op. Cit., p. 1

4. James Burns, *Revivals, Their Laws And Leaders*, p. 163, Baker Book House, Grand Rapids, Michigan, 1960. Originally published by Hodder and Stoughton, London, England, 1909.

5. Roland Bainton, *Here I Stand: A Life of Martin Luther*, pp. 47, 48, A Mentor Book, by arrangement with Abingdon Press, Nashville, Tennessee. Copyright, 1950 by Pierce and Smith, Twelfth Printing, 1964.

6. Cairns, Op. Cit., p. 299.

7. Bainton, Op. Cit., pp. 51-64

8. Burns, Op. Cit., p. 163

9. Bainton, Op. Cit., p. 128

10. Ibid., p. 134

11. Ibid., pp. 137, 138

12. James Burns, Op. Cit., p. 187

13. Bainton, Op. Cit., pp.140, 141

14. Burns, Op. Cit., p. 189

15. Bainton, Op. Cit., p. 144

16. 1 Timothy 6:12

17. Romans 8:31-39; Psalms 2:1-6

18. These lines are from Luther's hymn, "A Mighty Fortress Is Our God."

19. Edmund S. Morgan, *The Puritan Dilemma: The Story of John Winthrop*, pp. 134-154, Little, Brown and Company, Boston and Toronto, 1958

Chapter Seventeen

1. William R. Estep, *The Anabaptist Story*, p.1, Broadman Press, Nashville, Tennessee, 1963.

2. Latourette, Op. Cit., p. 1113

3. Ibid., p. 1076

4. Ibid., p. 1078

5. Ibid., p.1397, 1398

6. Ibid., p. 1398

7. Ibid., p. 1375

8. Soren Kierkegaard, *Attack Upon "Christendom" 1854-1855*, Translated and with an introduction by Walter Lowrie. For example, see p. 118. Beacon Press, Boston, 1944, by Princeton University Press, first Beacon Paaperback edition, 1956, by arrangement with Princeton University Press.

9. Leonard Verduin, *The Reformers And Their Stepchildren*, pp. 13-15, Baker Book House, Grand Rapids, Michigan, copyright 1964 by William B. Eerdmans Publishing Co. Reprinted 1980 by Baker with permission by copyright holder.

10. Ibid., pp. 276, 277

Chapter Eighteen

1. *The Chronicle Of The Hutterian Brethren, Vol. I*, pp. 43-46. Translated and edited by the Hutterian Brethren, copyright 1987, Plough Publishing House, Woodcrest Service Committee, Inc., Hutterian Brethren, Rifton, N.Y. 12471, U.S.A. Ste. Agathe, Manitoba, ROG 1Y0, Canada, Robertsbridge, E. Sussex, TN32 5DR, England.

2. Verduin, Op. Cit., pp. 21-62

3. Estep, Op. Cit., p. 1

4. Verduin, Op. Cit., pp. 63-94

5. Ibid., pp. 95-131

6. Ibid., pp. 132-159

7. Ibid., Ibid. pp. 160-188

8. Ibid., pp. 189-220

9. Ibid., pp. 221-242

10. Ibid., p. 223

11. Ibid., p. 243

12. Ibid., pp. 256-263

13. Ibid., p. 263

14. Ibid., pp. 265

15. Ibid., p. 265

Chapter Nineteen

1. Pierre Van Passen, *A Crown Of Fire: The Life and Times of Girolamo Savonarola*, p. 8. Scribners' Sons, New York, N.Y. 1960.

2. Revelation 18:23b, 24

3. Van Paasen, Op. Cit., p. 75

4. Francis A. Schaeffer, *How Should We Then Live? The Rise and Decline of Western Thought and Culture*, pp. 71, 72. Fleming H. Revell, Old Tappen, N. J. 1976.

5. Van Paasen, Op. Cit., p. 235

6. G.F. Young, *The Medici*, pp. 259-264. The Modern Library, Random House, New York, N.Y., 1933.

7. Genesis 25:19-23

8. G.F. Young, Op. Cit., p. 216

9. Daniel, chapters 2, 3, 4 detail Nebuchadnezzar's conversion; in chapter 7 he is represented in Daniel's vision as a lion who is made to walk uprightly like a man.

10. Van Paasen, Op. Cit., p. 13

11. Ibid., p. 14

12. Ibid., p. 27

13. Ibid., pp. 28-30

14. Ibid., pp. 32-37

15. Ibid., pp. 37-41
16. Ibid., pp. 42-47
17. Ibid., pp. 62, 63
18. Burns, Op, Cit., p. 132
19. Van Paasen, Op. Cit., p. 73

Chapter Twenty

1. Van Paasen, Op. Cit., pp. 88, 89
2. Ibid., p. 76
3. Burns, Op. Cit., p. 123. Quoted from *The Christ Face In Art,* p. 40
4. Young, Op. Cit., pp. 166-175
5. Ibid. p. 182
6. Ibid. pp. 179-183
7. Van Paasen, Op. Cit., pp. 91-96
8. Ibid., pp. 96-100
9. Ibid., pp 100-102
10. Ibid., 103-106

Chapter Twenty-one

1. Van Paasen, Op. Cit., pp. 116, 117
2. Ibid., p. 89, 115
3. Ibid., p. 77
4. Ibid., p. 116, 117
5. Ibid., p. 120
6. Ibid., p. 119
7. Ibid., p. 113
8. Ibid., p. 115
9. Ibid., p. 125
10. Ibid., p.133-135
11. Ibid., p. 139-152
12. Ibid., p. 153-159
13. Ibid., p. 163-168
14. Ibid., p. 168-169

15. Ibid., p.172

16. Ibid., p. 181, 183

17. Ibid., p. 183

18. Young, Op. Cit., p. 250

19. Van Paasen, Op. Cit., p. 182

20. Ibid., p. 178

21. Ibid., p. 221

22. Ibid., p. 173

Chapter Twenty-two

1. Van Paasen, Op. Cit., pp. 193-196

2. Ibid., p. 203

3. Ibid., pp. 204, 205

4. Ibid., pp. 207, 208

5. Ibid., pp. 208, 209

6. Ibid., pp. 212, 213

7. Ibid., pp. 213, 214

8. Ibid., pp. 215-223

9. Ibid., pp. 224-227

10. Ibid., p. 227

11. Ibid., pp. 228-232

12. Ibid., p. 236

Chapter Twenty-three

1. Van Paasen, Op. Cit., pp. 243-246

2. Ibid., p. 248

3. Acts 4:18-20

4. Hebrews 13:12, 13

5. Van Paasen, Op. Cit., pp. 261, 262

6. Ibid., pp. 264, 265

7. Burns, Op. Cit., p. 149

8. Van Paasen, Op. Cit., pp. 267-269

9. Ibid., pp. 270-287

10. Ibid., p. 292

11. Ibid., p. 301

12. Ibid., p. 305-315

13. Young, Op. Cit., pp. 309, 310

14. Ibid., pp. 323, 324

15. Ibid., pp 313-319

16. Martin, Op. Cit., p. 209

17. Young, Op. Cit., p. 324

18. Ibid., p. 330

19. Ibid., pp. 353, 354

20. Ibid., pp. 352, 353

21. Ibid., pp. 347-351

22. Ibid., pp. 358, 359

23. Ibid., p. 307

24. Martin, Op Cit., p. 227

Chapter Twenty-four

1. "Girolamo Savonarola: Was He A Saint?" by Antonio Gaspari, Inside The Vatican, May 1996

2. 1 Peter 2:6-9

3. Matthew 21:23-27

4. Eusebius, *Church History.* Book III, Chapters V,VI, VII, VIII, *Nicene And Post Nicene Fathers,* Op. Cit. Vol. 1, pp. 138-143.

5. 2 Samuel 21:1-9

6. *Vatican Council II, The Conciliar and Post Conciliar Documents,* General Editor, Austin Flannery, O.P., p. 809, Declaration On Religious Liberty, Costello Publishing Co., P.O. Box 9, Northport, N.Y. 11768.

7. Paul Johnson, *Pope John XXIII,* Library of World Biography, p. 134, Little, Brown and Co., Boston and Toronto, 1974. 8. Ibid., p. 170

9. Malachi Martin, *The Final Conclave,* pp. 339-350, Stein and Day Publishers, Scarboro House, Briarcliff Manor, N.Y. 10510, 2nd Printing, 1978.

10. Garabandal Prophecies, Video. St. Michael's Garabandal Center, 889 Palo Verde Ave., Pasadena, California 91104. E-Mail address: J-TIP@IX.netcom.com.

11. Malachi Martin, from a Personal letter to me, dated 2/11/95 in answer to a question I put to him about the prophecy.

12. Luke 18:18-27

13. 1 Peter 2:21

14. 1 Corinthians 11:31

15. 2 Corinthians 6:17, 18; Acts 2:40

16. John 15:18, 19

Chapter Twenty-five

1. Acts 13:1-3

2. Acts 14:26-28

3. 1 John 4:11, 12

4. John 13:35

5. 1 Corinthians 1:17-3:5

6. Edwin Hatch, D.D., Edited by A. M. Fairbairn, D.D. *The Influence Of Greek Ideas And Usages Upon The Christian Church*, Based on the Hibbert Lectures, 1888. Hatch died before the book was finished; his friend, Fairbairn, finished the book from Hatch's notes and edited it. Williams and Norgate, 14 Henrietta Street, Covent Garden, London, 1904.

7. Ibid., p. 353

8. Ibid., p. 350

9. Ibid., p. 353

10. Ibid., p. 162, 163

11. Ibid., p. 164

12. Ibid., pp. 113, 114

13. Ibid., pp. 136, 137

14. Ibid., p. 138

15. Ibid., pp. 169, 170

16. Ibid., p. 170

17. Ibid., p. 133

18. Athanasius, Bishop of Alexandria, 4th century, Op. Cit., p. 6.

19. Hatch, Op. Cit., p. 167

20. Ibid., pp. 167, 168

21. T. Austin-Sparks, *The Centrality Of Jesus Christ*, Vol. 1, pp. 32, 33. Seedsowers Publishing House, P.O. Box 285, Sargent Georgia 30275.

22. Ibid., p. 30

Chapter Twenty-six

1. John 13:35

2. John 13:34

3. Matthew 22:37-40

4. Deuteronomy 6:4,5

5. 1 John 4:7-12

6. Acts 20:35

7. John 13:1-17

8. John 14:9

9. Roland G. Usher, *The Pilgrims And Their History*, Macmillan, New York, N.Y. 1918.

10. Mother Teresa, *No Greater Love,* Edited by Becky Benenate & Joseph Durepos, p. 57. Copyright 1997 by New World Library, Novato, California 94949.

11. Romans 2:16

Chapter Twenty-seven

1. Juan Carlos Ortiz, *Call To Discipleship,* with Jamie Buckingham, p. 3, Logos International, Plainfield, N.H. 1975.

2. Wayne Jacobsen, *The Naked Church*, 3rd Edition, Body Life Publishers, 1998, p. 20. Jacobsen refers to an article by Charles Colson, "Jesus Is Lord," in the May 1985 issue of Charisma Magazine.

3. John 17:21

4. Ephesians 5:25-27, Revelation 19:7, 8.

5. Matthew 24:9-14

6. Dietrich Bonhoeffer, *Letters And Papers From Prison,* Op. Cit., pp. 27, 28,

7. Revelation 7:14

8. Hebrews 12:2

9. Isaiah 53:3

10. John 8:31, 32
11. Isaiah 60:1, 2
12. 2 Peter 1:19
13. 1 Peter 1:13

Chapter Twenty-eight

1. Luke 18:8
2. 1 Corinthians 4:5
3. Daniel 9:1-19
4. On Line, Dec. 95 - March 96. YWAM, P.O. Box 61700, Honolulu, HI 96839

Chapter Twenty-nine

1. Daniel 11:32-35
2. Matthew 24:13
3. John 10:14-16
4. Matthew 10:40-42
5. Matthew 25:31-46
6. 2 Thessalonians 1:3-5
7. 2 Thessalonians 2:13, 14
8. 2 Thessalonians 2:15
9. Jude 3
10. Galatians 3:15
11. Colossians 1:23
12. Hebrews 12:25-29
13. Luke 21:28
14. Luke 22:31, 32

Chapter Thirty

1. Isaiah 53:3
2. Luke 2:34
4. Newsletter: C.I.T.I. Prayer, November 1999, 8818 Weems Road, Manassas, VA. 20110, Bob Yarbrough, facilitator, BYARBRO724@AOL.COM

4. Newsletter: Michael and Jeanne Mears, October 1999, 2 Hanlen Ave., Waihi Beach, New Zealand 3060, mears6nz@xtra.co.nz David B. Barrett's Statistics Task Force is based in Richmond, VA.

5. Matthew 24:9-22

6. Matthew 5:44

7. Matthew 10:23

8. Romans 11: 25, 26

9. Revelation 12:10, 11

Chapter Thirty-one

1. Revelation 1:7

2. Revelation 6:12-17

3. 1 Corinthians 15:51-55

4. Revelation 11:15

5. 2 Peter 3:7-13

6. John 3:16

7. Isaiah 53:5,6, 10-12

8. Cecil F. Alexander (1818-1895) and George C. Stebbins (1846-1945), "There Is A Green Hill Far Away," *Hymns For The Family Of God*, Copyright by Covenant Press, 1973.

9. Matthew 16:24-27

10. 1 John 2:6

11. Hebrews 12:1-4

12. 1 Corinthians 15:45-54

13. Romans 5:1-5

Chapter Thirty-two

1. 2 Samuel 23:1-4

2. 2 Samuel 23:13-17

3. Numbers 3:29-31

4. 2 Samuel 6:1-15

5. Isaiah 55:8, 9

6. T. Austin-Sparks, *The School Of Christ*, pp. 13-14, a reprint by David Wilkerson, of a book published originally in London in 1964 by T. Austin-Sparks. David Wilkerson, c/o World

challenge, Inc. P.O. Box 260, Lindale, Texas 75771.

7. Isaiah 66:1, 2

8. Psalm 51:17

9. 2 Samuel 7:14-16

10. 2 Samuel chapters 11-20

11. Hebrews 12:11

12. Genesis chapters 37, 39-50 (Especially chapter 50, the final resolution.)

13. Jeremiah 10:23

Chapter Thirty-three

1. Acts 3:21

2. Luke 1:31-33

3. 1 John 2:15

4. 2 Peter 3:10-13

Epilog

1. Hebrews 12:26

2. Daniel 8:23

3. Matthew 24:21, 22

4. Daniel 7:7-14

5. Hebrews 12:27

6. Ephesians 2:2

7. 2 Corinthians 11:14

8. Matthew 15:13

9. Hebrews 12:28, 299.

10. 1 Corinthians 3:11-15

11. John Bevere, *The Fear Of The Lord*, pp. 21, 22, Creation House, Strang Communications Company, 600 Rinehard Road, Lake Mary, Fla. 32746, copypright, John Bevere, 1997.

Bibliography

Athanasius, Bishop of Alexandria, 4th century, *The Life Of Antony, And The Letter To Marcellinus,* Classics of Western Spirituality, Translation and Introduction by Robert C. Gregg. Copyright ©1980 by the Missionary Society of St. Paul, Paulist Press, Mahwah, N.J. 07430.

Augustine of Hippo, Epistle CLXXXV, *Nicene And Post Nicene Fathers, Vol. 4,* pp. 634-651, Hendrickson Publishers, Peabody, Massachusetts, 2nd printing, June 1995.

T. Austin-Sparks, *The Centrality Of Jesus Christ,* Vol. 1, Copyright © 1997 by Seedsowers Publishing House, P.O. Box 285, Sargent Georgia 30275.

T. Austin-Sparks, *The School Of Christ,* a reprint by David Wilkerson, of a book published originally in London in 1964 by T. Austin-Sparks. David Wilkerson, c/o World challenge, Inc. P.O. Box 260, Lindale, Texas 75771.

Roland H. Bainton, *Christian Attitudes Toward War & Peace,* Abingdon Press, Nashville, Tennessee, 1960, 16th Printing, 1988.

Roland H. Bainton, *Here I Stand: A Life of Martin Luther,* A Mentor Book, by arrangement with Abingdon Press, Nashville, Tennessee. Copyright © 1950 by Pierce and Smith, Twelfth Printing, 1964.

Dietrich Bonhoeffer, *The Cost Of Discipleship,* Macmillan Paperbacks, New York, N.Y. 1963.

Dietrich Bonhoeffer, *Letters and Papers From Prison,* Macmillan Paperbacks, Edited by Eberhard Bethge, Translated by Reginald H. Fuller, 1953, paperback edition, 1962.

Robert H. Bork, *Slouching Towards Gomorrah, Modern Liberalism and American Decline,* Copyright © Robert H. Bork, Regan Books, an Imprint of Harper-Collins Publishers, 1996, 10 East 53rd Street, New York, N.Y. 10022.

James Burns, *Revivals, Their Laws And Leaders,* Baker Book House, Grand Rapids, Michigan, 1960, a reprint. Originally published by Hodder and Stoughton, London, 1909.

Earl E. Cairns, *Christianity Through The Centuries,* Third Edition, Zondervan Publishing House, Grand Rapids, Michigan, 1958.

Harvey Cox, *The Secular City, Secularization and Urbanization in Theological Perspective,* Revised Edition, p. 2, Macmillan Company, New York, N.Y. 1965, 1966.

Jonathan Edwards, *Jonathan Edwards On Revival: A Narrative Of Surprising Conversions* (first published in 1736); *The Distinguishing Marks Of A Work of the Spirit of God* (first published in 1741); *An Account Of The Revival in Northampton, 1740-1742* (first published in 1965), The Banner Of Truth Trust, 3 Murrayfield Rd., Edinburgh, EH 12 6EL, P.O. Box 621, Carlisle, PA 17013, U.S.A., 1999.

Jacques Ellul, *The Subversion Of Christianity,* William B. Eerdmans, Grand Rapids, Michigan, 1986.

Lou Engle with Catherine Paine, *Digging the Wells of Revival, Reclaiming Your Historic Inheritance Through Prophetic Intercession,* Revival Press, An Imprint of Destiny Image® Publishers, Inc., P.O. Box 310, Shippensburg, PA 17257-2015-6, © Copyright 1998 by Destiny Image Publishers.

Samuel E. Ericsson, "Twelve Baskets Full" an audio tape series produced by Advocates International, 9691 D Main Street, Fairfax, Virginia 22301, advonet2@aol.com, phone, 703/764-0011.

William R. Estep, *The Anabaptist Story,* Broadman Press, Nashville, Tennessee, 1963.

John Neville Figgis, *The Will To Freedom, or The Gospel Of Nietzsche And The Gospel Of Christ,* Bross Lectures Delivered in Lake Forest College, Illinois, pp. 63-66, Charles Scribner's Sons, 1917, New York, N.Y.

Charles G. Finney, *The Promise of the Spirit,* Compiled and Edited by Timothy L. Smith, Bethany Fellowship, 6820 Auto Club Road, Minneapolis, Minnesota 55438, Copyright © 1980 Timothy L. Smith.

James W. Garrett, *The Doulos Principle, Called to be God's slaves,* Doulos Press, P.O. Box 50130, Tulsa, Oklahoma 74150, Copyright © 1999 James W. Garrett.

Edward Gibbon, *The Decline And Fall Of The Roman Empire,* an Abridged Version, Edited and with an introduction by Dero A. Saunders. Penguin Books, Middlesex, England and New York, N.Y. Copyright 1952 by Viking Press. Reprinted in 1985 by Viking Penguin.

Daniel Gruber, *The Church And The Jews: The Biblical Relationship.* Part I: The Historical Development of Anti-Judaic Theology. Serenity Books, Hagerstown, Maryland 21742-3595, Copyright © Dan Gruber, 1997.

Mark Hatfield (U.S. Senator, Rep., Oregon), *Between A Rock And A Hard Place,* a Key-Word Book, Word Books, Waco, Texas, 1976.

The Chronicle Of The Hutterian Brethren, Vol. I. Translated and edited by the Hutterian Brethren, Copyright ©1987, Plough Publishing House, Woodcrest Service Committee, Inc., Hutterian Brethren, Rifton, N.Y. 12471, U.S.A. Ste. Agathe, Manitoba, ROG 1Y0, Canada, Robertsbridge, E. Sussex, TN32 5DR, England.

Soren Kierkegaard, *Attack Upon "Christendom" 1854-1855,* Translated and with an introduction by Walter Lowrie, Beacon Press, Boston, 1944, by Princeton University Press, first Beacon Paperback edition, 1956, by arrangement with Princeton University Press.

Kenneth Scott Latourette, *A History Of Christianity, 2 Volumes,* Revised Edition, Harper Collins, Harper San Francisco, Copyright 1953.

Franklin H. Littell, *From State Church To Pluralism,* Macmillan, New York, N.Y., 1962, 1971.

Richard F. Lovelace, *Dynamics Of Spiritual Life, An Evangelical Theology Of Renewal,* Inter-Varsity Press, Downers Grove, Illinois 60515, Copyright © 1979 by Inter-Varsity Christian Fellowship.

Gordon MacDonald, *Rebuilding Your Broken World,* Oliver Nelson, a division of Thomas Nelson Publishers, Nashville, Tennessee, 1988.

Ramsay MacMullen, *Christianizing The Roman Empire, A.D. 100-400*. Yale University Press, New Haven and London, pp. 46, 47.

Paul Marshall with Lela Gilbert, *Their Blood Cries Out, The Worldwide Tragedy of Modern Christians Who Are Dying for Their Faith*, Word Publishing, Dallas, Texas, 1997.

Malachi Martin, *The Decline And Fall Of The Roman Church*, G.P. Putnam's Sons, New York, N.Y. 1981.

Malachi Martin, *The Final Conclave*, Stein and Day Publishers, Scarboro House, Briarcliff Manor, N.Y. 10510, 2nd Printing, 1978.

Justin Martyr, *Dialog With Trypho, Chapter LXXX. Ante-Nicene Fathers*, Vol. 1, Hendrickson Publishers, Peabody, Massachusetts, 2nd printing, June 1995.

Mars Hill Audio Journal, Tape #34, P.O. Box 7826, Charlottesville, Va. 22906-7826

C. Wright Mills, *The Causes Of World War III*, chapter 23, A Pagan Sermon, Balantine Books, New York, N.Y. 1958, 1960.

Edmund S. Morgan, *The Puritan Dilemma: The Story of John Winthrop*, pp. 134-154, Little, Brown and Company, Boston and Toronto, 1958

Benjamin Wills Newton, *Prospects Of The Ten Kingdoms Of The Roman Empire*, Third Edition, Revised and Abridged; Wembley, G.L.Silverwood Browne, 32 Hillcroft Crescent, England, 1955.

The Portable Nietzsche, Edited and Translated by Walter Kaufman, Penguin Books, Viking Press, 40 West 23rd St., New York, N.Y. 10010, U.S.A.

William Ramsay, *The Church In The Roman Empire, Before 170 A.D.* A reprint by Baker Book House, Grand Rapids, Michigan, 1954.

Leonard Ravenhill, *Why Revival Tarries*, Copyright © Leonard Ravenhill 1959, Bethany House Publishers, 11300 Hampshire Ave. South, Minneapolis, Minnesota 55438, 1997.

Francis A. Schaeffer, *A Christian Manifesto*, Copyright © 1981 by Francis A. Schaeffer. Published by Crossway Books, a division of Good News Publishers, Westchester, Illinois 60153.

Francis A. Schaeffer, *How Should We Then Live? The Rise and Decline of Western Thought and Culture.* Fleming H. Revell, Old Tappen, N. J., 1976.

Philip Schaff, *History Of The Christian Church, The German Reformation, 1517-1530*, Vol. 7, Hendrickson Publishers, P.O. Box 3473, Peabody, Massachusetts 01961-3473.

Nina Shea, *In the Lion's Den, A Shocking Account of Persecution and Martyrdom of Christians Today and How We Should Respond*, Broadman & Holman Publishers, Nashville, Tennessee, 1997.

Wilbur M. Smith, D.D., *World Crises and the Prophetic Scriptures*, Copyright © by Moody Bible Institute, 820 N. LaSalle St., Chicago, Illinois, 1950, pp. 169-172

Timothy L. Smith, *Revivalism and Social Reform, American Protestantism on the Eve of the Civil War*, The Johns Hopkins University Press, Baltimore and London, 1980, originally published by Abingdon Press, 1957.

Gordon F. Snyder, *Church Life Before Constantine, Ante Pacem*, Mercer University Press, Copyright 1985, 2nd Printing, 1991, The Seedsowers, PO Box 285, Sargent, Georgia 30275.

P.A. Sorokin, *Man And Society In Calamity*, E.P. Dutton and Company, Inc., New York, N.Y. 1942.

Terry Sullivan, *The Church Of The Empire Versus The Christian Church Of North Africa, 312-430 A.D.*, Copyright © Terry Sullivan, 1526 E. 35th Ave., Denver, Colo. 80205, 1997.

Tommy Tenney, *The God Chasers*, © Copyright 1998, Destiny Image Publishers, P.O. Box 310, Shippensburg, PA 17257-0310

Pierre Van Passen, *A Crown Of Fire: The Life and Times of Girolamo Savonarola*, Scribner's Sons, New York, N.Y. 1960.

Leonard Verduin, *The Reformers And Their Stepchildren,* Baker Book House, Grand Rapids, Michigan, Copyright 1964 by William B. Eerdmans Publishing Co., Reprinted 1980 by Baker with permission by copyright holder.

Richard Wurmbrand, *Tortured For Christ,* Living Sacrifice Book Co., P.O. Box 2273, Bartlesville, OK. 74005-2273, Copyright 1967 by the Voice of the Martyrs, Inc.

Philip Yancey, *What's So Amazing About Grace?,* Copyright © 1997 by Philip D. Yancey. Zondervan Publishing House, Grand Rapids, Michigan 49530

G.F. Young, *The Medici,* The Modern Library, Random House, New York, N.Y., 1933.